More advance praise for William Coplin's
How You Can Help

"This is a wonderful book. It will be enormously helpful to all individuals who want to make the world a little better. We often hear that people want to get involved but don't know how. This book will make it impossible for anyone to use that excuse anymore."
—Sara E. Meléndez, President and CEO of the Independent Sector

"Finally we have a realistic roadmap that can be used to leverage our charitable giving and our volunteer time in ways that will genuinely improve society. This book includes all the component parts that anyone—regardless of age, sex, income level, or political persuasion—can assemble into a powerful strategy that will truly make a difference."

How You Can Help

An Easy Guide to
Doing Good Deeds
in Your Everyday Life

William D. Coplin, PhD

Routledge
New York and London

Published in 2000 by
Routledge
29 West 35th Street
New York, NY 10001

Published in Great Britain by
Routledge
11 New Fetter Lane
London EC4P 4EE

Colin Powell photograph courtesy of AP/Wide World Photos;
all other photographs herein are used with express permission.

Printed in the United States of America on acid-free paper.
Designed and typeset by The Whole Works®, New York

10 9 8 7 6 5 4

Library of Congress Cataloging-in-Publication Data

Coplin, William D.
    How you can help : an easy guide to doing good deeds in your
everyday life / by William D. Coplin.
        p. cm.
    ISBN 0-415-92297-6 (pbk.)
    1. Voluntarism—United States.   2. Volunteer workers in social service—
    United States.   3. Social Services—United States.
    I. Title.
HN90.V64C695 2000   99-20659
361.3'7—dc21   CIP

To Those Who Proudly Accept
the Label

Contents

Preface   ix
Acknowledgments   xiii
Introduction   xv

PART ONE:
What Is a Genuine Do-Gooder?
   1: The Blessing and Curse of Mother Teresa   3
   2: The Mission   12
   3: Organize Thyself   19

PART TWO:
Ways You Can Help
   4: Effective Volunteering   31
   5: Donors Unite: You Have Nothing
       to Lose but Your Money   47
   6: Good Citizens and Watchdogs   60
   7: Careers That Serve Society   71

PART THREE:
Finding Nearby Windows
of Opportunity
    8: Families   97
    9: Neighbors   109
   10: Employees   118
   11: Consumers   131
   12: Investors   141
   13: Social Organizations,
        a.k.a. Packs   153
   14: Retirees   165
   15: Students   175
   16: Alumni   186

PART FOUR:
The Power to Create Change

17: Cooperative Problem Solving   197
18: Getting on the Agenda of Players   209
19: Problem Solving through Existing   220
    Organizations
20: Creating New Organizations   229

Appendix

  I: Resources: Contact Organizations   244
  II: Suggested Readings   253
  III: List of More than 100 Approved Charities   256

Preface

My father was fond of telling me that I was destined to be a teacher because, at the age of four, I was teaching older kids on my block how to tell time. He was right about this insight even though I did not realize it until I graduated from college. I became a college professor. Like most college professors, I taught in my field of scholarship. However, I underwent a major readjustment in my teaching mission sometime in 1967, when I was already a published and tenured associate professor at Wayne State University in Detroit. The change in mission happened suddenly. During a meeting of a consciousness-raising group I attended in the '60s (they were quite popular then), I received what I would call a wake-up call.

The group members decided to focus on me. When I told them that I was a college professor, several said, "So you get paid by undergraduates to write books so you can get tenure and make money." I was shaken by this comment coming from a group that I thought did not know much about colleges and universities. If they could see through the hypocrisy, how could I have missed it? I asked myself. The attack was especially hard to take because I had been a constant critic of the irrelevance of much classroom education ever since the tenth grade, when my history teacher would write facts on the board and tell the class to memorize them. I don't have anything against facts, but I do have something against learning only that which can be easily tested with a paper and pencil. Now I was telling students to learn the theories of international relations or American government so they could critique and contrast them to other theories in their little blue books. I was my tenth-grade history teacher not by conscious choice, but because I was too busy trying to become an academic superstar to think carefully about my teaching mission.

As a result of that interaction, I decided that my primary mission had to be teaching what would help my students succeed in life, according to their personal definitions of success, and succeed at being good citizens, according to the Declaration of Independence. I still wrote books and articles to keep my job and get raises, but I worked hard to make them secondary to my teaching mission, first at Wayne State University and later at Syracuse University. My goal is to help students develop the skills, attitudes, and understandings from the social sciences that they need to succeed in their careers and, equally important, how to be good citizens. And being a good citizen means, quite simply, helping to make society better.

The path from my early interest in teaching and my mid-twenties readjustment has led me to write this book. My goals are to help you understand how to define doing good, to organize yourself to do good, to find opportunities for doing good, and to encourage others to do good. The book also provides specific information on resources that you can tap into to decide where and what kind of doing good you want to pursue and how to be a more effective do-gooder. Much of this book is based on my personal experiences as a husband, father, neighbor, community member, citizen, and college teacher as well as my research on the infinite number of ways our society can be organized to help people do good.

My early recollections of doing good include asking for contributions to the American Cancer Society in front of the five-and-dime store as a middle-schooler and lobbying to get a baseball field in our neighborhood as a teenager. Throughout my life, I have volunteered and participated in a number of activities to help improve our society.

The bulk of my do-gooding experience has been as a college professor seeking to provide students with the skills and predisposition to make the world better through volunteering, citizen participation, and community problem solving. I was fortunate to become the director of the Public Affairs Program of the Maxwell School of Citizenship and Public Affairs at Syracuse University in 1976. The program offers courses through the College of Arts and Science designed to entice and even cajole students to do what they can to improve society. At the end of my introductory course, I lead the hundred-plus students into the foyer of Maxwell Hall and ask them to hold hands and repeat the Athenian Oath that is inscribed on the wall behind the statue of George Washington:

> We will ever strive for the ideals and sacred things of the city, both alone and with many; we will unceasingly seek to quicken the sense of public duty; we will revere and obey the city's laws; we will transmit the city not only as less, but greater, better, and more beautiful than it was transmitted to us.

Despite the feeling of awkwardness, they take the oath. To be admitted to the program's major, applicants must demonstrate to me that they are serious about leaving society better than they found it. After they graduate, I send the more than six hundred alumni of the program an annual reminder that asks, "What good have you done lately?"

I briefly list my other experiences so you might better understand where I am coming from when you read this book. Over the past 25 years, I have:

• Served as a coach of my daughters' little league softball team for several years.

• Established the Community Link Program in 1978, where students complete research projects for public agencies. According to the agencies, the value to the community has been in excess of $110,000 each year for more than a decade.

• With several colleagues in the mid-1980s, drafted a curriculum for the participation in a government course required by the New York State Board of Regents to prepare every high school graduate to become an active and responsible citizen.

• Worked since the late 1980s with more than 40 high schools throughout New York and New Jersey on teaching how to do good through problem-solving analysis and public service.

• Started two programs that allowed SU undergraduates to work with city youth to deliver products and services to members of the community. In the first program, called Teens Teaching Spanish, undergraduates worked with local Latino teens to tutor police and other public servants in the local Spanish dialect. The second program was called University Reach, which linked undergraduates with local teens to work on community projects. It received funding from the Mott and Kellogg foundations, Chase Bank, and Nationwide Insurance.

• Donated my summers of 1992 and 1993 to run six-week, full-day programs where more than 30 at-risk students were brought to campus to learn how to use computers and basic skills that would help them in high school.

• Organized a group of students that set up a university-wide volunteer center on campus. The center was the basis for the creation of the Center for Public and Community Service, which is a permanent university program today.

• Helped to organize and served as vice chair and chair of the Town of Manlius Coalition, Inc., a grassroots organization to educate citizens in the town about how to influence local government decisions and the positions of candidates in local government offices.

These experiences and my study of the field have driven me and given me the knowledge to write this book. I have learned a great deal about the role businesses, governments, and nonprofits play in improving our society and how current business techniques can help do-gooders work smarter and better. Most important, my direct contact with hundreds of people who serve society either as volunteers or as workers has taught me, by example, what it takes to be a genuine do-gooder. This contact has also convinced me that those of you who are already hard at work doing good need advice on how to make more of a difference and suffer less frustration. You need tools to assess and improve your attempts to help make a difference. I also know that many of you do not want to plunge into doing good because you are not sure how to help or you just haven't figured out how to match your talents and resources to society's needs. My hope is that this book will show you the way.

Acknowledgments

This book has benefited from the advice of many people. The tireless effort and steady insight of my editor, Ilene Kalish, at Routledge, were crucial. Ilene was brutal but honest in her comments and made this book much more than it otherwise could have been. The following students and staff at Syracuse University provided critical support: Tiffany Blair, who had to carry the ball over Christmas and down the final stretch; Laura Deschaines, who helped to rewrite some of the profiles; Carole Dwyer, Michelle Magnanti, Stephanie Pasquale, and Lisa Tobin, who conducted several interviews and wrote drafts of the profiles; Abbie Toner, who helped manage the research effort; Jessica White, who developed the charts and materials in the chapter on volunteers; Michelle Walker; Tom Webster; Laurie Shrall; and Michael Kent. Advice and support from several alumni were extremely helpful, including written comments from Gary Puddles, Laura Faery, Stacie Simpson, Kristin Weniger, Kiran Guadioso, and Chris Lavelle. Early readers of the manuscript helped to redirect me. They include Hamilton Armstrong, Frank Brieaddy, Valerie Falso, Tina Press, Noel Van Swol, and Barbara Wanger. Michael Kent and Melissa Sexton read a near final draft and provided useful suggestions that have greatly improved the manuscript. My children, Britt, Debbie, Laura, Doug, Judy, Richard, and Tilly, gave me encouragement and advice throughout. I thank Alice Halstead for her advice early on. Others: Jack Brill, Judy Hamby, Paul Hilton, Marty Nathan, Tom Nolton, and Alice Tepper Marlin, for providing advice on the chapters on corporate social responsibility; and Curtis G. Weeden of the Corporate Contributions Management Academy. Wendy Kopp and Rebecca Barreras provided information on Teach for America. Ajay Bhatt,

Rosaria Champagne, and Rocky De Florio, whose conversations early on helped me develop the idea of the book. Susan Weiner and Patricia Workman of the Independent Sector supplied information on nonprofits, and Dan Langan of the National Charities Information Bureau did the same for the chapter on donors. Judith Helein of AARP and Donna Anderson of the National Retiree Volunteer Center provided insight on the role of retirees in the volunteer sector. Several people from Literacy Volunteers of America, including Carol Gabler, Susan Anderson, Rebecca Levy, and Ellie Spence, helped in contacting outstanding volunteers. Also, thanks to Wendy Schaetzel Lesko for information on community-based learning and the Activism 2000 project, and to Carl Nash for his suggestions on the introduction. In addition to providing inspiration for the entire book, Ralph Nader alerted me to the role of some college alumni as a new source of public interest groups, and Chet Safian of Princeton '55 Inc. gave me an opportunity to observe the phenomenon firsthand.

My wife, Vicki, advised me throughout the process that "nothing worthwhile in life comes easy," which kept me going and actually is something every Genuine Do-Gooder should remember.

Introduction

The overall goal of this book is to rescue the term *do-gooder* so that it is a label everyone can proudly wear. As I see it, a Genuine Do-Gooder is someone who wants to help make America into the society envisioned in our Declaration of Independence—a society in which everyone has the opportunity for life, liberty, and the pursuit of happiness. Of course, this is no easy task. But I believe it is possible, and I want to say this clearly: It is possible to make things better in the world. It is possible for individuals to make a difference. I know, because I've seen it happen. You probably think it's possible, too. Perhaps you're not sure how you can help or what the best ways are to help. This book will give you concrete suggestions on how to:

1. Decide where you can have maximum impact as a volunteer, donor, and citizen;

2. Organize your own life so that you have the time to be a fulfilled, rather than frustrated, volunteer;

3. Use your volunteer time and energy efficiently;

4. Donate money to achieve your goals effectively;

5. Explore career options in business, government, and non-profit organizations where you can work full time at doing good;

6. Be a strategic employee, consumer, and investor who supports a socially responsible private sector; and

7. Pursue cooperative problem-solving strategies where you work and play.

This book will help you whether you want to spend a few hours a week as a volunteer, spend a small percentage of your income on helping others, or devote your life to helping others.

How to Use This Book

This book is written according to the principle "to hear is to forget; to see is to remember; and to do is to learn." This book provides more than just a vision of a better world; it also provides you with action principles, steps you can take to create change, contact information, profiles of Genuine Do-Gooders, and a wealth of ideas that may inspire you to do some good.

The book is divided into four sections. Part I will help you understand the basic characteristics of a Genuine Do-Gooder and enable you to make choices about how much you want to help as well as suggest where and what organizations you may want to help. Part II looks at how you can help by discussing the four roles of the Genuine Do-Gooder—volunteer, donor, citizen, and employee. Part III demonstrates the part-time opportunities for doing good that are easy for you to access. Part IV will provide you with guidelines and tools for getting other people and organizations to do more. The first part of the appendix provides a list of service or volunteer organizations with full contact information, including Web sites. The second provides a list of suggested readings that I have found useful in writing this book. The third provides a list of charities that meet the standards of the National Charities Information Bureau (NCIB), an organization that monitors charities for effectiveness and compliance with the law.

Each chapter has a similar organization designed to help you digest the information presented as easily as possible. Thus, each chapter contains the following elements: A Quiz introduces the topics covered in each chapter. Don't be scared by these quizzes, as you often won't know the answers until you've read the chapter: they are merely meant to start you thinking about the chapter topics. Throughout the chapters you will find Principles that will help you understand your role as a Genuine Do-Gooder or offer you suggested guidelines to follow. Each chapter ends with Quiz Results that provide you with the answers to the questions posed at the beginning of the chapter and serve as a summary of the chapter.

Sources

As a how-to guide, this book synthesizes information from a broad variety of sources. These include original interviews, published information from newspapers and books, and information provided by organizations and obtained from either publications or Web sites. A particularly valuable source of information on volunteers has been the Daily Point of Light Award descriptions, which I scanned for useful examples to illustrate specific points in the text. If you are interested in more information about these examples and thousands of others, please consult the Points of Light Foundation Web site, which is available at http://www.pointsoflight.org.

Each Web site in the list of organizations in the appendix was tested to make sure it is functioning and up to date. However, some organizations are more aggressive in updating their sites than others, so you may find that the information has not been updated or that the site no longer operates. For this reason, address, phone, and e-mail information have been provided wherever possible.

I have attempted to provide readers with the most complete and comprehensive resources as possible; however, the possibility of omitting important organizations is real. I have tried to include organizations that will support your efforts to do good in general but have not provided a list of the thousands of organizations dedicated to specific pursuits. A few are included for purposes of illustration, but the sources that are provided will help you find those organizations that work for the cause in which you are interested. Given those guidelines, I would appreciate hearing from all individuals or organizations that think they should be included in future editions of the book. I can be contacted at coplin@genuinedogooder.com.

Readers in Canada should find this book useful since Canada has thousands of organizations and opportunities for the Genuine Do-Gooder. For that reason I have listed a few of the key Canadian organizations in appropriate chapters and in the organization list in the second part of the appendix. However, space does not permit as lengthy a listing as has been included for the U.S. organizations. The Web sites of the Canadian organizations that are listed should give you access to the whole range of Canadian organizations.

One particularly useful Web site can be used to access the entire range of activities in the nonprofit and volunteer sector not only in this country and Canada, but also in more than a hundred countries.

Action without Borders
350 Fifth Ave., Suite 6614
New York, NY 10118
Tel. 212 843-3973   Fax 212 564-3377
http://www.idealist.org

Are You a Genuine Do-Gooder?

As I will discuss later, "doing good" is a way of life. In another sense, it's an attitude: you want to help. This does not mean that you are a busybody or a martyr, but someone who simply wants to improve things. Does this sound like you? Do you have the potential to become someone who works to improve society? The test below is designed to give you an insight into your potential. Take it now and score yourself.

Read each of the sentences below and indicate the extent to which you agree or disagree with the statement by circling the appropriate response.

Always (4)   Usually (3)   Sometimes (2)   Never (1)

1. I believe everyone should have equal opportunities to life, liberty and the pursuit of happiness.   4 3 2 1
2. I am angry about the lack of a level playing field in America, but I know that I can work to level it.   4 3 2 1
3. I am capable of serving others on a personal level without receiving any award other than self-satisfaction.   4 3 2 1
4. My parents and my peers are or have the potential to become Genuine Do-Gooders.   4 3 2 1
5. I donate five percent of my waking time and/or current income to help the less fortunate or to improve American society.   4 3 2 1
6. Money and material things are not the most important things in my life.   4 3 2 1
7. I am a courteous and responsible driver.   4 3 2 1
8. I don't litter and clean up after people who do.   4 3 2 1
9. I say "thank you" when people hold a door open for me.
   4 3 2 1

10. I give money to the homeless.   4 3 2 1
11. I would vote for a reasonable increase in the school
    budget even if I had no children in the school.   4 3 2 1
12. I have excellent time management skills.   4 3 2 1
13. I know my neighbors and have helped them when they have
    needed it.   4 3 2 1
14. At work, I stick up for colleagues whom I feel have been
    treated poorly.   4 3 2 1
15. My leisure time activities involve charitable
    projects.   4 3 2 1
16. I participate as much as I can in volunteer
    programs.   4 3 2 1
17. I know government leaders and seek to influence
    them to do the right thing for my community.   4 3 2 1
18. I do not purchase goods and services that do harm
    to the environment or society.   4 3 2 1
19. I am familiar with the idea of corporate social
    responsibility and use it when I buy products and make
    financial investments.   4 3 2 1
20. I am knowledgeable about the organizations to which
    I make charitable contributions and where I volunteer.
21. When I do good, I plan my activities and evaluate them on
    a continuous basis.   4 3 2 1
22. I believe I can build support for policies within
    different kinds of organizations.   4 3 2 1
23. I can name my congressperson, my mayor, and my school
    superintendent.   4 3 2 1
24. I obey the law.   4 3 2 1
25. I pay my parking tickets.   4 3 2 1

Scoring Key: Add up the points earned for each answer and apply the
following scale.
100–90=Very High Potential; 89–80=High Potential; 79–70=Modest
Potential; Below 70=You have some serious work to do.

Interpreting What Your Score Means

Don't expect to score in the high category. As long as you are
above 70, you have a good shot at becoming a Genuine Do-Gooder.
Scoring below 70 raises questions and suggests immediate remedial

work. Your score is only a snapshot of where you are now. After you read this book and if you undertake the actions suggested, your score will approach 100. I guarantee it.

Note that the scoring procedure weighs each of the twenty-five items equally. The presence of several questions on the same topic, in effect, gives extra weight to certain factors. There are several questions that look in part at your willingness to avoid doing harm to society and to sacrifice for society (numbers 4, 5, 6, 7, 9, 10, 11, 18, 19, 20, and 21) because these are critical character attributes required of anyone who seeks to be a Genuine Do-Gooder.

Are you surprised by your score? Don't worry if you didn't do quite as you expected. The point of the test is just to get you thinking about yourself and your everyday actions. Remember, doing good is an attitude. All it takes is the desire to help.

I

What Is a Genuine Do-Gooder?

1 The Blessing and Curse of Mother Teresa

INTRODUCTION

Mother Teresa is the premier Genuine Do-Gooder of the 20th century. By the time she died in 1997 at the age of 87, her public persona and her private deeds had perhaps made her the perfect do-gooder. She was both a rower, someone who held the dying poor in her arms, and a steerer, someone who engineered a movement that established 127 orphanages, 213 free dispensaries, 54 leprosariums, and 60 free schools. Her commitment was total, her motives pure, and her spirit tireless.

Mother Teresa is a very tough act to follow. Therein lies the problem for the rest of us who want to be Genuine Do-Gooders. As a model, Mother Teresa is both a blessing and a curse.

Principle 1.1: **Part-time do-gooders are welcome**

One curse of Mother Teresa for Genuine Do-Gooders has been the mistaken notion that they must give as much as she did to improve society. Don't be fooled into thinking, "If I can't be like Mother Teresa, I might as well tend only to my own garden."

As far as the size of your commitment, Mother Teresa is far from a workable role model. Rather, you need to look at the more reasonable standards established by the life and work of millions of Genuine Do-Gooders who give five, ten, or fifteen hours a week to help the disadvantaged, write a few checks each year to their favorite causes, or have careers in such fields as teaching and health.

I'd like to introduce you to someone I know well, someone who to me exemplifies an ideal do-gooder. Her name is Michelle Walker, and she works with me to help people in our community every day. She is one of many more reasonable models to follow.

Michelle Walker: "I just knew . . . it was up to me"

Michelle Walker heard the call to public service at an early age. Each day Michelle's mother sent her to the grocery store. On her way, Walker's mother also told her daughter to check in with several elderly neighbors to see if they also needed food. "By the time I got to the store," Walker remembers, "I had four or five different lists and four pockets of money."

In her teens, Walker provided another service: reading the mail for neighbors who weren't able to do it themselves. "I didn't realize this was a community service," says Walker. "I just knew my neighbors didn't have the resources. It was up to me."

Years later, she is still helping those who don't

have the resources. Since 1996, she has been director of community programs for the Syracuse University Public Affairs program, working with students to discover and nurture their spirit of public service. She's pretty good at it: last year some 125 students put in more than 19,000 hours of community service at 40 agencies (equaling a minimum wage value of more than $88,000).

Walker is also deeply involved in East-side Neighbors in Partnership, an organization that provides affordable and decent housing to lower-income folks and renovates some of Syracuse's once elegant homes now in disrepair. She is also vice president of the 17th Ward Democratic Committee, a position that allows her to stay invested in the local politics of her community. As busy as Walker is, she still finds time for her family, tennis lessons, and finding bargains in the shopping malls. She doesn't consider herself a "saint"; instead she says, "I honestly don't believe you can live anywhere—city, country, or suburb—and not contribute to the welfare of your community."

If you do not have as much time to devote as Mother Teresa or even Michelle Walker, how much is enough? And can money be a substitute for time? Ultimately, you are the only one who can decide this. In my book, I consider giving five percent of your time or money sufficient to earn you the status of Genuine Do-Gooder.

The point is that limited commitments are good enough for most of us. The average volunteer in this country gives a little more than four hours a week. Five percent is just above this average. At least 40 million people who have full-time jobs and family responsibilities volunteer each week. Genuine Do-Gooders can make varying commitments that range from a total one like Mother Teresa's to a full-time one like Michelle Walker's, to a part-time one like Ellie Spence's of Marin County, California, whose contribution is described in the profile below. Spence has volunteered all her life, but rarely more than an average of five hours a week.

Ellie Spence: Sunday morning do-gooder

Prior to her retirement last year, Ellie Spence was an eighth-grade English teacher who worked 55 hours a week on average (time spent at school plus her work at home grading papers and preparing activities for students). Every Sunday morning for eight years, she would volunteer from 8 A.M. to noon in the visitor center of the Marin County Jail. She would provide refreshments and a welcoming ear to the family members who came to see their loved ones. Ms. Spence felt her services were needed because the jail personnel were brusque with the visitors, many of whom were having a hard time dealing with the surroundings and the situation of those they were visiting. The experience was deeply rewarding for someone who describes herself as a "rescuer."

When the jail closed, she went to the Literacy Volunteers of Marin County and was trained as a literacy volunteer. The Marin County organization is a local chapter of Literacy Volunteers of America (LVA), which has hundreds of local chapters throughout the United States. LVA affiliates are a perfect place for the busy person to volunteer because they have an excellent training program and require a commitment of only about three hours a week after the initial training. Spence chose as her new volunteer site the new county jail. She now helps inmates improve their reading and writing skills.

Now that she has retired, Spence has added a couple of more limited volunteer commitments. She works two hours a month at a church thrift shop and three hours a month at a shelter for the homeless. She spends most of her time with two part-time jobs and visiting with family, especially her grandchildren. However, volunteering is an important part of her life and something she is deeply committed to. That is all we can ask of a Genuine Do-Gooder. For more information on Literacy Volunteers of America contact:

Literacy Volunteers of America
635 James Street
Syracuse, NY 13203
315 472-0001
www.literacyvolunteers.org

It's important that you not overestimate the amount of time and money you can give to helping others. My advice is to think of ways to give your time and money to fit into your life as conveniently as possible. Accepting this viewpoint is one way to avoid being immobilized by standards so high that only someone like Mother Teresa could match them.

Principle 1.2:   **It's okay to have mixed motives**

The second curse of Mother Teresa is that it is hard, if not impossible, to have Mother Teresa's purity of purpose. As I'm sure you know, why people do good is a favorite topic around the dinner table. Religious leaders, politicians, philosophers, and psychologists have suggested numerous reasons for why we help others. My aim is not to convince you of one theory over another, only to emphasize that your motives need not be pure.

Motivating Source of Doing Good

1. Religion, or God made me do it.
2. Psychological need, or my insatiable desire for approval made me do it.
3. Upper-class mores (a.k.a. noblesse oblige), or it is my duty.
4. Guilt, or I got more than I really deserved.
5. Birth order, or I was the oldest child and had to take care of my little brothers and sisters.
6. Rational calculation, or I knew that I would get a payback in the form of actual or symbolic services before my time was up.
7. Role models, or I wanted to be just like _____.
8. Reflex, or I just can't not be helpful.
9. Cultural, or I learned it from the traditions of my ethnic group, my country, or some other definable group to which I belong.
10. Genetics, or I got it from my relatives.
11. Individual competition, or I needed to beat others at raising funds, serving meals, or collecting merit badges.
12. Group competition, or I wanted my company, town, city, state, ethnic group, university, family, bowling league, school, or nation to be #1.
13. The fun of participation, or I enjoy working with other do-gooders.
14. Education, or I learned it in school.
15. Empathy, or when people suffer, I suffer.
16. Money, or I make a living doing good.
17. Immediate circumstances, or I had no other choice but to rescue the cat from the burning house.

18. Early age pattern, or I started doing good things when I was young and just cannot break the habit.
19. Life-changing crisis, or I want to make sure that what happened to me does not happen to others.

Mother Teresa's motivation was fueled by her commitment to her religion. She was also deeply influenced by the volunteer work she did with her mother when she was a child. Your motivation can be mixed. We know from research that people who do good at an early age, like Michelle Walker, are likely to continue doing good throughout their lives. Yet many people also take up the call to do good even if they have not done so in the past. Doing good for the sake of doing good may be the hallmark of Mother Teresa, but doing good because it brings fame, fortune, and pleasure is okay too. What's important is the amount of time and money devoted to doing good and the competence of the do-gooder in helping others at any level.

In many conversations with people about this book, I have been challenged on my view that motives for doing good do not have to be pure. The idea that someone gets paid for doing good or that people do good to receive praise troubles many people. But I maintain that being a Genuine Do-Gooder does not require sainthood. It only requires that you help improve society in one way or another. Why you help make society better is much less important than that you do your best to help.

Principle 1.3: Do-gooders are tough and pragmatic

Too many people are ashamed to admit that they are do-gooders. They don't like the label for the same reason that good students frequently like to hide their academic success from their peers. This reticence is caused by many things—some benign, others not. The most common benign reason is that people do not want to be accused of seeking praise since doing something good should be a reward in itself. Another is that the publicity could lead to a flood of bothersome requests.

The not-so-benign reasons are more revealing about the challenges all do-gooders face. Do-gooders are often thought of as naive optimists. Many ask, why would anyone in their right mind make sacrifices for the benefit of strangers, society, future generations, and those down on their luck? That question is at the heart of why Genuine Do-Gooders are in such short supply and why they face such an uphill battle.

When I began writing this book, I assumed that the term *do-gooder* had a negative connotation. In fact, the purpose of this book is to rescue the term from the ridicule that it receives. I believe the secret to improving society from top to bottom is to have more people do good and admit to doing it. People need to stand up and say, "I am a Genuine Do-Gooder, and I am proud of it." If this happens, more people will learn of each other's good works, and the world will be better for it.

In writing this book, I met with much more resistance than even I imagined. When I mentioned to people that I was writing a book about Genuine Do-Gooders, they frequently thought it was a bad idea. A few got the point immediately, but most were controlled by the knee-jerk stereotype that doing good is for hopeless idealists. One of my friends said, "I assume your book is a work of fiction."

But then a funny thing happened. Many of the people who talked to me about the subject started behaving in a curious way. After saying that they themselves were not do-gooders, they proceeded to tell me all of the things they did to help others and society. "But," they would assure me, "I'm no do-gooder."

Why all of this cynicism and ambiguity? The answer lies in our culture and our history. We are both pragmatic and idealistic, in that order. Our ideals are always tempered by what is possible. We like to be right, but we must be successful.

Doing good is wrongly considered to be more about the ideal than about success and power. It is considered to be more about standing up for what is right and restoring justice in the face of those who have power than about playing a powerful role in the business and government of society. Doing good is viewed as something in which intentions are more important than results. Nothing can be more sinful than that, for a nation built on free enterprise.

Here is where Mother Teresa's life can serve to encourage the hesitant to see themselves as Genuine Do-Gooders and wear the title proudly. In a word, Mother Teresa was a powerhouse. This tough little woman showed that do-gooders can drive hard bargains and get remarkable results. She could never be accused of being naive, ineffective, or in denial. Mother Teresa may have placed the curse of total selflessness on us do-gooders, but her life clearly demonstrates that doing good is not the naive idealism that has given the term a bad name.

Her selflessness and total dedication to the poor gave her a power base, but she had a can-do orientation that makes her a model to be followed by all Genuine Do-Gooders. Though she started with nothing, the organization she founded, the Missionaries of Charities, now has 1,800 missionaries in India and 25 other countries. She accomplished her goals through a combination of toughness, clarity of focus, and the skills of a great negotiator. She was pragmatic, but she never lost sight of her ideals.

There are many stories I could share with you of how she succeeded in the face of overwhelming odds. Here are some of my favorites. She was given a free rail pass from the government of India, and badgered them into giving her a flight pass also. She stopped the military government of Guatemala from turning her inner-city mission into a shopping mall. She could play the media to help her raise support, which is one of the major reasons that most work she did outside of India was done in the United States, and particularly New York City. She used her access to the media to give lectures to support her positions, even the controversial ones, such as her firm stand against abortion. She established 6 small hospices for AIDS victims in New York City and 27 centers across the United States. She was what all Americans value above everything else, a successful and powerful doer.

The words below come from a sign on the wall of Shishu Bhavan, a children's home Mother Teresa established in Calcutta. On one level, they express the deep idealistic commitment to doing good that we associate with Mother Teresa, who is surely destined for sainthood. On another level, they could have been written by Benjamin Franklin or other paragons of American pragmatism.

Anyway*

People are unreasonable, illogical, and self-centered,
LOVE THEM ANYWAY
If you do good, people will accuse you of selfish, ulterior motives,
DO GOOD ANYWAY
If you are successful, you will win false friends and true enemies,
SUCCEED ANYWAY
The good you do will be forgotten tomorrow,
DO GOOD ANYWAY

* Mother Teresa, *Mother Teresa: A Simple Path* (New York: Ballantine Books, 1995), p. 185.

Honesty and frankness make you vulnerable,
BE HONEST AND FRANK ANYWAY
What you spent years building may be destroyed overnight,
BUILD ANYWAY
People really need help but may attack you if you help them,
HELP PEOPLE ANYWAY
Give the world the best you have and you'll get kicked in the teeth,
GIVE THE WORLD THE BEST YOU'VE GOT ANYWAY

These are not the words of someone who is in denial about the realities of a society that needs improving. They are the words of a powerful and successful person who sees those realities and demands of herself and others that something must be done. That is Mother Teresa's legacy for the Genuine Do-Gooder and a blessing that we should build on.

QUIZ RESULTS

1. The more one gains personally from giving time and money, the less genuine the act of doing good.
Answer: No. It is not important for self-sacrifice to be the only motivation for doing good. You can even earn a living doing good as millions of clergy and doctors do every day. What's important is the quantity and quality of the act.
2. Genuine Do-Gooders need to spend only a fraction of their time and money on improving society.
Answer: Yes. Contributing at least five percent of your waking hours or income is enough to make you a Genuine Do-Gooder. Total devotion of time and energy to doing good is impossible for most. Do not make the mistake of not giving because you feel you cannot give enough.
3. Genuine Do-Gooders should refrain as much as possible from letting others know what they are doing.
Answer: No. It is very important that you let people know you are a Genuine Do-Gooder and that you are proud of it. It will show that you have put to rest your own reticence about doing good, and it may inspire others to do the same.

2 The Mission

QUIZ

1. A do-gooder helps others to enjoy life, liberty, and the pursuit of happiness.
Circle one: Yes No Not Sure

2. The primary cause of poverty and other social ills is the failure of individuals to take advantage of the opportunities that exist.
Circle one: Yes No Not Sure

3. Do-gooders should participate extensively in debates over definitions, priorities, and alternative policies so they make sure they do the right thing.
Circle one: Yes No Not Sure

INTRODUCTION

John Kenneth Galbraith is a well-known academic economist who has taught at Harvard since the 1940s. Galbraith's career is not typical of an economist. He has worked in government and chosen to write books accessible to the American public, and not just to his academic colleagues. His book *The Good Society: The Humane Agenda,* published in 1995, provides a map for the Genuine Do-Gooder. Galbraith writes:

> The essence of the good society . . . is that every member, regardless of gender, race or ethnic origin, should have access to a rewarding life. . . . Individuals differ in physical and mental ability, commitment and purpose, and from these differences come differences in achievement and in economic reward. . . . In the good society, however, . . . no

one, from accident of birth or economic circumstance, may be denied these things; if they are not available from parent or family, society must provide effective forms of care and guidance.*

Galbraith's quote is an affirmation of the Declaration of Independence, no more and no less. Everyone should have equal access to:

1. Life, or physical survival in the face of threats from foreign attack, crime, accident, disease, or a harmful environment.
2. Liberty, or the freedom to do or say anything that does not directly threaten others.
3. Pursuit of happiness, or the chance to achieve what each individual perceives as a good life given his or her capacity to use existing resources.

Equal access does not necessarily mean that everyone enjoys equal levels. It means that there must be a level playing field so that the chance of a healthy and long life, liberty, and the pursuit of happiness are not denied by reason of birth.

The contemporary reality of our society is an increasingly slanted playing field, which pushes us away from, rather than toward, the good society. Income and mortality rates for different ethnic groups and different geographical areas vary greatly. People of color and inner-city and rural residents have shorter, less healthy lives and make less money than Caucasians and suburbanites. According to a 1997 public health study, a black male in Detroit can expect to live 64 years compared to 72 years for a white Michigan male. The study also found a 14.5-year disparity in the average life span between men from Washington, D.C., and nearby high-income Fairfax County, VA.** All too frequently, a citizen is denied opportunities due to discrimination by gender, race, religious affiliation, sexual preference, or socioeconomic class. In the good society, such a difference in life expectancy would approach zero. Moving toward the good society requires that we level the playing field without threatening the achievements of those who have already earned them.

I see the mission of the Genuine Do-Gooder as taking actions, big and small, to move America closer to the goals of the good society. This mission statement serves as a compass directing us toward what needs to be done.

*John Kenneth Galbraith, *The Good Society: The Humane Agenda* (New York: Houghton Mifflin Co., 1995), p. 23.
** "U.S. Life Expectancy: Study Shows Regional Variations," *Health Line*, Dec. 4, 1997.

Principle 2.1: Help others to live fuller lives

Genuine Do-Gooders work to level the playing field for all members of society. They do this in thousands of ways depending upon their place in society and their interests and capabilities. They do it in one-on-one relationships like Mother Teresa's missionaries or, like Tammy Kissell Fields, they do good in a combination of ways as both rowers and steerers. They do it through working for big organizations like the Salvation Army or small organizations like a local library. They do it by typing a mailing list for a library fundraiser or serving as a foster grandparent to a newborn. They do it through lobbying for campaign finance reform or working on the board of directors of a community center. As you meet many Genuine Do-Gooders throughout this book, you will see that the settings and jobs are infinite.

Tammy Kissell Fields: Role at school is top priority

Tammy Kissell Fields, who is now in her late thirties, advises us to "look no further than the nearest school. Whatever your hidden talents, the school can use you. Just reading a book is always appreciated." Fields works monthly in a classroom on art projects at her son's school. She also chairs the school's advisory committee, sits on the district Compliance Monitoring Committee, which monitors the integration agreement with the Office of Civil Rights, and is on the board of directors of the Florida Rural Legal Services. However, she says, "I know my committee and board work makes a difference, but I feel like I've accomplished something every time I leave the classroom after an art project. Hugs from the children and 'When are you coming back?' melt my heart."

The acid test of whether or not your actions can be classified as doing good, then, depends on whether you help one or more individuals have a better chance for:

1. A long and healthy life.
2. Freedom of choice and expression.
3. Ample opportunities to pursue their own happiness.

All Genuine Do-Gooders share this common mission. However, they may disagree on precise definitions of the words "life, liberty, and the pursuit of happiness."

Principle 2.2: **Don't stop with talk: Walk!**

Recognizing that definitions are open to different interpretations and that Genuine Do-Gooders can attach different priorities to the goals of the good society does not reduce the usefulness of our mission statement. Doing good is an inherently ambiguous activity, and uncertainty cannot be avoided if you want to make a difference.

The key is to not get bogged down over disagreements. Talking about our problems should never be an end in itself. For example, research can provide some evidence on what works and what does not. But research rarely provides conclusive evidence of success or failure for any given policy because so many complicated factors must be taken into consideration. Research on the impact of Head Start programs, which are designed to provide pre-kindergarten education to the disadvantaged, is far from conclusive. Research and reports conducted by Head Start found that the programs' participants get early literacy and verbal skills they would not have obtained otherwise. A legislative study on Dayton, Ohio, schools, on the other hand, found Head Start graduates to be no better prepared for kindergarten than similar risk groups with no pre-schooling. Congress's watchdog agency, the General Accounting Office, even questions whether Head Start reports accurately evaluate the programs' achievement of school and social readiness.*

Does this mean you shouldn't support Head Start programs in your area? My advice is to visit them and decide for yourself. Remember that research can help guide the action of the Genuine Do-Gooder, but while research is more useful than uninformed discussions, it can consume large amounts of money and human capital, some of which could be put to better use by direct action. Talk and research should be viewed as the fertilizer that can lead to action. Discussion of the causes of problems in our society and what to do about them can stimulate growth and creative action. Too much discussion, like too much fertilizer, will destroy the action at its very roots. It is better to take action like the thousands of Points of Light honorees have year after year. As mentioned earlier, throughout the

---

* "Head Start Can Take Hit, Even Get Better," *Dayton Daily News*, June 5, 1998, city ed.: 14A.

book I will refer to the Points of Light honorees. The profile below introduces you to this important organization that honors those who take action.

Awards focus spotlight on good deeds

The Points of Light Foundation was established in 1990 to encourage volunteerism at the national level. Its mission is to "engage people more effectively in volunteer community service to help solve serious social problems." The Points of Light Foundation fulfills its mission by providing leadership, training, programs, and publications to people in the public and private sectors to encourage volunteer action in local community service efforts. It has three major awards programs:

The President's Service Awards—the "highest honor given by the President of the United States to outstanding individuals, families, groups, organizations, businesses and labor unions engaged in voluntary service to help solve serious social problems."

The Daily Points of Light Award—cosponsored by the Points of Light Foundation, the Corporation for National Service, and the Knights of Columbus, this award "honors and publicizes daily those who have made a commitment to connect Americans through service to help meet critical needs in their communities, especially those needs focused on youth."

Awards for Corporate Excellence in Community Service—"recognizes businesses for the excellence of their overall employee volunteer program."

For more information about the Points of Light award programs, write or call:

The Points of Light Foundation
1400 I Street, NW, Suite 800
Washington, DC 20005
Tel. 202 729-8184
http://www.pointsoflight.org

Action, however, even based on solid research, is not sufficient by itself. It must be followed by careful, consistent, and serious evaluation of its results. These evaluations, as we have already seen with respect to studies on the Head Start program, are not definitive. Instead, the evaluations can only contribute to another cycle of talk and research and then adjusted action. Think in terms of a triangle that consists of talk and research, action, and evaluation of the results of that action as depicted below. The Genuine Do-Gooder should devote time to all three corners of the triangle. Talk and research, action, and evaluation should eventually lead to better results as adjustments are made based on the continuous cycling among the three.

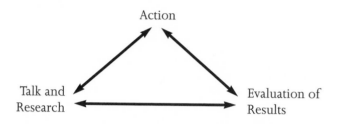

Action

Talk and Research

Evaluation of Results

Principle 2.3: **Respect the right of others to differ**

Given the uncertainty we have just discussed, Genuine Do-Gooders are likely to find themselves in intense struggles with each other. For example, consider movie star Charleton Heston, president of the National Rifle Association, and Sarah Brady, whose husband, Jim Brady, was paralyzed in an attempted assassination of President Ronald Reagan in 1982, and who now heads an organization seeking to control the purchase of handguns. They may be bitter opponents but they are both Genuine Do-Gooders. In this case, the root of the disagreement is that Heston gives a higher priority to liberty and Brady attaches more importance to the preservation of life. There is no possibility of a general resolution to their disagreement, but compromise over specific policies is possible.

Genuine Do-Gooders can be found throughout the political spectrum. The ideological and policy position of those working to improve opportunities for life, liberty, and the pursuit of happiness in America is not relevant in determining whether or not an individual is a Genuine Do-Gooder. The concept is nonpartisan and nonideological.

There is one very critical proviso, however. Every Genuine Do-Gooder must respect the right of others to participate in the processes that promote the good society. Extremists who attempt to silence and intimidate those they disagree with cannot be considered Genuine Do-Gooders. This includes those who use or threaten to use violence and those who use more subtle forms of intimidation to silence their opponents. Part of the definition of a Genuine Do-Gooder is that they will do no intentional harm to others or to society. Individuals who fail to respect the diversity of missions do harm directly to those whom they disrespect and to the very foundation of our democratic society.

QUIZ RESULTS

1. A do-gooder helps others to enjoy life, liberty, and the pursuit of happiness.
Answer: Yes. The basic mission of any do-gooder is to help othershave a better chance to enjoy life, liberty, and the pursuit of happiness. Ultimately, the responsibility still rests with individuals to help themselves, but the Genuine Do-Gooder can work to level the playing field.

2. The primary cause of poverty and other social ills is the failure of individuals to take advantage of the opportunities that exist.
Answer: No. All personal suffering is some combination of society's conditions and the individual's mistake. Any attempt to make a general statement about which is the primary cause is a waste of time. In any given situation, the environment may have played a larger role than the individual or vice versa. Participating indefinitely in such arguments may be an excuse for talking about, rather than acting on, the problem.

3. Do-gooders should participate extensively in debates over definitions, priorities, and alternative policies to make sure they do the right thing.
Answer: No. Uncertainty over the consequences of the actions of do-gooders, whether tutoring a child or shaping environmental policy, must be the accepted reality of the Genuine Do-Gooder. Looking for definitive lists of causes and policies that always work is okay, but only if limited by the need to act and then to evaluate the results of those actions.

3 Organize Thyself

1. Genuine Do-Gooders must sacrifice their careers and their opportunity for fun in order to have the time to do good.
Circle one: Yes   No   Not Sure

2. There are countless windows of opportunity for you to do good.
Circle one: Yes   No   Not Sure

3. Genuine Do-Gooders must fight injustice wherever they see it.
Circle one: Yes   No   Not Sure

INTRODUCTION

You need to decide how much time you want to devote to doing good. Some people spend their entire lives or large chunks of their time, perhaps as much as 20 hours a week, making society better. Think about your life and your commitments; whatever time commitment you make should involve thoughtful planning.

Think of your life as a tapestry in which four types of thread are woven together. The four threads are: work, family, play, and doing good. How you weave these threads together, and which threads you use the most, must be of your own design. I would not presume to tell you how to design your tapestry, but I can provide you with some guidelines.

Principle 3.1: **Weave doing good into your life**

Your service to others can range from the five percent minimum to every waking minute.

You can make different choices about how much you want to serve for different stages of your life. In your twenties, thirties, and forties you may spend the bulk of your time working and raising a family but have some time for doing good and playing. From your fifties on, you may have more "free" time for activities outside work. If you want to do more for others than you are now doing, you should study your current activities and see if you can make some choices that will give you additional time. If that is not possible, you should do some planning and training now so that when you move to the next stage of your life you will be ready and able to do more.

Spending more than 40 hours a week doing good requires that you retire or find a career that fulfills your need to do good. The 40-hour cutoff point is, like all such guidelines, arbitrary. Some may spend slightly more than 40 hours a week on average and still have a full-time job. Others might find anything over 20 hours a week of volunteer work too much if they hold a full-time job. However, as you approach the 40-hour-per-week limit, you will find it increasingly difficult to meet your job and family responsibilities.

There are two ways to do good for more than 40 hours a week and not sacrifice your work and family. One is to get one of the millions of business, government, and nonprofit jobs that serve society in such fields as education, health, criminal justice, and the environment. That is what Michelle Walker and millions of others have done. Choosing a career where you get paid to do good full time will be discussed in chapter 7, where we will briefly describe the wide range of careers available and how to get information on them. Your other option is to retire and take on a full-time volunteer commitment, a topic that will be discussed in chapter 14. Retirement assumes that you have the financial resources to do so regardless of your age.

There are just not enough hours in the day for you to devote more than 40 hours a week to doing good if you work in most private sector jobs. You will burn out, failing as a do-gooder, worker, or both. Don't despair at that decision. Accept it so that you can make the most of the time you can devote to doing good.

Tyrone Gaines, whose profile appears below, spends close to

40 hours a week working to improve his community. Gaines is driven to devote almost as much time and energy to his cause as he spends on his family and job.

Tyrone Gaines: Hoops, "trash busters," and grannies

Tyrone Gaines, who is the Daily Point of Light Award Winner for July 27, 1998, puts 2,000 hours a year (nearly 40 hours a week) into doing good while holding down a job as a full-time information systems operator at Baltimore Gas and Electric. Many of the Daily Point of Light winners who have full-time jobs give more than the five-hour minimum.

Gaines volunteers to make his neighborhood a better place to live. In 1971, when Gaines was 16, he started a basketball league in an effort to unite the community following the murder of a 12-year-old. Today, more than 200 players, ages 7 to 35, participate in the Reservoir Hill Rivalry Community Basketball League, funded primarily by Gaines's personal income. From that base, he has developed other volunteer programs, including "Trash Busters," the Granny Committee, and the Reservoir Hill Coalition, which raises money for community events.

Gaines is at the upper limit of time commitment for someone who has a job and family responsibilities. If you approach that limit, you need to think seriously about a change in career. You could try to get a paid position in a local Boys and Girls Club or establish your own nonprofit organization and seek government funding. Short of that, you need to make sure that your time commitment does not get in the way of your other responsibilities.

Doing good can be woven into work or play. You don't have to earn a living serving society in order to do good. In fact, Scott Liebert has provided us with a list of his good deeds in the profile below, demonstrating that doing good can be fun and can also help your career. Liebert has his own independent insurance agency; but as you can see, he spends as much as 10 hours a week in some activity that serves to improve society.

Scott Liebert: A life of community service

This is a list that Liebert, one of my 1978 alumni, responded with when I sent a call out to selected alumni to ask them how they are doing good.

- Serve as member of the New York Blood Bank Gallon Club.
- Headed various committees for Rotary Club for more than 10 years.
- Served as president of the local Rotary Club.
- Served on board and as president of the local Independent Insurance Agents Association.
- Served as board member for the Rockland Council for Young Children.
- Served as board member for the Rockland Community College Foundation.
- Served as co-chairman of Build Nanuet Highview Wooden Playground.
- Serve as an usher once a month in my church.
- Donate my employees' time, with their consent, to deliver Meals on Wheels once a month.
- Served as board member of the United Way of Rockland County.
- Served as vice president of the board of the Meals on Wheels of Rockland County.
- Served on the advisory board of St. Thomas Aquinas College.
- Decorate my home on Halloween extensively for the fun and joy of the local children.

Doing good, therefore, does not necessarily have to conflict with your work, family, or play. You can do good full time, by retiring, or getting a job that pays you to do so, or you can spend between 5 and 40 hours a week doing good. You can weave doing good into the tapestry of your life. The point to remember is to decide what's right for you.

Principle 3.2:   Search for opportunities nearby

Where do you want to help? Your family, your town, your workplace, and your social activities will provide nearby windows through which you can give your time or your money. "Nearby" may mean you are geographically near, but the window of opportunity may also be close to you because of a shared purpose.

Your nearest window is your family. You can play a large role in your own family by fulfilling your obligations to them. In many cases working to improve conditions for your family will lead you to work on community conditions. This is especially true if you have children. Your support for their education could lead you to become active in their school, or your support for their participation in sports could lead you to manage league activities.

After your family, your nearest windows of opportunity are where you live, where you work, and where you socialize or participate in educational or spiritual activities. From these immediate bases, you can move to nearby political windows; first at the local level and then at the state and national levels. The opportunities presented by nearby windows are unlimited and are described in Part Three.

Starting nearby makes sense for several reasons:

1. You will already know something about the setting, so you can more easily determine what needs to be done and how.
2. You will have more opportunities for strong and frequent interactions with the members and leaders of the organization, making it more likely that your voice will be heard.
3. You are likely to see success and failure more clearly if you start nearby, because you interact at a personal level with those affected by and those causing the change.

The nearby-window principle can feel constrictive at first, because it means skipping the charm and excitement of working on far-away windows right away. Worrying about global hunger, civil war in Sudan, or global warming is important and necessary for all of us. However, you can't do much more than give money to organizations that deal directly with these problems. It is important to concentrate your efforts on closer issues that you understand and can access directly through critical players.

Sticking to nearby windows will help you avoid abstract discussions that lead nowhere. For example, instead of debating with your neighbors at the Sunday barbecue whether or not money can make a difference in improving urban education throughout the United States, you should discuss whether or not it would make a difference in a nearby school district. The tone and content of the debate would become more productive. Would you donate your time and effort? Would you vote for a state representative who was calling for redistribution of aid that would potentially reduce funds in your own district?

The nearby-window principle does not mean you are helpless to act against far-away problems. During the the era of apartheid, for example, college students and corporate stockholders put pressure on the South African government by lobbying their own organizations to cease investing in or doing business with South Africa.

Principle 3.3: Steerers should know how to row

What kind of help do you want to give? Are you interested in creating a new organization? Helping an existing one? Do you want to tutor a child in math or do you want to found a program that recruits math experts in your community to help tutor kids at the local elementary school? In other words, do you want to be a rower or a steerer?

Rowing requires concentrated efforts and specialized skills where the focus is on specific repetitive tasks. Steering requires the analysis of information and the integration of different viewpoints to be applied when making decisions in a changing environment. For an organization to serve its purpose, decisions must be made by steerers and then acted upon by rowers.

In most cases, the distinction needs to be maintained to avoid disorganization and inefficiency. Waiters in a restaurant do not generate the menu. Stockers in a grocery store do not decide where to shelve the chicken soup. Similarly, managers in a restaurant do not wait on tables and grocery store owners do not stock shelves. Rowers who take it upon themselves to steer and steerers who spend too much of their time rowing upset the normal functioning of organizations. Each is required to act in their capacity to execute the mission of the organization. Mutual respect and appreciation of the interdependence between rowers and steerers is a prerequisite to improving conditions at any level of society.

The distinction is critical in deciding how to make your contribution to improving society. The demands of rowing are different from the demands of steering for the four roles of the do-gooder: volunteer, donor, citizen, and paid employee. These four roles are discussed in the next four chapters, but it would be helpful to discuss briefly what kinds of activities are associated with them for both rowers and steerers.

Rowers who volunteer do the repetitive things like tutoring a child, reading to the elderly, distributing food at a food pantry, or soliciting funds. Rowers who are donors send in their checks. Rowers fulfilling citizen roles might serve as election observers or work on a government-sponsored clean-up. A Social Security caseworker or a laboratory technician at the Centers for Disease Control may be people who "row" for their cause.

Steerers who volunteer might serve on a board of directors or head a committee to raise funds. As donors, steerers seek to shape and evaluate the policies of the organizations to which they donate. As citizens, steerers work for candidates on their campaigns or serve on planning boards. Careers in steering might include directing a non-profit organization, heading a government department, or managing the fundraising activities of a charity.

One of the pitfalls of do-gooders is the mistaken belief that steering is more important than rowing. This forces many people who would be perfectly good rowers to become perfectly ineffective steerers. Keep in mind that both types of activities are necessary and worthwhile.

The relationship between rowers and steerers can be enhanced greatly if steerers have an intimate knowledge of the rowers' tasks. The best way to do this is for the steerers to emerge from the ranks of rowers and, on occasion, pitch in as a rower. Business leaders who want their sons and daughters to take over their businesses apply this principle when they require their children to learn the business from the ground up. Steerers emerging out of the ranks of rowers increase the likelihood of two things—that steerers will make better decisions by knowing what is necessary to row effectively and that rowers will support the decisions of the steerers because they know the steerers have "been there."

Reuben Greenberg: Always an on-duty do-gooder

Reuben Greenberg is good at combining rowing and steering in a meaningful way. As police chief of Charleston, South Carolina, most of the time he steers by setting policies. However, he believes that the most effective steerers are those who continue to row on occasion. He believes in never asking others to do something you would not do. His ultimate integration of rowing and steering occurred when, as he was driving to the scene of an accident, Greenberg bumped into another car and, when all was said and done, wrote himself a ticket.

Greenberg continues to be "on duty" even when he is off duty. He directs traffic or works one-on-one with a parent of a troublesome teenager. He is constantly thinking about how to "put the crooks out of business," and will try different strategies to do just that. His primary operating principle is that just as he holds himself responsible for his own performance, he holds those who break the law responsible for their own behavior.

Principle 3.4:   Focus, focus, focus

Excuse the repetitiveness of this principle, but many do-gooders need to be hit by a two-by-four to get their attention on this focus thing. Focus means:

1. Clearly defining a limited goal.
2. Identifying measures for determining your successes and failures.
3. Making the commitment in time and energy to do what needs to be done.

Reuben Greenberg stayed in the same job despite numerous opportunities to "move up" so that he could concentrate on reducing crime in Charleston. In addition, his strategy on reducing crime maintained a strong emphasis on juveniles and young adults.

Without proper focus, you may take on too many causes and will most likely end up doing more harm than good. For example, at the rowing level, you may move too quickly from one volunteer job, such as tutoring middle school students, to another job, leaving in your wake some very disappointed and disenchanted students. At the steering level, you may serve on too many boards to guide the organizations effectively and responsibly. Over-committed board members simply can't keep track of their organizations. You need to pick a cause and stick with it, rather than starting projects and failing to follow through.

The greatest change agents of the 20th century—Mother Teresa, Mahatma Gandhi, Martin Luther King, Jr., and Nelson Mandela—showed a willingness to stick to a few goals and to pursue them over long periods with great personal sacrifice. Other leaders with accomplishments in particular fields like medicine, environmental protection, and civil rights have had the same kind of dedication. You may not match the accomplishments of these major do-gooders, but, if you focus your efforts on a nearby window and work hard at both rowing and steering, you will accomplish much more than you ever imagined. As Mother Teresa once told someone who wanted to follow her to India to do good, "Do the right thing in front of you."

QUIZ RESULTS

1. Genuine Do-Gooders must sacrifice their careers and their opportunity for fun in order to have the time to do good.
Answer: No. It is possible to weave these threads into a tightly woven tapestry. The choices you make will determine how many trade-offs you make in order to spend time on doing good.

2. There are countless windows of opportunity for you to do good.
Answer: No. Genuine Do-Gooders avoid going into areas where they do not have strong knowledge and experience. They build up their expertise as a base for broader impact.

3. Genuine Do-Gooders must fight injustice wherever they see it.
Answer: No. The key is to focus on your primary mission. This may mean ignoring other problems, but it is the only viable strategy for solving problems effectively.

II

Ways You Can Help

4 Effective Volunteering

I N T R O D U C T I O N

Chris Zorich was a star defensive lineman for the Chicago Bears, but he is a serious Genuine Do-Gooder. He supports nationwide programs, but mainly his focus is on his nearby window of the Chicago area. As a volunteer and donor, he is both a rower and a steerer.

Chris Zorich: A firm foundation in giving

Chris Zorich was born and raised on Chicago's South Side, and spent nearly his entire professional career playing for the Chicago Bears. He has formed the Christopher Zorich Foundation, which helps those in need by fostering a sense of community caring that crosses all religious, racial, and economic boundaries.

For Zorich, 1991 was a year of ups and downs. He graduated from the University of Notre Dame and was selected in the National Football League draft by the Chicago Bears. Those accomplishments were overshadowed, however, by the untimely passing of his mother, Zora. Two years later, he formed the foundation in her honor.

Annually, CZF endorses several programs, each with different purposes. As a memorial to his mother, Zorich provides financial assistance to Chicago-area students through the Zora Zorich Scholarships at Notre Dame University, Lewis University in Romeoville, Illinois, and the Chicago Vocational Career Academy, Zorich's high school alma mater.

Among his many projects are:

• Care to Share Family Food, which delivers food to families twice a year.
• Love Grows Here, inspired by his mother, which gives gifts like flowers, cosmetics, and personal care items to low-income women.
• School Is Cool, which allows Zorich to speak to students about the importance of staying in school.

According to his foundation's literature, his efforts have assisted more than 50,000 individuals. Zorich has worked as a rower, counseling youth, and he has worked as a steerer by directing his foundation and by sitting on the boards of several charitable nonprofits. He has received more than 50 humanitarian and public service awards.

He continues these activities today even though at 30 he is a first-year law student at Notre Dame Law School. Clearly, Zorich has made doing good a personal lifestyle.

Zorich is like thousands of people in all walks of life and from every corner of the country who give their time to help others. They may not have the public visibility and the financial resources that he does, but they have the commitment, the heart, the drive, and the power to make a difference in their world.

The Independent Sector, an organization based in Washington, DC, that represents a coalition of voluntary agencies, foundations, and corporate giving programs, indicates that the equivalent of $201.5 billion in volunteer services were performed in 1995, up from $182.5 billion in 1993. It estimates that 93 million adults and

13 million young people, or close to 50 percent of the eligible population, volunteers 4.2 hours a week on average.

The 4.2-hour average clearly indicates that most volunteer work is done as part of an already fully packed life. The key is to make the most of your time volunteering and to find opportunities that will satisfy your needs for volunteering in the first place.

Principle 4.1:   Search as you would for a job

Where do you want to help? Deciding what organization to volunteer for may at first seem overwhelming. There are so many wonderful organizations that can use your help that at first it may be difficult to choose. In their book *By the People: A History of Americans as Volunteers*, Susan J. Ellis and Katherine H. Noyes describe in detail how people who assumed responsibilities through concrete actions have had a huge impact on the United States.

Below is Ellis and Noyes's list of 15 areas in which volunteering takes place. Selected examples drawn from their book are provided for each of the areas; they are far from comprehensive, but they should give you a good place to start.

Fields and Places of Volunteer Activity*

LABOR AND EMPLOYMENT
- Unions: volunteers serve as representatives and local shop stewards, and also sponsor community service projects.
- Mutual benefit: organizations offer employees group travel rates and aid in times of crisis.

AGRICULTURE AND FOOD
- Farmers' and ranchers' cooperatives: volunteers share information, coordinate marketing and pricing, and plan social activities.
- Youth groups: volunteers provide agricultural education and recreational outlets for young people.

BUSINESS AND INDUSTRY
- Trade associations: people volunteer in organizations of the same industry to deal with mutual problems.
- In-kind services and donations: corporations or individual businesses extend help by fund-raising or donations.

---

* Adapted from chapter in Susan J. Ellis and Katherine H. Noyes, *By The People: A History of Americans as Volunteers* (San Francisco: Jossey-Bass, 1990), pp. 315–37.

COMMUNICATIONS
• Public access television: communities produce their own cable television shows on public service issues.
• License review: volunteers decide whether to approve broadcasting license applications for the FCC and on the local level.

PUBLIC TRANSPORTATION
• Public transportation advocacy: groups pressure for more and better bus and subway services.
• Commuters: volunteers lobby for improved transportation services, and car and van pools.

RELIGION
• Missions: volunteers serve as missionaries at home and abroad.
• Religious education: church members volunteer to educate children at Sunday schools and in youth groups.

RECREATION AND LEISURE
• Sports enthusiasts: volunteers seek to improve parks and facilities as well as form recreational clubs.
• Parks and forest service: volunteers repair shelters, maintain trails, patrol campgrounds, and raise money.

CULTURAL ARTS
• Public commissions and trusts: volunteers serve as trustees, advisers, and board members.
• Arts support: individuals and businesses give money and technical advice to performing arts groups.

ENVIRONMENTAL QUALITY
• Conservation: volunteers work the protection of the wilderness and endangered wildlife.
• Animal protection: groups work to protect animals from abuse and scientific experimentation.

JUSTICE
• Prisons and institutions: volunteers act as visitors, activity leaders, instructors, and counselors.
• Delinquency prevention: volunteers work to prevent juvenile crime by offering recreational activities, leadership development programs, and counseling.

PUBLIC SAFETY
• Volunteer fire companies: men and women are involved in running the company, fundraising, and combating fires.

- Police support: citizens handle nonemergency functions, assist at public events, patrol streets, and form neighborhood watch-dog agreements.

MILITARY

- Veterans projects: volunteers organize services to aid veterans with jobs, counseling, medical support, and Memorial Day programs.
- Community service: volunteers in the armed forces assist in holiday programs, projects, and youth education.

INTERNATIONAL CAUSES

- Relief efforts: activities to raise goods and money for crisis situations overseas.
- Technical aid: volunteers give their technical expertise to underdeveloped nations through organizations such as the Peace Corps.

POLITICAL AND SOCIAL ACTION

- Town government: citizens are active in public office, committees, and block associations.
- Consumerism: citizens engage in efforts to help, protect, and benefit the consumer.

HUMAN SERVICES

- Hospices: volunteers help terminally ill patients and their families.
- Public health: men and women help with immunization campaigns, serve on poison prevention teams, staff hotlines, and ensure the provision of free medical services.

Given the number and variety of volunteer activities, you owe it to yourself and to those who benefit from your efforts to search for volunteer opportunities just as you would search for a job.

As a volunteer you are investing your free time, which is your only nonrenewable resource, in something that must, when all is said and done, give you satisfaction. Ideally, that's the same criterion for choosing a job. The difference is that salary is not a consideration, which allows you to be even more selective with your decision. And selective you should be; too many times plunging into a volunteer opportunity without carefully thinking through the decision can lead to frustrating results.

To help you plan your search, think in terms of the triangle presented below. There are three points you should consider. First, you must decide what mission you would like to work toward. Next you should determine what activities you enjoy. Finally, you should consider characteristics of the agency with which you would like to volunteer. These three points require you to think about what you want to accomplish as a volunteer and match that to an opportunity that is available.

The Volunteer Search Triangle

Activities You Will
Be Doing

Mission of
the Organization

Characteristics of
the Ideal Agency

Although the three points of the triangle are all connected, the most important point is deciding what mission you would like to work toward. Defining the mission you are interested in will help to narrow the agencies you would like to volunteer for and the activities you will do. For example, are you interested in finding a cure for cancer, caring for the elderly, or helping young people learn to read? If you are interested in helping young people learn to read, you might volunteer at a local library by organizing a reading hour for children or you might volunteer at an elementary school as a reading tutor. Below is a list of some popular missions. You can use it to help you determine where your volunteering interests lie.

Possible Missions and Opportunities for Involvement

FIGHTING DISEASE
• Education
• Service
• Fundraising

FIGHTING HUNGER
• Crop walk
• Soup kitchen
• Harvesting

IMPROVING LITERACY
• Advocacy for children, teens, adults
• Tutoring for children, teens, adults
• Mentoring for children, teens, adults

AIDING THE SICK
• Hospitals
• Red Cross
• Hospice care

PROMOTING THE ARTS
• Museums
• Theaters
• Local schools

IMPROVING HOUSING
• Advocacy for homeless
• Renovation/building
• Yard and community work

IMPROVING THE ENVIRONMENT
• Clean-ups
• Advocacy
• Education

IMPROVING ELDERLY CARE
• Nursing homes
• Alzheimer's organizations
• Hospitals

HELPING WOMEN
• Women's shelters
• Domestic violence prevention
• Hotlines for victims

HELPING CHILDREN
• Day care
• Recreation/activities
• Crisis center

HELPING THE DISABLED
• Mental/physical therapy
• Companionship
• Advocacy

IMPROVING EDUCATION
• Tutoring/mentoring
• Teacher aids
• PTA

The activities you undertake as a volunteer will be partially determined by your ideal mission, although most activities can be used to support different missions in different agencies. For example, if you enjoy cooking, you could prepare food for bake sales at a nearby school, serve as a cook in a homeless or elderly shelter, or prepare food on holidays and special occasions for needy families. If you enjoy planning special events, you could organize a local sports team, organize a crop walk, raise money for your mission, or organize a local church to donate food to a pantry.

Types of Volunteer Activities

ADMINISTRATION
• Board member
• Committee/consultant
• Facilitator

CLERICAL/OFFICE WORK
• Receptionist
• Bookkeeper
• Computer operator/
data entry
• General office aide
• Library aide
• Mailings handler
• Registrar
• Researcher
• Typist
• Word processor

COMMUNICATION
• Conference/workshop
planner
• Graphic designer
• Newsletter designer
• Photographer
• Public relations aide
• Public speaker
• Publicity flack
• Writer
Counseling
• Arbitrator/mediator
• Advocate

• Crisis/hotline staffer
• Drug/alcohol counselor

FOOD SERVICE
• Food server
• Kitchen help
• Menu planner

HEALTH SERVICES
• Blood collection aide
• Blood pressure screener
• Patient escort
• Rehabilitation worker
• Health educator

PEOPLE
• Liaison/group leader
• Mentor
• Support provider
• Victims assistance worker

CRAFTS
• Arts/drawing aide
• Calligrapher
• Flower arranger
• Knitter
• Seamstress
• Woodworker

DISASTER TEAMS
• Ambulance driver
• Firefighter
• Medical emergency technician

Once you have determined the mission you are interested in and the activities you would like to do, you need to find an agency where you would enjoy volunteering. First you should consider volunteering in "nearby windows." This would allow you to have greater understanding and power because you would be trying to do good in a setting with which you are familiar. Many people enjoy volunteering with friends, also another plus to starting nearby. If nothing else, volunteering nearby will save on transportation since you are already in that area for other reasons. Part III of this book suggests types of opportunities you may find through your family, neighborhood, social organizations, place of employment, and other avenues.

If you would prefer to expand your horizons and look beyond nearby windows, but are not sure how to go about it, follow these steps:

1. Contact the agencies in your area that match people who want to volunteer with the agencies that need volunteers. Check the phone book.

2. If you are unable to locate a volunteer coordination agency, get help from a great service provided by the Points of Light Foundation. Call 800-VOLUNTE[er] (865-8683) and choose option 1, which will require you to enter your zip code. You will receive the phone number of the volunteer center working with the foundation in your area. If you would like some general ideas on where to volunteer without the help of a coordinator, press 3.

3. You can also use the Volunteer Match Service. Visit its Web site at http://www.volunteermatch.org.

4. An increasingly popular approach has been developed by City Cares of America, which has Care groups in more than 24 cities (and growing) across the United States. Recognizing the increasing time required for work and other commitments, City Cares provides specific projects from existing nonprofit organizations. The Web site below will lead to the City Cares organization closest to you.

   City Cares of America
   PO Box 7866
   Atlanta, GA 30357
   Tel. 404 875-7334
   http://www.citycares.org

5. You may want to start a new activity on your own. If so, first search for similar projects from around the world. Begin with

the publications of Ignite the Community Spirit, 500 West Roy, W. 107, Seattle, Washington 98119, 206 283-4385, or visit its Web site at http://www.gstech.com/ignite. Its newsletter, *I Can,* and two books, *Ignite the Community Spirit: 300 Creative Ideas for Community Involvement* and *301 Ways to Turn Caring into Action,* which is a compilation of three years of the *I Can* newsletter, will give you plenty of ideas and directions on how to go about starting something new. More on creating new organizations appears in chapter 20 of this book.

6. If you have a computer connected to the Internet and would like to volunteer from you home, look into "virtual volunteering," which allows you to help anywhere in the world through your computer. Visit the Volunteer Match and click on virtual volunteering to learn about thousands of opportunities for any cause you can think of.

Regardless of whether you decide to work near your home or in a different location, you should consider the characteristics of the ideal agency with which you would like to volunteer. The agency you work for will have characteristics that you may or may not like. You may find its location inconvenient. You may or may not like the people. You may prefer a tightly organized operation or one that is more open-ended. All of these features can be classified as "agency characteristics" and need to be incorporated in your decision making. Characteristics that you should consider are listed below. Use this to help find the best place for you.

Considerations in Choosing an Agency

ASK YOURSELF: If I were going to volunteer at an organization, what characteristics of that organization would be most important to me?

AGENCY MANAGEMENT
• Volunteer coordinator available
• Job descriptions available
• Training available
• Size and age of agency

TIME COMMITMENT
• Holidays
• Seasonal
• Mornings
• Afternoons
• Evenings
• Weekends
• Short-term (less than six weeks)
• Long-term (six or more weeks)
• One-day special projects/events

LOCATION
• Urban or rural
• Public transportation
• Parking
• Handicap accessible

WHO YOU WOULD BE WORKING WITH	• By yourself
• For presidents	• In groups
• For managers	• The elderly
• For supervisors	• Adults
	• Teenagers or children

You also need to make sure that the agency will make good use of your time. Ask if there is a volunteer training program and if there are specific job descriptions at your agency. Talk to the volunteer coordinator to see if you can communicate easily and can get in touch with him or her without playing telephone tag. This research will help you avoid disappointment and frustration. However, you will need to tolerate some weaknesses of agencies because too often they are underfunded, understaffed, and dealing with problems that can be overwhelming. Nevertheless, it is better to enter your volunteer activity with realistic expectations than to have no idea about what you will be facing.

The Independent Sector has provided tips for volunteers, which appear below:

Ten tips on volunteering wisely*

1. Research the causes or issues important to you. You may want to start your volunteer experience with an organization that you are already donating money to or one that deals with issues you feel strongly about.
2. Consider the skills you have to offer. Many volunteer opportunities require a person to be familiar with certain equipment, therefore choose a position that allows you to incorporate your skills and personality.
3. Would you like to learn something new? Nonprofit organizations have demonstrated a need for people who are dedicated and willing to learn new skills. This gives you a chance to enhance your abilities, but be sure that you are willing to commit to the responsibilities involved.
4. Don't overcommit your schedule. Life is hectic, so be careful not to overschedule your time and end up shortchanging the organization you are trying to help.
5. Nonprofits have questions, too. Remember that it is in an organization's interest to make certain you have the skills,

*Toolkit on Volunteering, #2 in the Giving Voice to Your Heart series (Washington, DC: Independent Sector, 1997) and Give Five brochure (Washington, DC: Independent Sector, 1998).

time, and interest that best match those of a nonprofit. So don't be weary if they ask you for an interview or for background information.

6. Consider volunteering as a family. Family involvement with a nonprofit organization not only helps others. It teaches children values and skills, and brings the entire family closer together.

7. Virtual volunteering? Computer access to the Internet can open a wide range of opportunities for volunteers, especially if your time is limited.

8. I never thought of that! Volunteer opportunities available in your community: local theaters, shelters, recreation centers, prisons, parks, halfway houses, or even fraternal organizations.

9. Be a year-round volunteer. We all need to be aware that making our communities, our nation, and our world a better place is a year-round job that always needs your support.

10. Give voice to your heart through your giving and volunteering. Enthusiasm, sincerity, and humor are priceless gifts that will make volunteering a pleasurable and memorable experience.

Principle 4.2: Don't let agencies abuse you

As a homeowner, you would not tolerate the furnace running full blast in the middle of winter while the windows are wide open. As a Genuine Do-Gooder, you should not tolerate wasted volunteer time or energy. If you have done any volunteering, you know that volunteer abuse can be a problem.

At the rowing level, for example, you volunteer at an inner-city school. You are told to arrive at the school at 8:30 A.M. You arrive on time, but the coordinator does not show up until 9:15. The coordinator tells you to go to Mrs. Smith's room and get Johnny out of class so that he can be given special help in math. You knock on the door, and the teacher says, "Who told you to take Johnny? He needs to stay here." Mix-ups such as this are bound to happen occasionally. However, in too many volunteer sites around the country, this type of mix-up is common.

Volunteers can also be abused at the steering level. They can be placed on boards of directors in order to raise money or provide high-power contacts and then not be listened to. They are treated badly when meetings are canceled at the last minute, when agendas are not developed for meetings, or when requests are made to have decisions rubber-stamped without providing the necessary information. Steerers can be abused when they are asked to provide professional legal and accounting services and then are not provided with access to the records and staff that they need. These examples illustrate how volunteers, who were enticed to serve because they would have a role in steering an agency, are treated like a commodity to be used for the staff's purposes.

Why are volunteers abused? The answer lies partially in the attitude deeply embedded in our culture that "you get what you pay for" or that there is "no such thing as a free lunch." This attitude leads people to question the skills and motivations of volunteers. Volunteers, as Ellis and Noyes point out, are "perceived as do-gooders, meddlers, radicals, or those foolish enough to work for nothing" and their work is not respected.

Volunteers are also abused by agencies because the agencies themselves lack effective management and adequate resources to fulfill their mission. They often fail to allocate enough resources to use volunteers effectively. Since volunteers are viewed as "free," agencies are inclined to pay more attention to paid personnel, to the clients they serve, and to their funding sources. Even if volunteers are fully appreciated, the agency may be so understaffed, compared to the challenges it faces, that it cannot provide adequate support.

As a Genuine Do-Gooder you have an obligation to fight volunteer abuse. Here are three guidelines to follow:

1. Follow Principle 4.1 and search for your volunteer position as you would search for a job and treat your volunteer position as if it were a job.
2. Work for an agency whose staff treats volunteers as valued workers.
3. If the agency fails to make good use of its volunteers, demand that they do so or leave that agency and inform its leaders why.

This last guideline suggests "tough love" for causes that are near and dear to you. It won't be easy, but it is the only path for the Genuine Do-Gooder. Below is a list of the characteristics of an efficient nonprofit agency. Few agencies follow all of the guidelines, but you should use the list as a guide to determine where your volunteer effort will be the most effective. The list is based on a study Susan J. Ellis completed for the United Way, entitled *Volunteer Management Audit*, to help agencies improve their use of volunteers.

Procedures of agencies that use volunteers well*

Agencies that get the most out of their volunteers will:

1. Create written job descriptions for all volunteer positions. Provide volunteers with a detailed description of all expectations, duties, and goals required of them. Remember to update job descriptions annually, as well as to revise assignments.
2. Follow up each volunteer applicant within 30 days of the interview. Inform all applicants immediately so that their energy is put to use in the agency or in other resources.
3. Provide a standardized orientation in order to help all volunteers become familiar with the purpose, structure, and policies of the agency. Be sure to put the key policies and requirements in writing so that they are conveyed consistently to everyone.
4. Provide training for all volunteers based on each job description. Training not only helps develop and increase the skills of volunteers but continued in-service training also helps move volunteers into new assignments.
5. Give recognition to members of the staff who work well with volunteers. Work to improve performance of staff members who are weak in this area.
6. Provide feedback to volunteers based on the quality of their work. Seek opportunities to share the accomplishments of volunteers with the community.
7. Keep confidential personnel records for each volunteer. Keep individual performance reviews within these records, where volunteers are evaluated by their supervisors.
8. Treat all volunteers equally. Treat volunteers as part of their staff and give volunteers their full trust and acceptance.
9. Encourage the opinions, views, and suggestions of volunteers. Volunteers should receive respect for their opinions.
10. Provide an orderly work environment for volunteers. Be sure that their environment is conducive to work and worthy of the job being completed.

If you work for an agency that follows most of these guidelines, you are likely to be an effective volunteer and to enjoy volunteering. You need to keep these guidelines in mind in your search for volunteer positions and in your reactions to agency activities.

---

*Susan J. Ellis and Katherine H. Noyes, *By the People: A History of Americans as Volunteers* (San Francisco: Jossey-Bass, 1990), p. xii.

Principle 4.3: Don't abuse your agencies

Before you feel too sorry for the abused volunteer, you should realize that volunteers are not always abusees; they are frequently the abusers. Volunteers can act just as irresponsibly as the agencies they serve. At the level of rowing, volunteers serving others sometimes have the attitude that if they volunteer, they have the right to back out on their commitment at any time. They may make a commitment for three hours a week working for Meals on Wheels in January, but when April rolls around decide that the commitment conflicts with planting flowers in the garden or with playing golf. At the steering level, the members of a board may not show up for meetings, fail to read preparatory materials provided to them in advance, or avoid asking difficult questions. They might agree to serve on too many boards so that they can feel good or promote their businesses. When volunteers suspect that the agency's executive director is doing evil things, monetarily or otherwise, they may ignore the signs.

Think of yourself as a "professional" do-gooder. You can enjoy the antics of the child you are tutoring or feel great about putting on a successful fundraiser, but your volunteer effort, even at the most mundane level, should be taken seriously. It carries with it an implicit contract that you are trustworthy and committed. Always try to:
1. Arrive on time and fulfill your commitment to others.
2. Understand your role by knowing the objectives and goals of the agency and firmly establish what is expected of you.
3. Give an evaluation of the agency and its programs in order to improve the service.
4. Work hard.
5. Respect the rights, values, and privacy of all parties involved.

The problems you want to tackle as a volunteer are too important not to take at least as seriously as you take your job. Your compensation, however, is much more than monetary. Volunteering can be fun and a great way to make friends, but most of all, it is deeply satisfying to help others.

QUIZ RESULTS

1. Use job search strategies when choosing where to volunteer.
Answer: Yes. You need to consider the mission, the activities you will be doing, and your capacity to

perform well when selecting a volunteer position. The same is true when seeking a job.

2. With careful research, you can tell which agencies are likely to mistreat their volunteers.

Answer: Yes. Ask questions about the agency you are considering volunteering for.

3. High performance standards should be more important for paid workers than for volunteers.

Answer: No. The only difference between a job and a volunteer position is that you are paid at the former. Take your volunteer commitments seriously.

5 Donors Unite: You Have Nothing To Lose but Your Money

QUIZ

1. Genuine Do-Gooders must give at least five percent of their income.
Circle one: Yes No Not Sure

2. Making sure your donations get to the promised destination is time consuming and nearly impossible.
Circle one: Yes No Not Sure

3. Steering the organizations you donate to can be a complex task, but it can be done.
Circle one: Yes No Not Sure

INTRODUCTION

Edith and Henry Everett have had successful careers as investment bankers. They have given millions of dollars over the years to a variety of specific programs and causes. Three of their programs are described in the profile below to illustrate how a clear focus and careful follow-through can yield great results.

The Everetts: Highly leveraged giving

Edith and Henry Everett target their giving much as investment bankers target their investing. A prime example of a donation investment is the Everett Summer Fellowship Program, which creates summer internships for college students to work at nonprofit organizations. Some of the organizations that serve as placement are:

- Center on Budget and Policy Priorities in Washington, DC
- Child Welfare League of America in Washington, DC
- Shorebank Corporation in Chicago
- Josephson Institute of Ethics in Marina Del Ray, California
- Tobacco Products Liability Projects in Boston

The internships carry a cost-of-living stipend that has a triple impact. First, it gives students a meaningful learning experience. Second, it generates a spirit of public service among the recipients. Third, it guarantees the flow of strong candidates for summer positions to the underfunded nonprofits. This kind of well-managed program exemplifies the power of thoughtful giving.

Other examples of gifts from the Everetts that show their commitment to high-quality contributions include the establishment of the Dance Theater of Harlem, now known as the Everett Center for the Performing Arts, and a $1 million pledge toward the endowment campaign to support Teach for America. This organization, described in chapter 20, has had a remarkable impact on education in areas of poverty.

How rich you are is not the point here. For example, Thomas Cannon, a retired postal clerk, has given more than $96,000 in the form of $1,000 checks to individuals in need, although the most he has ever earned annually is $32,000. He gives his money to strangers, most of whose good works he reads about in the newspaper. "I give money away to reward and inspire those who work selflessly for others," he is quoted as saying in the Give Five organizational pamphlet of the Independent Sector. Like the Everetts, Cannon carefully picks his spots for critical social investments.

Principle 5.1: **Give the amount you want**

The American Association of Fund Raising Counsel reports that $143.5 billion was donated to charities in 1997. If you want to get a picture of how big and complex the world of donations is, read any issue of *The Chronicle of Philanthropy,* a bimonthly publication, or check out its Web site, which is sometimes open to nonsubscribers. Both contain articles about charity and philanthropic organizations. To subscribe, write

Chronicle of Philanthropy
1255 Twenty-third Street, NW
Washington, DC 20037
http://www.philanthropy.com

Information on philanthropic activities in Canada can be obtained by contacting

Canadian Centre for Philanthropy
425 University Ave.
Toronto, ON, Canada, M5R 2C4
Tel. 416 579-2293
http://www.ccp.ca

The amount of money you give to charity is a personal decision. I recommend that you try to give five percent of your personal income; this percentage is also suggested by the Independent Sector, a well-known and first-rate nonprofit organization that studies and supports voluntary organizations, foundations, and corporate giving programs.

For another perspective for those of you who think about such things, Claude Rosenberg is an investment manager who has created a Web site to help you decide on an affordable level of donations without impairing your net worth. You provide your financial information and the site tells you how much you can give and still maintain your current financial position.

Newtithing Group
Four Embaracadero Center, Suite 3700
San Francisco, CA 94111
Tel. 415 274-2761   Fax 425 274-2756
http://www.newtithing.org

Still, how much you give is up to you. You need to be comfortable with your decision. Hence, there is no requirement that you donate anything to be a Genuine Do-Gooder.

Principle 5.2: **Give to the needy, not the greedy**

You may have heard the Latin phrase "caveat emptor," which means "buyer beware." Genuine Do-Gooders who donate need to conduct what might be called "due diligence," a phrase used to describe the responsibility of corporation officials to seriously investigate a possible investment or company they are planning to take over. Likewise, you should make sure your money goes to the cause for which it is intended.

Due diligence required

There are plenty of fly-by-night charities where 80 to 90 percent of every dollar donated goes in the pockets of professional solicitors. For example, most law enforcement and fire department associations are not charities but membership organizations for which contributions are not tax deductible. Fundraising for these associations is commonplace; they usually have contracts with phone solicitation companies that keep 80 cents or more of every dollar raised, leaving the organizations with 20 cents or less. A report by the attorney general of California on charities operating in that state indicates that about 33 percent of receipts from paid solicitors actually went to the charities. The attorney general of New York published a study in October 1998 called *Pennies for Charity: Telemarketing by Professional Fund-Raisers*, which showed charities actually losing money because commissions are paid through uncollected pledges. For example, the Presbyterian Hospital in the City of New York lost $142,144 to DMC University Inc. as a result of uncollected or unpaid pledges, showing no net gain from their fundraising efforts.* These arrangements are the most frequent targets of action by attorneys general and state charity officers.

It is not just high marketing costs you need to watch out for. Downright stealing exists. The most celebrated case in recent history is the former president of the United Way of America, William Aramony, who served from 1970 to 1992, ultimately resigning under heavy pressure from local United Way agencies. He retired due to

*Dennis Vacco, New York State Attorney General, *Pennies for Charity: Telemarketing by Professional Fund-Raisers*, October 1998, p. 21.

reports of abuse of his expense account and questions of financial impropriety. Evidently, his annual salary package of close to half a million a year was not enough. In 1995, he was convicted of 20 different criminal acts and sentenced to a seven-year prison term.*

The United Way has been seriously hurt by this incident and so have all major nonprofits. Once the issue of trust is raised, the process of restoring it is very difficult. The United Way has taken major steps to clean up its act, and vigilance throughout major nonprofits is now stronger than it has ever been. Nevertheless, as discussed in the next section, there are steps you can take to protect your donations.

Unfortunately, you will not get much help from the government. Only 16 states actually ask for professionally audited financial statements from the charities operating in their state, according to a 1998 newsletter published by the American Association of Fund-Raising Counsel, Inc. They are Connecticut, Georgia, Illinois, Maine, Maryland, Massachusetts, Michigan, Minnesota, Mississippi, New York, Pennsylvania, Rhode Island, Tennessee, Virginia, West Virginia, and Wisconsin. The rest either do not ask for any financial statement or accept those that have not been independently audited. Some of the states may take other steps to ensure the integrity of the charities, but they do not take this all-important one. If you are a Genuine Do-Gooder in one of those states, put this book down right now and call your state representative to draw attention to this problem.

Make sure your donations are used for charity

Help from nongovernmental agencies is readily available. The only thing you have to do is know who they are and how to take advantage of their services. Here are several ideas on how to protect your giving from those who do harm to our charitable institutions.

1. Contact the National Charities Information Bureau (NCIB). This organization has been helping donors since 1918 and has the most comprehensive set of services for national charities. Check out the NCIB guidelines on how to choose a charity that does what it promises. The NCIB rates charities according to standards in such areas as: the structure of the Board of Governors; how much of the funds collected goes to program activities rather than to administrative expenses and fundraising costs (70

*Charles E. Shepard, "United Way Head Resigns Over Spending Habits," *The Washington Post*, http://www-tech.mit.edu/V112/N9/united-way.09w.html

percent indicates a well-managed organization); and the use of generally accepted accounting principles. Four times a year, the NCIB publishes an updated list of those charities that conform to these standards and those that do not. If you are planning to give to a national charity and it is not on this approved list, you need to get more information on that charity before giving. The appendix lists all charities that appeared on their February 15, 1999, list of organizations that met their standards. For more information, contact the NCIB at:

> NCIB
> 19 Union Square West
> New York, NY 10003
> Tel. 212 929-6300
> http://www.give.org

The NCIB rating procedures works like this. More than 300 charities are evaluated according to the standards. Those charities that pass all nine are listed monthly. Information on those that do not meet the criteria are also listed. For example, in the summer 1998 NCIB Wise Giving Guide, the American Cancer Society satisfied all nine standards, while the United Cancer Research Society did not meet the standards for the board of governance, annual reporting, accountability, and budget. Some charities, such as the Toys for Tots Foundation, did not answer the NCIB request for information—not a good sign. With so many charities that meet the NCIB standards, why give your money to ones that do not or are so disorganized or fearful of the consequences that they will not comply with the NCIB requests? Those that do not meet all standards at least require more investigation on your part.

2. Contact the Better Business Bureau (BBB). The national association maintains a Web site that contains philanthropy information, and your local Better Business Bureau may rate charitable organizations in your city.

> Philanthropic Advisory Service of the Council
> of Better Business Bureaus, Inc.
> 4200 Wilson Blvd.
> Arlington, VA 22203-1804
> http://www.bbb.org

NCIB Tips for Givers*

Ask any charity that requests contributions to send you information that tells you:
- its exact name (some sound-alike groups can be confusing);
- its purpose (e.g., finding a cure for a disease, or caring for people who suffer from the disease);
- how the group attempts to achieve its goals (its own research, making grants); and
- how much of your dollar is used for charitable purposes (NCIB standards call for a minimum of 60 cents out of each dollar).

Some things to be leery of:
- high-pressure calls and mail solicitation that emphasize emotional content but contain little substance;
- charities that won't send written material;
- phone calls and letters telling you that you have won money or a valuable prize from a charity; and
- callers who want to send someone over to pick up your contribution; insist on using the U.S. mail.

Some very important don'ts:
- Don't give cash, and don't give out your credit card number. Write a check made payable only to the charity.
- Don't respond to letters that say you have pledged money unless you are 100 percent certain that you did.

---

3. Contact Guidestar. This Web site is a clearinghouse of information on nonprofit organizations. It is a free service for individual donors, institutional donors, and nonprofits that provides information on thousands of charities, news in philanthropy, and advice on managing a nonprofit. Write or call Guidestar and request information on the charity you are considering.

Guidestar
1126 Professional Drive
Williamsburg, VA 23185
Tel. 757 229-4631
http://www.guidestar.org

*National Charities Information Bureau Home Page: http://www.give.org

4. Consult with the United Way in your area. State and local charities are not covered by NCIB or the national BBB, but you can still obtain information. One relatively credible method is to find out whether or not the agency is a United Way agency. The United Way was established to help donors avoid constant solicitations and provide them with a place to donate that monitors how funds are used. Most United Way agencies are likely to be a good place to donate (despite the Aramony episode), but in any community they will typically constitute fewer than 25 percent of the jnncharities. For more information on the United Way, contact the agency at:

> United Way
> 701 N. Fairfax Street
> Alexandria, VA 22314
> Tel. 703 836-7100
> http://www.unitedway.org

5. Read special reports by state governments. Several states have issued reports periodically. The following might prove helpful to you even if you do not live in those states since many charities operate in more than one state but not necessarily on a national level. The reports include:

> *Pennies for Charity: Telemarketing by Professional Fund-Raisers,* October 1998
> Former Attorney General Dennis Vacco
> 120 Broadway
> New York, NY 10271
> Tel. 212 416-8050

> *Where Have All the Dollars Gone?*
> Consumer Division, Attorney General's Office
> 109 State Street
> Montpelier, VT 05609
> Tel. 802 828-3171   Fax 802 828-2154

> *Washington State Report*
> Office of the Secretary of State
> Charities Program
> 505 E. Union Ave.
> PO Box 40234
> Olympia, WA 98504
> Tel. 800 332-4483

Attorney General's Summary of Results of Charitable
Solicitation by Commercial Fundraisers
Attorney General's Office, Public Inquiry Unit
1300 I Street, Suite 125, PO Box 944277
Sacramento, CA 94244
Tel. 916 322-3360

6. Conduct your own research. If the four sources mentioned above are not helpful, you should ask for an annual report of the organization and look for an audited financial statement. If you cannot get a report or it lacks an audited financial statement, you need to be on the alert and follow up by calling members of the board or asking people you trust if they have knowledge about the agency. You can also obtain the Internal Revenue Service 990 form, which every incorporated charity has to submit yearly.

7. Refuse to give to charities that do not respect the Donor Bill of Rights, which is on the next page. This bill of rights was developed by the American Association of Fund-Raising Counsel (AAFRC), Association for Healthcare Philanthropy (AHP), Council for Advancement and Support of Education (CASE), and the National Society of Fund Raising Executives (NSFRE). Endorsed by the Independent Sector, National Catholic Development Conference (NCDC), National Council for Resource Development (NCRD), and the United Way of America.

The Genuine Do-Gooder who makes contributions has a responsibility not to support charities that do not make good use of the contribution. The larger the percentage of money going to fundraising, the less the power of the dollars you give. Money that goes to support administration rather than program activities directly may also represent a loss of your giving power especially if it exceeds 40 percent. The best way to protect against wasting your charitable dollars is to investigate the organizations to which you donate.

Principle 5.3: Big givers need to steer

Giving money beyond a certain threshold (which varies by size of the receiving organization) requires that you try to do some steering. The nature of the steering can vary. If you as an alumnus give a large unrestricted gift to your university, why not ask for a detailed report on how the money was spent? Better yet, why not stipulate that

A Donor Bill of Rights*

1. To be informed of the organization's mission, of the way the organization intends to use donated resources, and of its capacity to use donations effectively for their intended purposes.
2. To be informed of the identity of those serving on the organization's governing board, and to expect the board to exercise prudent judgment in its stewardship responsibilities.
3. To have access to the organization's most recent financial statements.
4. To be assured their gifts will be used for the purposes for which they were given.
5. To receive appropriate acknowledgment and recognition.
6. To be assured that information about their donations is handled with respect and with confidentiality to the extent provided by law.
7. To expect that all relationships with individuals representing organizations of interest to the donor will be professional in nature.
8. To be informed whether those seeking donations are volunteers, employees of the organization, or hired solicitors.
9. To have the opportunity for their names to be deleted from mailing lists that an organization may intend to share.
10. To feel free to ask questions when making a donation and to receive prompt, truthful, and forthright answers.

money go into the general scholarship fund or to plant roses in front of the administrative building? We will have more to say about alumni in chapter 16. The point here is that if you give a large amount of money, you should keep track of where it goes, or place conditions on how it is spent.

Philanthropists who want to steer are like parents who provide substantial support for their college-age child and hope that their child will go to class, and party only on the weekends. A parent could attempt to use their financial support to set a student on the correct path in one of several ways:

1. Require periodic reports that, if acceptable, would trigger a flow of money into the student's checking account.

* "A Donor Bill of Rights," http://www.cslnet.ctstateu.edu/attygenl/donright.htm, p. 1.

2. Threaten cuts of five percent of spending money, for every
tenth of a point under a 3.0 GPA.
3. Make vague and distant threats like, without a 3.0 you will
have to pay part of your college costs next year.
4. Make vague promises like, "You get a car if you do well."
5. Relax and say, "I trust you and know you will always do
your best."

Just as there is no best way for parents to keep their son or
daughter from being one of the more than 48 percent* of students
who do not graduate from college in five years, philanthropists need
to make sure their money is being well spent. They can require a report
of outcomes and attach monetary rewards and punishments to those
outcomes; they can make vague and distant threats; or they can relax
by expressing deep confidence in the staff of the organization they
are supporting. The best situation would be if, like parents, they did
not have to steer at all. In this scenario, philanthropists would have
close and open communication with the staff as they work together
toward the same goal.

The depth of the problem of trying to ensure that agencies
use money in the way intended by the donor is illustrated by the
continuing struggle the United Way faces in trying to monitor the use
of money it allocates to be sure the money is used effectively. United
Way chapters support approximately 45,000 agencies in communities around the world and spend a great deal of staff time and energy making sure that the agencies do what they say they are going
to do.* Although there is usually good faith on both sides, many agencies do not provide adequate and reliable information, so the United
Way cannot make sure the agencies keep their promises to donors.
The United Way is usually slow to react, like most parents, because
they would prefer that the agencies develop internal processes for
keeping these promises. In extreme cases, the United Way makes
and carries out threats, which means that it has already failed to steer
but is hopeful that providing a lesson will increase its influence in
the future.

Over the past five years, philanthropists and the United Way
have increasingly demanded more information on performance. They
want to receive information on the results of their funding decision.
Similarly, if you give a large gift to an organization you should:
1. Check its fundraising and administrative practices as well as
financial standing;

*United Way Home Page, "1998 United Way Facts," http://www.unitedway.org/uwfacts98/uwfs9801.html.

2. Know enough about the programs to target your gift to a specific purpose;

3. Understand how the agency measures the success of the program to which you are donating and reach an agreement on how you will receive information on the degree of success at least once a year; and

4. Concentrate your giving so that you have time to investigate the results of your gifts.

As we have suggested, steering through large donations is about as difficult as getting your children to do what you think is good for them. You may be unsuccessful and in some cases you may not really be competent to judge, but you should try. This may mean that you give larger sums of money to fewer causes so you have the time to perform due diligence.

Two sources that will help those of you who wish to make a significant donation to a philanthropy are both by Christopher Mogil and Anne Slepian, entitled *We Gave away a Fortune* and *Welcome to Philanthropy*. Both are available from the Impact Project, which you can e-mail at impact@efn.org.

For those of you who want to give to special local causes, see if there is a community foundation in your area. These organizations, more than 500 in the United States and a large number in Canada, allow you to receive a tax deduction for your donations and to direct your donations to specific local causes. To see if there is one in your area, contact in the United States:

Community Foundation Locator
Council on Foundations
1828 L Street, NW
Washington, DC
Tel. 202 466-6512
http://www.cof.org

In Canada, contact:

Community Foundations of Canada
301-75 Albert Street
Ottawa, ON, Canada, K1P5E7
Tel. 613 236-2664   Fax 613 236-1621
http://www.community-fdn.ca

QUIZ RESULTS

1. Genuine Do-Gooders must give at least five percent of their income.

Answer: No. You should give whatever you want.

2. Making sure your donations get to the promised destination is time consuming and nearly impossible.

Answer: No. Just use the resources suggested in the chapter and in the appendix. It will not require constant vigilance but a yearly checkup.

3. Steering the organizations you donate to can be a complex task, but it can be done.

Answer: Yes. It is complex because steering can take place in a variety of ways. These vary from specifying how your money is spent to asking for annual reports to communicating frequently with officials of the nonprofit.

6 Good Citizens and Watchdogs

1. Genuine Do-Gooders must abide by the law.
Circle one: Yes No Not Sure

2. Opportunities for volunteering that allow you to help perform government services and shape government decisions are limited.
Circle one: Yes No Not Sure

3. The watchdog function is the most critical role of the citizen who seeks to be a Genuine Do-Gooder.
Circle one: Yes No Not Sure

4. The best way to advocate for a change in government policy is to get the right politicians elected.
Circle one: Yes No Not Sure

INTRODUCTION

When she was in seventh grade, Barbara Wagner asked for a piece of pie in the school cafeteria and was told that only faculty could purchase the homemade pies. Outraged that school cooks were baking only for the faculty, she took her cause to the student council. The next day students were buying the pies.

Now 68 years old, Wagner is the watchdog in my little village, Fayetteville, New York (population 5,000). As you can see by the profile below, she still fights for the public good. She is also a dedicated volunteer who plants trees and flowers for the village, a donor who gives generously to all kinds of causes, and most important, she is an active citizen keeping close tabs on what government officials do.

Barbara Wagner: The ultimate watchdog

Barbara Wagner is an example of the Genuine Do-Gooder as a watchdog for her community. Over the past two decades, her watchdog activities have made her village a better place to live. Wagner is driven by the view that the public interest must be protected against corruption and the unfair application of the law. Her deep belief that the government must serve all people equally and that laws must be followed moves her to action.

Most of her efforts start with the complaints of residents who have neither the skill nor the stomach to confront authorities. She helps all citizens protect their own interests so that authorities make decisions that benefit the entire community. Two or three times a year, groups of residents will call about proposals to rezone areas of the village that would change the character of the property that they had invested in. Or they will ask her help to stop the building of public facilities in inappropriate places; for example, a skating park for teenagers along a dangerous single-lane country road. In these cases, she coaches the residents on what to do and helps them write, print, and distribute fliers to get a good showing at the public hearing. She may not agree with the residents' position, but she wants to make sure their voices are heard as part of the democratic process.

Wagner has the following message for aspiring watchdogs: "Be eternally optimistic, idealistic, resilient, realistic, secure within one's self, and persistent, and have a basic belief in the rights of others." She embodies all of these ideals.

Acting as a constructive watchdog over the government is an important part of being a citizen. A citizen is more than the definition you were given in elementary school: stay out of trouble and salute the flag. Citizens need to keep an eye on the government and make noises when it does not serve the interests of the entire community.

We will return to the qualities of a watchdog and Wagner in

the last section of this chapter. But before we do that, we need to examine two other principles that can enhance your power as a citizen.

Principle 6.1: Be a law-abiding citizen

First and foremost, it almost goes without saying, abide by the law. Not much more needs to be said about this except that when you pay your income taxes, wear your seat belt, and conform to local, state, and federal laws we all win.

There is no excuse for breaking the law, except in the very rare occasion that you think the law is unjust or frivolous. If you seriously question a law, as a do-gooder you may be inclined to try civil disobedience. But civil disobedience should come only after spending considerable time and energy to get the law changed through the legislative process. Second, and again it almost goes without saying, being a good citizen means being polite, courteous, and fair to everyone.

Principle 6.2: Volunteer for the public good

Being a good citizen also means doing things for the public good. They are voluntary, but not normally viewed as official volunteer activities. They can be informal, such as calling the police department if a stop sign has been knocked down, or formal, such as serving out your jury duty. Without these acts of civic caring, our quality of life would deteriorate, and government would have to grow even larger to clean up our messes or to enforce more laws.

Formal volunteer activities occur when the government requests volunteers for specific tasks, like serving on the zoning board or serving as a volunteer at the local library. These activities are also critical to improving society. They can be as complicated, important, and serious as working as a volunteer in a fire department or ambulance service or as simple as picking up trash on Earth Day. Natural disasters are met with significant numbers of volunteers who assist governments in dealing with life-threatening emergencies. Governments often set up boards of citizens as temporary committees (e.g., a task force to decide where to build a new library), planning and zoning boards, or as site-based school committees.

Government agencies at all levels, from your local community to the federal government, need the help of volunteers. The following sections will give you information on the available local and federal opportunities.

Local government opportunities

Each local government has a large number of volunteer and semi-volunteer (offering small monetary compensation) positions, examples of which are listed below. To find out about your area, call the office of your mayor, city manager, town supervisor, or county executive.

- Common Local Government Opportunities
- Civilian Review Board
- Commission for Women
- Community Cleanup Days
- Conservation Advisory Council
- Economic Development Advisory
- Human Rights Council
- Landmark Preservation Board
- Metropolitan Commission for Aging
- Model Neighborhood Corps
- Parade Committee
- Parks and Recreation Association
- Planning Board
- Resource Recovery Agency
- Tree Commission
- Volunteer Fire and Ambulance Service
- Zoning Board

In some of these programs, you need to be invited to participate. For example, the Civilian Review Board and the Planning Commission are usually appointed and may even carry a small stipend, but they are basically volunteer positions. Indicating that you are interested in serving to the appropriate department head or elected officials could get you the invitation. Other programs are strictly voluntary and you can join them by directly contacting the agency that sponsors the program.

Uncle Sam Wants Your Time

The federal government has initiated many volunteer programs over the past few decades. The list below provides a glimpse of the range of rowing opportunities offered by the U.S. government, and volunteer programs organized by the federal government and offered throughout the United States. While you serve on these programs in you own locality, they are supported by federal money and can be identified by contacting the national offices, which will then direct you to the local programs.

AMERICA GOES BACK TO SCHOOL (Department of Education)
• This is a nationwide movement started to encourage family and community involvement to improve children's learning. To help, you can join, start, or support a partnership in your community that focuses on improving children's learning. For more information, call 800-USA-LEARN or visit the Web site at http:// www.ed.gov/Family/agbts/.

FOSTER GRANDPARENTS PROGRAM (Corporation for National Service)
• Foster grandparents devote their volunteer service to children with special or exceptional needs. They offer emotional support to child victims of abuse and neglect, tutor children who lag behind in reading, mentor troubled teenagers and young mothers, and care for premature infants and children with physical disabilities and severe illnesses. For more information visit their Web site at http://www.fostergrandparents.org or call your local volunteer coordinating source.

NATIONAL 4-H COUNCIL (Department of Agriculture)
• The goal of 4-H is to extend agricultural and home economics education to rural youth by organizing boys and girls clubs. The 4-H serves youth through "learning by doing" in organized clubs, special interest or short-term groups, school enrichment programs, instructional TV, camping, or as individual members. You can become a group leader or serve as a resource person for the 4-H. For more information, contact National 4-H Council at 7100 Connecticut Avenue, Chevy Chase, MD 20815, tel. 301 961-2866, or visit its Web site at http://www.fourhcouncil.edu.

NEIGHBORHOOD NETWORKS (Department of Housing and Urban Development)
• This program encourages the development of resource and computer learning centers in privately owned HUD-insured and -assisted housing. Local businesses, nonprofits, educational institutions, faith-based organizations, civic organizations, foundations, hospitals, community clinics, and federal and state government agencies, among others, can all take part in this initiative. For more information, contact U.S. Department of Housing and Urban Development, Neighborhood Networks, 9300 Lee Highway, Fairfax, VA 22031-1207, tel. 888 312-2743, or visit its Web site at http://www.hud.gov/nnw/nnwindex.html.

THE RETIRED AND SENIOR VOLUNTEER PROGRAM
(Corporation for National Service)
• RSVP volunteers choose how and where they want to serve—
from a few hours to more than 40 hours a week. It allows older
adults to find the types of volunteer service opportunities that
they are interested in. For more information, visit the Corporation for National Service Web site at http://www.cns.gov or call
your local volunteer coordinator.

SERVICE CORPS OF RETIRED EXECUTIVES (Small Business
Administration)
• The SCORE Association is a nonprofit association dedicated to
entrepreneur education and the formation, growth, and success
of small businesses nationwide. Members serve as counselors,
advisers, and mentors to aspiring entrepreneurs and business
owners. These services are offered at no fee. For more information, call 800 634-0245 or visit the Web site at http://www.
score.org.

SENIOR, YOUTH, AND VOLUNTEER PROGRAMS (U.S. Forest
Service)
• This program provides assistance in natural resources protec-
tion and management programs. It offers individuals and
sponsored organizations the opportunity to contribute their
talents and services to help manage the nation's natural resources.
For more information on this program, contact the U.S. Forest
Service, Auditors Building, 201 Fourteenth Street, SW, at
Independence Ave., Washington, DC 20024, or visit its Web
site at http://www.fs.fed.us/people/programs.

AMERICANS FOR INDIAN OPPORTUNITY (Department of
Interior)
• This organization can use the services of volunteers regardless
of skills either in its offices or on Indian reservations. They are
devoted to issues relating to tribal leadership and governance.
They also create coalitions among tribes and between Indians
and non-Indians to enhance the cultural, social, political, and
economic self-sufficiency of tribes. For more information, contact Americans for Indian Opportunity, 681 Juniper Hill Road,
Bernalillo, NM 87004, tel. 505 867-0278.

VOLUNTEERS IN PARKS (National Park Service)
• The primary purpose of the VIP program is to provide a way
for the National Park Service to accept and use voluntary services

from the public. For more information, visit the Web site at
http://www. nps. gov/volunteer.

Principle 6.3:   Mixed breeds make the best watchdogs

Watchdogs are those who work to make sure government
officials follow the law and make good on their promises to all citizens whom they represent. Given the need for our society to provide
a more level playing field, the watchdog role is one of the most important functions of the citizen as a Genuine Do-Gooder. However, it takes
a special person who has the right combination of traits and character to get the job done. To be a powerful watchdog, you should be a
mixture of:

- A bloodhound sniffing out corruption;
- A retriever keeping eyes and ears on the public interest;
- A terrier digging out the facts with excruciating persistence;
- A sheepdog organizing people to fight for their rights and
a better society; and
- A Rottweiler barking vigorously when danger is suspected.

These breeds all have stamina and are accustomed to hard work.
Shaping government actions is not simply whining about laws or venting to whomever will listen. You need to attend government meetings, read newspaper articles about the issue, and talk with your representatives and other government officials. Genuine Do-Gooders
educate themselves first, and then attempt to talk to those in power
to shape legislation and government decisions. It is a long, arduous
process.

Watchdogs also must have a strong self-image because they
are constantly under attack. Those in power do not like to be criticized, so they call watchdogs naysayers. The criticism can become
more intense and personal as the watchdog begins sniffing out
the right trail. For these reasons, time spent as a citizen watchdog is
a highly valued activity of the Genuine Do-Gooder.

Principle 6.4:   Advocate causes to improve society

We have seen how citizens can work to help others, change
policies, and serve as watchdogs in their communities. As a citizen,
you can do good in still more ways. You can become an advocate supporting causes that you think are critical to promoting life, liberty, and
the pursuit of happiness throughout society. Your role of advocate for

a better society can be directed at any level. Locally, you can work to get the reading program improved at your school. At the state level, you may pressure for new laws to deter drunk driving. At the national level, you may lobby for campaign finance reform. Internationally, you may encourage your senator to push for more financial support for the United Nations.

Advocacy for the citizen as Genuine Do-Gooder means getting those in power to take the actions you think are necessary to improve society or, at the very least, getting them to give more attention to problems that you are concerned with. When all is said and done, politicians are in the business of responding to the pressure that comes from those who elect them. Some politicians may ignore those pressures or fail to read them correctly, but our government's actions are ultimately determined by those who lobby with the most power and persistence. If individuals on the side of improving society do not exert the necessary pressure, those on the side of special interests will dominate policy change.

It is a fact of life that special interests play a powerful role in forming policy. The Genuine Do-Gooder's role is to bring a broader perspective to the politicians who must decide among the special interests. You can do this in two specific ways. The first is to help to elect politicians who you think will support your views. The second is to apply pressure once the politicians are in power. The latter is almost always more important than the former, but both are necessary.

It is very easy to find ways to support politicians that you want to elect. You can donate money, serve as a volunteer, or simply get out and vote. Of course, it is a lot more difficult to tell which politician will push your agenda once he or she gets into office. This requires study on your part: talking with the candidates and their supporters, and, if they are incumbents or have served before, checking out their voting records. The following organizations provide information on voting records at the national level. Be sure you figure out where the organizations are coming from before you use their rating. They always have a viewpoint.

AIDSACTION—Capitol Hill Votes
1906 Sunderland Place, NW
Washington, DC 20036
Tel. 202 530-8030
http://www.aidsaction.org/hillvotes.html

American Civil Liberties Union—National Freedom Scorecard
125 Broad Street, Eighteenth floor
New York, NY 10004
Tel. 212 549-2585
http://scorecard.aclu.org/

Christian Coalition—Congressional Election Scorecard
1801-L Sara Drive
Chesapeake, VA 23320
Tel. 757 424-2630   Fax 757 424-9068
http://www.cc.org/scorecards/98ES/es98.html

League of Conservation Voters—National Environmental
Scorecards
1707 L Street, NW, Suite 750
Washington, DC 20036
Tel. 202 785-8683   Fax 202 835-0491
http://www.lcv.org/scorecards/

Public Citizen Congress Watch
215 Pennsylvania Ave., SE
Washington, DC 20003
Tel. 202 546-4996   Fax 202 547-7392
http://www.citizen.org/congress/

State PIRGS-Congressional Scorecards
29 Temple Place
Boston, MA 02111-1350
http://www.pirg.org

Women's Voting Guide
PO Box 20594
New York, NY 10021-0071
Tel. 212 396-3457
http://womenvote.org/scripts/Categories.asp?
type=incumbent

Placing pressure on elected officials and their staff is
essential even if "yours" win. You can communicate with elected
officials individually by making personal phone calls or writing personal letters. You can find the phone numbers and addresses of your
representatives by looking in the blue pages of the phone book. If
you are not sure who the representatives are, contact your local government office. Look also to those organizations that provide basic

information about government; they can also assist in suggesting ways to exert pressure on elected officials:

Join Together
441 Stuart Street
Boston, MA 02116
Tel. 617 437-1500   Fax 617 437-9394
http://www.jointogether.org

League of Women Voters
1730 M Street, NW
Washington, DC 20036
Tel. 202 429-1965   Fax 202 429-0854
http://www.lwv.org/~lwvus/

Project Vote Smart
One Common Ground
Philipsburg, MT 59858
Tel. 406 859-8683 or 888 VOTE-SMART   Fax 406 859-8680
http://www.vote-smart.org

Finally, you can support those public interest groups described in chapter 7 that share your viewpoints. There are more than 300 of these groups operating at the national level, representing a wide variety of positions and topics. The best source to locate the public interest organizations that might fit your interests is Public Interest Profiles (Washington, DC: Congressional Quarterly, Inc., 1998). There are even more state and local groups that advocate for specific public interests, some of which are affiliated with the national organizations. It is best to start with the national and ask for help in finding the local organizations.

QUIZ RESULTS

1. Genuine Do-Gooders must abide by the law.
Answer: Yes. Sorry to state the obvious, but this one is essential.

2. Opportunities for volunteering that allow you to help perform government services and shape government decisions are limited.
Answer: No. There are millions of opportunities, many of which are underserved, especially in our cities.

3. The watchdog function is the most critical role of the citizen who seeks to be a Genuine Do-Gooder.
Answer: Yes. Watching out for your own interests will keep politicians from running over them.
4. The best way to advocate for a change in government policy is to get the right politicians elected.
Answer: No. Politicians must listen to all sides even if they truly agree with your position. Therefore, the best way to advocate a specific government policy is to apply pressure to those politicians in power. Threatening to support an elected official's opponent may help you more than actually getting that opponent elected.

7 Careers That Serve Society

1. For-profit businesses cannot provide careers for Genuine Do-Gooders.
Circle one: Yes No Not Sure

2. Careers in doing good will pay less on average.
Circle one: Yes No Not Sure

3. Careers in doing good require a higher standard of behavior than other careers.
Circle one: Yes No Not Sure

INTRODUCTION

Ralph Nader has been a career do-gooder since 1964. He earned his degree from Harvard Law School in 1958, but decided to distance himself from his private law practice in 1964 when he worked as a consultant on auto safety for the assistant secretary of labor. Since then he has made a living as a professional lobbyist for consumers and the American public, dealing with such issues as occupational safety and public disclosure. Not only has he been a highly effective and visible lobbyist for safer consumer products, he has also helped to create dozens of other public interest lobby groups.

Ralph Nader: An inspiration in activism

Ralph Nader, founder of modern consumer advocacy and one of *Life* magazine's most important people of the 20th century, says he likes to think of himself as a Johnny Appleseed, "getting public interest groups started and letting them grow on their own."

An activist for more than 30 years, Nader has some advice for aspiring do-gooders. For those who do not know where to start or feel they cannot make a difference on their own, his advice is to look at history. "If we know our history, that almost all things we love about the country started with just one or two people—whether it was the abolition of the slave movement, the trade union movement, consumers, civil rights, environmental movements—everything starts with one or two."

If you lack the energy to start a group to slay the modern-day monsters, Nader advises joining an existing one. Chances are high that the group you join may be one of the many Nader helped establish. This list includes more than 50 groups, centers, and projects. The full-time activist still heads the Center for Study of Responsive Law.

Nader has learned many things from his experiences, including that being an activist requires a certain personality. "You have to know not to be discouraged, to be resilient when things don't work as you planned," Nader reflects. He also cautions to control moral indignation so as not to interrupt the strategic logic necessary to get things done.

The words he speaks today echo those he spoke in 1972 when referring to his own efforts: "I'm an activist. If you're an activist you orchestrate, you do things that play back to strengthen one another." This perspective helped Nader win the war he waged against the auto industry in his book, *Unsafe at Any Speed*. The 1965 book exposed fatal defects in General Motors's compact Corvair. Whereas the book may have sparked some interest, actually keeping on top of Congress directly from Washington, he says, is what led to passage of the Motor Vehicle Safety Act and Highway Safety Act in 1966. Nader has been effective on many transportation and consumer issues because he has the information, drive, and skill to lobby those in power.

Full-time careers in doing good do not have to be as all-consuming as Ralph Nader's career has been. Just as we did for Mother Teresa as all-around do-gooder, we want to avoid the curse of Ralph Nader. Still, his standards of working hard and competently to improve society give all career do-gooders something to shoot for.

Principle 7.1: Try a career of doing good on for size

My experience as a college professor who advises students in a College of Arts and Science major called"policy studies," illustrates the importance of assessing how well a career in doing good fits you. To be admitted into the major, students must convince me that they have a commitment to making the world better. Many of my students are passionate about the Athenian Oath—to leave society "not less, but greater, better, and more beautiful than it was transmitted to us." Yet as they approach graduation, some grow increasingly conflicted over whether or not they should take a job that pays approximately $25,000 annually working for a nonprofit or get hired by, say, a consulting firm at $40,000 a year.

I have seen this conflict work both ways. Some students who take the money find out they are unhappy and change their career direction. Some students who take a public service job get their fill of it and eventually go after the money. Many students who take moneymaking jobs find ways to do a great deal of good from within their company and outside of it.

A career in doing good is different from the roles of volunteers, donors, and citizens described in the three previous chapters. This section is written for those of you who are thinking about a career in doing good, either right out of college or as a change from what you are currently doing. Trying a career on for size will help you think seriously about getting paid to do good on a full-time basis. There are three steps you take to try a career on for size: research, volunteering, and internships.

Research

There are two methods that can be used when conducting research about potential careers: library and Internet searches, and informational interviews. These sources, some of which are listed below, provide background information on career fields as well as details on different government and nonprofit agencies. The Internet provides search engines that will help you to find organizations related to your field of interest and will give you important facts on your research. It is also important to seek out people already in your career field of interest. You should meet with these people and conduct informational interviews.

Volunteering

One of the best ways to explore a career in doing good is to volunteer for a cause that you support. For instance, you might apply your trade as an accountant at a nonprofit agency, or volunteer to serve on the financial board of a nonprofit agency, or offer to provide some advice on the agency's tax return. If your target is a government job, volunteer to work on the budget committee or offer free consulting services.

Internships

A more elaborate way to try on a new career is to take advantage of the increasing number of paid temporary positions, often referred to as internships, that are available both in government and nonprofit agencies. These internships can run from a few months up to two years. They are designed primarily for college students or recent college graduates. If you are a student or alumnus, contact your college career service or internship office. You can seek information about internships that are related to your decided field of interest from these sources:

1. Consult directories of internships. There are hundreds of books and manuals about seeking internships in almost any field. These are available at a number of bookstores, libraries, and university career centers. They will provide you with organization and company internship listings, contact information, and any requirements. Some examples of these resources are:

Reham Botros and Nancy R. Bailey, *National Directory of Internships (1998–1999 Edition)* (Needham Heights: Simon & Schuster, 1998)

Mark Oldman, *America's Top Internships: 1999* (Princeton: Princeton Review, 1998)

Peterson's Internships 1999: More than 50,000 Opportunities to Get an Edge in Today's Competitive Job Market (Peterson's Guides, 1998)

2. Consult books on public interest research organizations and leadership directories. Approximately 300 descriptions of public interest research groups in the United States are available in *Public Interest Profiles. Leadership Directories* provides contact information for hundreds of leaders around the country. You can contact these people or groups to inquire about internships. Some may or may not have formal internship programs, but often a position can be arranged if it doesn't already exist.

Foundation of Public Affairs, *Public Interest Profiles* (Washington, DC: Congressional Quarterly, 1998)

Leadership Directories (New York: Leadership Directories)

3. Go directly to federal, state, or local government agencies. To find an internship within the government, you may seek out any agency related to your chosen field. Usually, the agency's human resources department will be able to provide you with internship information. Agency Web sites usually provide internship information or contact information.

4. Internet: There are several Web sites designed to help in the search for internships. Most allow you to choose a specific field and geographic area in which they will search for internship opportunities. Some examples of Web sites are:

Rising Star Internships
http://www.rsinternships.com.

Princeton Review Internship Find-O-Rama
http://www. review.com/career/find/intern.cfm

The Non-Profit Career Center supported by Action without Borders
http://www.idealist.org

5. Go to existing programs. There are numerous well-established internship programs that are available to those seeking career experience. Most of these have Web sites with a great deal of information on their programs. Some examples of these existing programs are:

> Americorps
> Tel. 800 942-2677
> http://www.americorps.org.
> The CORO Foundation
> One Whitehall Street, 10th Floor
> New York, NY 10004
> Tel. 212 248-2935   Fax 212 248-2970

> The Washington Center for Internships
> and Academic Centers
> Tel. 800 486-8921
> http: //www.twc.edu

6. Seek out information at local universities. Most universities and colleges have career service centers, which provide resources for finding internship opportunities since many organizations send internship postings and other related information. Also, these resource centers will have books and other forms of assistance to help you find an internship.

Principle 7.2:   Do-good careers are plentiful

You can find a career that will make you into a serious Genuine Do-Gooder in business, government, or a nonprofit organization. The lines between these three types of organizations are becoming increasingly blurred as business gets into some areas like trash removal that government used to do by itself, and governments and nonprofits become more businesslike. However, it is still useful to make the distinction in order to help you understand the choices available if you want a career that is dedicated to improving society.

Businesses

There are many profit-making organizations and careers that seek to promote a safe and long life, protect liberty, and improve opportunities to pursue happiness. If you work for an organization that places the clients' and society's interests above the profit motive, you can count a substantial percentage of your work time to doing good. An overview of these careers and organizations are provided below and grouped according to fields.

Health

By definition, careers in health are dedicated to doing good because they seek to enhance life. Doctors, nurses, pharmacists, and medical researchers get paid not only to preserve life, but also to improve the quality of life. Not all of these positions are well paying, but those that require training and skill provide a reasonable standard of living.

Law

All lawyers and judges, as well as paralegals and stenographers, are, by definition, in a career that does good because they are dedicated first and foremost to maintaining the second value of the Declaration of Independence—liberty. They also seek to protect life and help people in their pursuit of happiness. They preserve the individual freedom of speech and choice against arbitrary and capricious actions of the government, other institutions, and other individuals. The mission of the legal profession is noble.

If you read the newspapers, watch television, or ever had the misfortune of running into an unscrupulous lawyer, you know that not all lawyers are true to this mission. There is no need to try to decide what percentage of lawyers act in their careers to serve society rather than themselves. There are many lawyers that meet and even exceed the standards of doing good, like Leigh Steinberg, who is both a lawyer and a premier sports agent, two careers you might think to be almost antithetical to the concept of doing good.

Leigh Steinberg: Lawyer, sports agent, do-gooder

Leigh Steinberg, who represents big-time athletes like Troy Aikman and John Starks, insists that every contract negotiated for his players includes a clause that requires the athlete to give back to his or her own hometown, high school, university, or to national charities and foundations. As a result, more than $50 million has been contributed to various charities and scholarships nationwide. Just like his millionaire superstars, Steinberg follows his own rules and gives both his time and his money to organizations such as Children Now, Children's Miracle Network, the CORO

Foundation, Starlight Foundation, his high school, and his alma mater. You can visit Steinberg's Web site at http://www.steinbergandmoorad.com.

Media

Careers in the media, including both news and entertainment, can also be viewed as careers for doing good. The media serve not only to preserve the freedom of information, a major component of liberty, but also can work to save lives and to create a more level playing field for all Americans to pursue happiness. In fact, the newspaper industry was frequently referred to as the "Fourth Estate" of government (executive, legislative, and judicial are the first three) as early as the 18th century. There is no question that without a free press, there could be no democracy.

Aside from its political impact, the media also have a social and economic impact that can and has helped improve society. For example, prime time TV during the 1960s helped to break down the stereotypes about African-Americans held by many white Americans. News programs that show acts of heroism and charity expose people to levels of doing good that make them want to be involved. The work of media celebrities who create and support charities, like Oprah Winfrey's Angel Network, helps to build the supply of do-gooders. For information on Oprah's Angel Network, write to PO Box 81888, Chicago, IL 60681, or check the Web site at http://www.oprah. com/angelnet/angelnet.html.

Like lawyers, members of the media do not always enjoy a positive reputation in America today, and for similar reasons. Too many times it appears that the media are driven by the desire to make money, not the desire to serve the needs of the good society. The negative attitude may be well deserved in many cases, both with respect to the media's role in providing information and its even larger role in providing entertainment. The media can do good, but they can also do harm. As a Genuine Do-Gooder, you can work for companies that place a particular emphasis on doing good.

Insurance and financial companies

Most people do not think of insurance and financial companies as private machines for doing good, but that is their mission. In our complex world, where government has limited ability to steer, insurance and financial companies are critical to the organization and survival of our society. They stimulate new business, they protect the rights of consumers, and they provide enough stability so that business can operate with some stable expectations.

Privatized careers

Business opportunities for doing good are growing as a result of the transfer of jobs primarily from the government but also from the nonprofits to profit-making businesses. This transfer process, referred to as "privatization," is based on the reasonable assumption that profit-driven organizations are more efficient, more responsive to customers, and more likely to be self-funding than those not driven by profit. Like all reasonable ideas, the practice of privatization sometimes works and sometimes does not. In any case, privatization is creating new jobs that you can pursue as a Genuine Do-Gooder. The list below describes some of these jobs fields.

Businesses That Take on Public Roles

AMBULANCE AND FIRE SERVICES
• Rural/Metro is a publicly owned business that makes a profit by providing ambulance and fire services. It started in Phoenix, Arizona, when a newspaper reporter who had no fire protection in his community bought a fire truck and persuaded his neighbors to pay for fire protection services. Today, according to its Web site, Rural/Metro is one of the largest ambulance companies in North America providing "911" and general transport services.*

ENVIRONMENTAL MANAGEMENT
• The largest private business in this area is Waste Management, which has recently outperformed all major corporations. The corporation has more than 17,000 employees and posted more than $2.5 billion in sales in 1997 for services like trash removal, cleanup after natural disasters, and hazardous waste disposal.**

PRIVATE SECURITY SERVICES
• The number of private security jobs, which include positions in prisons and other criminal justice areas, is likely to increase over the next few decades. One of the world's largest private

*Rural/Metro Home Page, "History," http://www.ruralmetro.com/who/history/index.html.
**Hoover's Online, http://www.hoovers.com/annuals/15374af.html.

security companies, which earns more than $1 billion in annual sales, is Pinkerton World Security. Pinkerton employs more than 47,000 people worldwide and has more than 225 offices.*

EDUCATIONAL SERVICES
• Several companies are offering to run schools for districts and make a profit, including the Edison Project, which is the most well known. In addition, there are for-profit businesses in areas like office administration, computer network management, driver training for tractor-trailers, and services like Sylvan Learning Systems, which provides tutorial services to existing educational institutions.

JOB TRAINING
• The welfare reform movement, which has been under way for some time, has spawned a desire in businesses to design training programs that help people maintain their jobs, learn new skills, and get off of welfare. For example, one of the largest corporations that is helping employees to get off and stay off of welfare is Lockheed Martin, which has gone beyond securing its traditional defense contracts to obtain contracts to do what government training programs used to do: train the unemployed so they can get jobs.

CONSULTING COMPANIES
• Many consulting firms, like Andersen Consulting and Arthur Andersen (don't mix the two up), do a lot of work that government used to do. For example, they may develop a new information system for the IRS and then run it for several years until government workers can take it over. Or they may study how a state Department of Motor Vehicles handles its customers and develop new procedures.

Government

Both dedicated teachers, whose job is to level the playing field for all Americans, and local police, who seek to protect life and property, are pursuing careers as Genuine Do-Gooders. The same is also true for janitors in public buildings, lifeguards at public swimming pools, and the thousands of researchers and engineers working to improve the lives of others.

*Pinkerton World Security Home Page, "Corporate Fact Sheet," http://www.pinkertons.com/company/html.

Although not always appreciated by a public that is stingy with its tax dollars, government officials do remarkable things for this country. The Council for Excellence in Government gives awards each year for new programs that are developed, frequently in cooperation with business and nonprofit organizations, to solve social problems. George F. Bond Jr. and Alan T. McKenzie, described in the profile below, won an award for providing health care to uninsured patients in Buncombe County, North Carolina.

Government and business team up

George F. Bond Jr., director of Buncombe County Health Center in North Carolina, and Alan T. McKenzie, executive director and CEO of Buncombe County Medical Society Corporation (a 700-member professional association of physicians), developed the BCMS Project Access for uninsured patients. The project provides an integrated network of free clinics, hospitals, pharmacies, and private, primary, and specialty physician volunteers. More than $3.5 million in free care is provided through this project and related activities.

Government jobs can be extremely rewarding not just for those who create programs, like Bond and McKenzie. Teachers and police who serve the public can blend their need to earn a living and their desire to do good. A 1998 Sloan Public Service Award winner, Enda Muriel, for example, works at Bellevue Hospital in New York City as a mainstay of a program that serves more than 2,000 HIV/AIDS patients a year. According to her award write-up, Muriel "helps to plan and maintain medical treatment as she follows patients' clinical progress" and she provides counseling and comfort to patients and their families. Working for the government at either the steering or rowing levels is not without its down side, but it is essential to the survival of our society.

The following list* presents a number of federal and local government offices that you might work for. State organizations are not included because almost all of the federal offices have their state counterparts. You can tell the mission of each office by its title; you will need to seek out the individual agency to find out what type of programs and services it offers.

*From Daniel Lauber, *Government Job Finder* (River Forest: Planning/Communications, 1992).

Federal government

General Accounting Office
Government Printing Office
U.S. Tax Court
Office of Management and Budget

Department of Agriculture
Department of Commerce
Department of Defense
Department of Education
Department of Energy
Department of Health and Human Services
Department of Housing and Urban Development
Department of the Interior
Department of Justice
Department of Labor
Department of State
Department of Transportation
Department of the Treasury
Department of Veterans Affairs

Environmental Protection Agency
Equal Employment Opportunity Commission
Federal Emergency Management Agency
General Services Administration
National Aeronautics and Space Administration
Office of Personnel Management
Panama Canal Commission
Securities and Exchange Commission
Small Business Administration
Tennessee Valley Authority
U.S. Information Agency
U.S. Postal Service

Local government

County Attorney
School Boards
County Executive
Department of Extension and Continuing Education
Department of Health
Electoral Board and General Registrar
Community Mental Health, Mental Retardation,
  and Substance Abuse Services Board

Park Authority
Library
Social Services
Community Corrections
Office of Consumer Affairs
Office of Economic Development and Tourism
Office of Emergency Services
Juvenile Detention Home
Office of Management Information and Audit
Office of Personnel
Office of Planning
Office of Project Management
Office of Telecommunications
Office of Youth
Development Administration Department
Finance Department
Fire and Rescue Services Department
General Services Department
Police Department
Public Works Department

The Bureau of Labor Statistics estimates the number of local, state, and federal jobs at approximately 20 million, or more than 15 percent of the entire work force. This number is not likely to shrink significantly over the long run.

In addition to traditional government jobs, there are many political jobs that come from working on a winning election campaign, or working for or being appointed by an elected official. By definition, working as or for an elected official is also getting paid to do good. Despite the negative opinions you might have of politicians in general, their mission is very clear: to represent the interests of the people who elected them and to work to improve our society.

The number of appointed staff positions of our federal and state elected officials is much larger than most people realize. Part of the American system of politics is the spoils system, in which newly elected officials bring in their own people to the top layers of the bureaucracy. When a new administration comes to Washington, numerous jobs are up for grabs in the executive branch. The legislative branch also has a large number of positions that are constantly turning over.

The following resources will help you get started exploring careers in government:

USAJOBS: Provides listings from the U.S. Office of Personnel Management. http://www.usajobs.opm.gov.

U.S. Federal Government Agencies Page: Guide to federal Web sites and links to helpful pages. http://www.law.vill.edu/Fed-Agency/fedwebloc.html.

Daniel Lauber, *Government Job Finder*. River Forest: Planning/Communications, 1992.

Nonprofit Organizations

Nonprofit organizations are tax-exempt because they serve the public good. Close to 7 percent of the workforce is now employed by nonprofit agencies. The types of careers are as varied as they are in the other two sectors, which makes them difficult to describe in a few pages. The discussion here will give you an overview of the types of opportunities available.

Nonprofit organizations can be divided into five types:

1. Religious institutions
2. Educational institutions
3. Charities and foundations
4. Providers of products and services
5. Public interest lobbies

You should be familiar with the first three but probably need some background on the last two.

Providers of products and services

A large number of nonprofits serve the needs of those who cannot pay prices that would generate profits. The primary target of these products and services are the poor, but middle-class and even upper-class families might be confronted with a natural disaster or a devastating and prolonged illness for which they would require outside assistance.

Below is a list of the areas in which typical nonprofits provide products and services. This list will give you an idea of the types of causes that serve as the mission for the nonprofit. You will note that they run the entire gamut of activities that touch upon the lives of all Americans. Following are some fields that are home turf for nonprofits*:

* List adapted from Richard Steckel and Jennifer Lehman, *In Search of America's Best Non-Profits* (San Francisco: Jossey-Bass, 1997), pp. 187–188.

- Arts, culture, humanities
- Educational institutions and related activities
- Environmental quality, protection, and beautification
- Health: general and rehabilitative
- Mental health, crisis intervention
- Diseases, disorders, medical disciplines
- Medical research
- Crime, legal-related
- Employment, job-related
- Food, agriculture, and nutrition
- Housing, shelter
- Public safety, disaster preparedness, and relief
- Recreation, athletics, leisure
- Youth development
- Human services
- International foreign affairs and national security

The following source can be used to explore careers with nonprofits that provide services.

IMPACT ONLINE: Nonprofit job listings and other useful information. http://www.impactonline.org.

Good Works: Provides information on nonprofit jobs as well as access to nonprofit job listings. http://www.essential.org/goodworks/.

Terry McAdam, *Doing Well by Doing Good: The Complete Guide to Careers in the Non-Profit Sector* (The Taft Group). Provides insight and information on deciding on and finding a career in the nonprofit sector.

Richard Steckel and Jennifer Lehman, *In Search of America's Best Non-Profits* (San Francisco: Jossey-Bass, 1997). Provides a great deal of information about nonprofits, including a section on careers and finding a job.

Canadian Non-Profit Resource Network: Provides information on jobs in Canada. http://www.waterloo.org/cnrn.

Access: Useful information for the nonprofit career search. http://www.accessjobs.org.

The Nonprofit Career Center: Provides an extensive list compiled by Action without Borders. http://www.idealist.org/career.html.

Public interest lobbies

Genuine Do-Gooders can lobby for the public interest. Lobbying groups exist for every issue imaginable, from children's rights advocacy (Children's Defense Fund) to environmental issues (Greenpeace USA). Chances are that if you feel that something is a serious issue, others probably share your view, and there is likely to be a lobbying group operating for your interests somewhere in the country. On the facing page is just a small sample of the thousands of lobbying organizations that exist in many fields.

Lobbying organizations advocating similar agendas often differ greatly in size, budget, and political influence. Most of the major lobbying organizations keep headquarters in Washington, DC, but this does not mean their efforts are solely concentrated on national issues. Many of the larger organizations operate in state capitals and major U.S. cities.

The following sources can be used to explore careers in public interest lobbying:

Foundation of Public Affairs, *Public Interest Profiles* (Washington, DC: Congressional Quarterly, 1998): Provides general and contact information on more than 300 public interest groups.

Environmental Career Opportunities: Newsletter providing more than 600 jobs monthly, including environmental lobbying and environmental nonprofits. For more information, visit the newsletter's Web site at http://www.ecojobs.com.

Access: Web site providing information on careers and organizations dealing with public lobbying. http://www.communityjobs.org.

The Fund for Public Interest Research: Web site providing information on jobs in the public interest sector: http://www.FFPIR.org, or contact them at PO Box 120-271, Boston, MA 02112-0271, Tel. 617 292-8050.

Principle 7.3: Do-good careers pay less on average

In general, pursuing a career in doing good will pay less than a similar job somewhere else. The marketing director of a local United Way with a $15 million budget, for example, will be paid less than 70 percent of the salary of the marketing manager at a private

A select list of public interest groups by field

BUSINESS/ECONOMIC
- Co-op America
- U.S. Chamber of Commerce

CIVIL/CONSTITUTIONAL
RIGHTS
- American Civil Liberties Union
- Children's Defense Fund
- National Association for the Advancement of Colored People

COMMUNITY/GRASSROOTS
- Mothers Against Drunk Driving
- Center for Community Change
- United States Public Interest Research Group

CONSUMER/HEALTH
- American Foundation for AIDS Research
- National Coalition on Health Care
- National Safe Workplace Institute

CORPORATE ACCOUNTABILITY/RESPONSIBILITY
- Business for Social Responsibility
- Council on Economic Priorities
- Investor Responsibility Research Center

ENVIRONMENTAL
- Greenpeace USA
- National Audubon Society

- National Wildlife Federation
- Sierra Club

INTERNATIONAL AFFAIRS
- American Committee on Africa
- Human Rights Watch
- Institute for International Economics

POLITICAL/GOVERNMENTAL
PROCESS
- Arab American Institute
- Common Cause
- Fund for a Conservative Majority

PUBLIC INTEREST LAW
- Alliance for Justice
- National Legal Center for the Public Interest
- Trial Lawyers for Public Justice

RELIGIOUS
- American Jewish Congress
- Interfaith Center on Corporate Responsibility
- National Conference of Catholic Bishops/United States Catholic Conference

THINK TANKS
- American Enterprise Institute
- The Brookings Institute
- The CATO Institute
- The Urban Institute

company with $15 million in sales. You could be the executive director of a local community center, responsible for a $2 million budget and make less than $50,000 a year in 1998. Lower pay is part of the deal not just because salaries for comparable jobs are less, but also because there is less room for job advancement. The pattern is even true for many business careers for do-gooders. Lawyers who fight for the rights of the poor or the average consumer, for example, will on average make less than those who take on more lucrative cases.

There are, however, significant exceptions to this pattern. Some government jobs pay well at higher levels of management and carry good pension benefits. Some top managers working for nonprofits are making six-figure incomes. This is true for nonprofit hospitals, foundations, research institutes, and universities. Well-managed organizations usually pay reasonable salaries for most positions. Boards who have expertise in developing viable organizations usually direct them, which means, among other things, that they know it takes money to get and retain good people. A 1997 report by Towers Perrin indicated that CEOs of major national nonprofits had average salaries in excess of $160,000 per year and that office managers, a position that does not require a college degree, made an average of $42,000 a year.

Despite these exceptions, the choice of a career that serves to improve society will require some financial sacrifice that makes sense only if you are committed to the cause. If you are not ready to make those sacrifices, you can still do a lot to help society in your roles as volunteer, donor, and citizen.

Principle 7.4: Always put the mission first

If you choose such a career—as a doctor, government meat inspector, or a charity fundraiser, for example, you must put the mission of the organization above your own interest and the survival of the organization itself. This requirement plays out differently in business, government, and nonprofit organizations.

Businesses

Businesses with a do-good mission are confronted daily with the choice between making as much money as possible and remaining true to their mission. The biggest danger is the practice of what is called "creaming," where you service only those segments of the population that are profitable to service. For example, insurance businesses might avoid coverage in inner cities, or private schools might take only high-achieving students. The inevitable pressure toward creaming might ultimately do harm to the public good, especially with respect to the goal of leveling the playing field. The profit motive will also create pressures to cut corners by, for example, understaffing. As a Genuine Do-Gooder, you don't want to be part of an organization that promotes a nonlevel playing field.

There are other inherent conflicts facing the Genuine Do-Gooder who chooses a career in a business that works to improve society. The conflicts apply whether you are in business for yourself or work for an organization. If you are a lawyer, you and your law firm must place the legitimate needs of all of your clients above your drive to make money. If you are a doctor, you and your hospital or medical practice must make sure your patient load does not exceed your capacity. If you are a media manager, you and your network must commit to truth above all else. If you are a banker or insurance company manager, your company ultimately must be more concerned about the general ramifications of your decisions for society as a whole than your profit.

If you work for a business that provides traditional government services, you are obligated to give the same or better quality services at equal or lower cost than your predecessor. The failure of your company or yourself to honestly serve your clients in order to keep profits high or to get a raise is more than just bad business. It violates the public trust you and your company accepted when you went into that business.

Government

Government careers have the same conflict as businesses seeking to do good. Working to enhance your position and hence your salary or to enlarge the budget of your department will come into conflict with the mission of your department to serve society. Your military unit may seek to maintain its base even though it serves no function in national defense or you may not challenge the illegal activities of your direct supervisor because you fear it may hurt your career advancement.

Government workers have an additional burden. They sometimes do not receive the support or respect, even from elected officials, that the large majority of them deserve. The reasons for this are related to the kinds of jobs government workers have to perform, like collecting taxes, enforcing the law, and trying to meet the needs of the entire society. Despite the bad press, the majority of government workers live up to their job descriptions. Many bring so much enthusiasm, dedication, and ingenuity to their government work that they make a huge difference in peoples' lives. For example:

• Ann Brown, who is chair of the U.S. Consumer Product Safety Commission, and Marc. J. Schoem, director of Recalls and Compliance Division for the Commission, created the Fast-Track Product Recall Program to encourage companies to move quickly to recall potentially unsafe products from the market before they injure or kill people.

• Jean Hatfield, program service manager, and Kathy McLellan, youth service outreach specialist, developed a program to provide day-care providers with preplanned packages of activities for the children they cared for in Johnson County, Kansas.

• Linda Rosenstock, MD, director of the National Institute of Occupational Safety and Health of the U.S. Department of Health and Human Services, joined forces with Mike Acott, president of the National Asphalt Pavement Association, to reduce worker exposure to hazardous fumes by inventing a ventilation system designed by the government and used by manufacturers.

These individuals and many more were recognized by the Council for Excellence in Government in their 1998 Innovations in Government Award Program. Many award programs for outstanding government service are offered by the government as well as business and nonprofit organizations. They include:

The Council for Excellence in Government
1301 K Street, NW, Suite 450 W
Washington, DC 20005
Tel. 202 728-0418 Fax 202 728-0422
http://www.excelgov.org

The Alfred P. Sloan Foundation's Program
630 Fifth Ave., Suite 2550
New York, NY 10111-0242
Tel. 212 649-1649 Fax 212 757-5117
http://www.sloan.org

National Center for Small Communities
444 N. Capitol Street, NW, Suite 208
Washington, DC 20001
Tel. 202 624-3550
http://www.natat.org/ncsc/

Governing Public Officials of the Year Award
1100 Connecticut Ave., NW, Suite 1300
Washington, DC 20036
Fax 212 862-0032

Nonprofit Organizations

Working for a nonprofit raises the same conflict between your own self-interest and the mission of the organization. Your own integrity will be the determining factor, just as it is for the businessperson who works in a field that seeks to improve society and the government official who is committed to a career that improves society.

However, nonprofit workers face an additional conflict. You have neither the discipline of business profits nor the checks and balances of government to keep you on the right path. You will need to ask yourself continually if what you are doing is best for the organization and the mission it pursues.

To get an idea of the kind of achievements that those in the nonprofit sector achieve, you may want to study the activities of the winners of the John W. Gardner Leadership Award. This award is provided by the Independent Sector to "recognize living individuals who build, mobilize and unify people, institutions or causes." For more information, contact:

The Independent Sector
1200 Eighteenth Street, NW, Suite 200
Washington, DC 20036
Tel. 202 467-6100 Fax 202 467-6101
http://www.indepsec.org

This means holding your organization to very high standards. Given poor funding and the dependence on gifts from people and from the government, your nonprofit can make the mistake of trying to do too much with too few resources. You have a duty not to let that happen. You must maintain your focus and the focus of your organization.

Public interest lobbies

Since public interest lobbies are basically in the business of sales, they must make sure that they do not oversell themselves. Although they must remain steadfast in their positions, they should avoid swallowing their own message to such an extent that they cannot compromise. Since lobbyists always have to tell their targets that what they want is what's good for the country, self-delusion is a perpetual problem. Even more important, they must avoid actions that threaten the integrity of the process through which they seek to influence elected officials. Genuine Do-Gooders who work for public interest organizations should never threaten or seek to destroy other public interest groups. Their efforts should be directed at influencing elected officials, not winning at all costs.

QUIZ RESULTS

1. For-profit businesses cannot provide careers for Genuine Do-Gooders.
Answer: No. Careers in doing good are not reserved for nonprofits and the government. Many for-profit businesses and lucrative professions have as their primary mission life, liberty, or the pursuit of happiness. In fact, there may be more jobs in for-profit business that have a mission of doing good than there are in the government and nonprofit organizations.

2. Careers in doing good will pay less on average.
Answer: Yes. The gap may be narrowing and there are some high-paying jobs, but on the whole the average is lower than for careers outside of doing good.

3. Careers in doing good require a higher standard of behavior than other careers.
Answer: Yes. In businesses that do good the mission may get in the way of profits or the survival of the agency. The Genuine Do-Gooder must always choose the mission first. This is not the case for businesses that do not serve to improve society; their owners and managers tend to place profits above everything

else. However, for-profit companies can give some resources to improving society as part of their sense of social responsibility, but only those gifts do not seriously undermine the profitability of the business.

III

Finding Nearby Windows of Opportunity

8 Families

QUIZ

1. Trying to improve conditions for your child leads to opportunities to do good for society.
Circle one: Yes   No   Not Sure

2. Volunteering to improve conditions for your child is a win-win situation.
Circle one: Yes   No   Not Sure

3. Making a commitment to support groups that help you deal with family challenges can be a direct path to making a major impact on society.
Circle one: Yes   No   Not Sure

INTRODUCTION

As we will see throughout this section, there are an endless supply of nearby windows of opportunity for doing good. Your family is probably the easiest outlet for finding nearby windows, and so I will begin this section by turning to family. The activities you undertake with members of your family and the ways in which you support them as they pursue life, liberty, and happiness will inevitably lead you into contact with a variety of organizations and opportunities through which you can do good. Perhaps the most common example of this is how parents, like Robert Gonnam, get involved in their children's sports programs.

Robert Gonnam: Soccer dad and then some

When Robert Gonnam's daughter Michele was a child, she was an avid soccer player. Her interest gave Gonnam the perfect window of opportunity to blend three driving forces in his life: his children, his love of sports, and his life-long devotion to teaching and guiding children. Gonnam became the coach of his daughter's team, and father and daughter enjoyed years as player and coach. But when his daughter aged out of the soccer league, Gonnam did not stop coaching. To date he has coached more than 334 soccer teams ranging from eight-year-olds to adults, and has pioneered training programs for several towns. He has also created referee programs and offered free clinics for kids who want to improve their soccer skills. Gonnam's daughter opened the door for her father, but it was he who seized the opportunity to do good as a soccer dad extraordinaire.

Whether putting on a holiday show for the community, working as a volunteer in the school your child attends, creating a neighborhood watch group, or joining a support group to help a family member deal with a crisis or serious illness, choosing to do good for your children or other family members always has a triple effect. You can help yourself and your loved ones, improve a small piece of society, and set an example for your family.

Principle 8.1:   Parents must set an example

If you are a parent, you know that children have a tendency to turn their parents' lives upside down. While this tendency is sometimes overwhelming, if not painful, it also has an up side. Parenthood opens up many nearby windows of opportunity for being a volunteer, a donor, and a good citizen.

Parenting, when done right, is an intensive and comprehensive experience. As a parent who whole-heartedly accepts the responsibility of raising a child, you will become so involved in shaping that child's environment that you will have no choice but to become active. The more you embrace opportunities for doing good for the sake of making a better place for your child, the better you will be as a parent. You will be demonstrating to your child through your actions the importance of doing good, and you will be making a better social and physical environment in which your child will develop.

Your work in parent-oriented volunteer activities serve as a model for your child, and a study by the Independent Sector shows that 65 percent of adults who volunteer did so as youths; studies have consistently shown that youths who are active in school groups, student government, and religious organizations are much more likely to volunteer than those who are not. Genuine Do-Gooders need to get their kids involved as early as possible. Here are some suggestions for how you as a parent can encourage your child to become a Genuine Do-Gooder:

1. Volunteer as a family. The best way to get your children to volunteer is to be a role model. For example, 1997 Daily Point of Light Award winners Dale and Angie Anderson put on a Christmas show with their children in their back yard for more than 10,000 people, involving the whole family in serving the community. Less ambitious family projects might include:
   - Cleaning up the roadside on Earth Day;
   - Participating in a walk-a-thon together;
   - Serving meals to the homeless on a holiday;
   - Organizing safe areas for trick-or-treating on Halloween; and
   - Putting up luminaries during Christmas season.

Volunteering as a family provides your children with a good model for improving society and a hands-on learning experience simultaneously. If that's not enough to persuade you to volunteer as a family, consider this: it is a lot cheaper to spend two hours cleaning the local park than it is to take the family to a movie!

The inspiration for volunteering as a family is sometimes initiated by the child, not the parent. Ted Gross was walking his three-year-old daughter in Manhattan when his daughter noticed a homeless man huddled inside a carton. She said to her father, "That man's cold, Daddy. Can we take him home?" Gross recalls, "It was a shock of recognition that I had a new kind of responsibility for myself, for him, but probably most of all for her." Out of that experience came the Common Cents program, described in chapter 15, which organizes schoolchildren to collect and distribute money to organizations that aid the homeless, and other needy organizations.

2. Lobby your schools to increase opportunities for volunteering. The growing movement to encourage, academically reward, and, at the high school level, even require students to serve their community is something that parents should encourage. Some parents and educators fight this trend on the grounds that it coerces service and is therefore not volunteering, or that it takes time away from academic work. If they are fighting this trend because they are concerned about the good of society, then they are entitled to their opinion. Feel free to join them. But if you agree that service helps to educate children on how to become responsible adults and good citizens, lobby for more time and resources to encourage volunteer activity.

3. Be active in your child's school as a rower. Studies demonstrate that parental involvement is an important key to the performance of children as students. The most successful schools are those in which parent involvement is plentiful, and the least successful schools are those in which it is not. You need to support your child's school with such volunteer activities as raising money for school trips, serving as a tutor or volunteer on the playground or in the cafeteria, or attending open houses.

4. Be active in your child's school as a steerer. You can play a strong role in the governance of your child's school by participating on official school committees like the Site-Based Planning Committee, by being active in the Parent-Teachers Association (PTA), and supporting candidates for the school board. There are several national organizations that you may want to contact and perhaps join that will help you play a positive role in the school. They are:

Parents for Public Schools (PPS)
PO Box 12807
Jackson, MS 39236-2807
Tel. 800 880-1222   Fax 601 982-0002

National Associations of Partners in Education (NAPE)
901 Pitt Street, Suite 320
Alexandria, VA 22314
Tel. 703 836-4880

National PTA
330 N. Wabash Ave., Suite 2100
Chicago, IL 60611
Tel. 312 670-6782 or 800 307-4PTA   Fax 312 670-6783

Principle 8.2:   Be positive in your parental efforts

The most intense and common type of volunteering you will face as a parent occurs during the K–12 years. It is also the time when you are likely to find yourself in some difficult situations. It is a good idea to be aware of some of the risks you might face during these years:

1. Your child drags you into an activity, and you are only a half-hearted participant.
2. Your child drags you into an activity that you really enjoy, but then your child decides it is uncool.
3. You cannot treat your child fairly when working with a group of children either because you lean over backwards to be fair and mistreat your own child or you lean over forward and mistreat the other children.
4. You cannot stand the parents of the other children, or, conversely, the other children's parents cannot stand you.
5. You only worry about creating better conditions for your own child—and ignore the concerns of other children.
6. You damage your relationship with your children by becoming too involved and invading their space.

Genuine Do-Gooders take volunteer activities associated with their children very seriously because of the significant benefits that can accrue from a good experience as well as the enormous risks presented by the opportunities. Parents can almost guarantee positive volunteer experiences with their children by following the same principles that all acts of doing good follow; namely, that they do no intentional harm and that they contribute to the general good. Parents can ensure that they follow these principles by thinking about the following questions each time they make a decision as a donor, volunteer, or citizen: Will my action improve society or serve only the interests of my own child? When giving, is it for a good cause that I would give to even if my child were not involved? When volunteering, am I building a stronger organization that will continue to thrive long after my child moves on? When I lobby for a program in a school, will that program meet a generally unmet need or simply help my child?

These questions are not meant to suggest that you should ignore the interests of your child. They are posed so that you maintain the kind of balance required of the Genuine Do-Gooder—a balance between your own self interests, your child's interests, and the interests of society. The questions help you to do this by making you move beyond your immediate interests to think about the long-term good of society. If you can do this, you will have set a good model for your child and you will avoid the kind of hostility and selfishness we sometimes see when parents become overprotective and overcompetitive as volunteers.

Principle 8.3:　**Move from your family to the world**

The challenges of parenthood, as well as other family matters, frequently create stress and problems. Ultimately, this stress and these problems bring you to nearby windows that can lead to quite a lot of doing good. For example, Mothers Against Drunk Driving, which has more than 600 chapters nationwide, has had a major impact on legislation and education in this country. The organization was originally started by a small group of California women in 1980 after the death of a 13-year-old girl from a hit-and-run accident. The selected list* on the next page provides similar examples of support groups that have national and international scope, and all of which resulted from a challenge faced by one particular family.

---

*From Barbara J. White and Edward J. Madara, *The Self-Help Sourcebook*, Denville: Northwest Covenant Medical Center, 1998.

Selected List of Support Groups for Parents

ACES (Association for Children for Enforcement of Support) helps parents who have custody of their children and have difficulty collecting child support payments.Location services on nonpayers are available as well.

ACES c/o Geraldine Jensen
2260 Upton Ave.
Toledo, OH 43606
Tel. 800 537-7072
http://www.childsupport-aces.org

Dad-to-Dad brings at-home fathers together through children's play groups, field trips, dads' night out dinners, and a monthly newsletter. Provides information and referrals, as well as phone support and literature.

Dad-to-Dad c/o Curtis Cooper
13925 Duluth Drive
Apple Valley, MN 55124
Tel. 612 423-3795

FEMALE (Formerly Employed Mothers at the Leading Edge) provides support for women who have left the full-time work force to raise their children at home, as well as for all women dealing with transformation between paid employment and at-home mothering.

FEMALE
PO Box 31
Elmhurst, IL 60126
Tel. 630 941-3551

Full-Time Dads provides networking and support for fathers (married or single). Provides a forum for sharing information, resources, and experiences through a bi-monthly journal.

Full-Time Dads c/o James McLoughlin
379 Clifton Ave.
Clifton, NJ 07011
Tel. 973 772-9444

MADD focuses on effective solutions to drunken driving and underage drinking problems. The organization is made up of mothers, fathers, sisters, friends, and others who are willing to support people who have experienced the pain of this senseless crime.

MADD
511 E. John Carpenter Freeway, #700
Irving, TX 75062-8187
Tel. 212 744-6233
http://www.madd.org

MOPS (Mothers of Pre-Schoolers) is a fellowship of mothers of preschoolers (birth to first grade) that offers a nurturing, caring environment with a spiritual focus.

MOPS
1311 S. Clarkson Street
Denver, CO 80210
Tel. 303 733-5353
http://www.mops.org

MUMS National Parent to Parent Network provides mutual support and networking for families dealing with children with rare birth defects, chromosomal abnormalities, and medical or undiagnosed conditions. Also matches families with extremely rare disorders.

MUMS
150 Custer Court
Green Bay, WI 54301
Tel. 920 336-5333

National Foster Parent Association is a support, education, and advocacy group for foster parents and their children. Resource center for foster care information.

National Foster Parent Assoc.
9 Dartmoor Drive
Crystal Lake, IL 60014
Tel. 800 557-5238

National Organization of Mothers of Twins Clubs is a forum for mothers of multiple births to share information, concerns, and advice on dealing with their unique problems.

National Org. of Mothers of Twins
PO Box 23188
Albuquerque, NM 87192-1188
http://www.nomotc.org

National Organization for Men seeks equal rights for men, and uniform national divorce, custody, property, and visitation laws. Offers educational seminars, lawyer referrals, and a quarterly newsletter.

National. Org. for Men
11 Park Place
New York, NY 10007
Tel. 212 686-MALE
http://www.tnom.com

P-FLAG (Parents and Friends of Lesbians and Gays) advocates equal rights for lesbian, gay, transgender, and bisexual people.

P-FLAG
1101 Fourteenth Street, NW, Suite 1030
Washington, DC 20005
Tel. 202 638-4200
http://www.pflag.org

PWP (Parents without Partners) educational nonprofit organization of single parents, either divorced, separated, widowed, or never married.

PWP
401 N. Michigan Ave.
Chicago, IL 60611-4267
Tel. 800 637-7974

Tough Love International is a self-help program for parents, kids, and communities dealing with the out-of-control behavior of a family member. Parent support groups help parents take a firm stand to help kids take responsibility for their behavior.

Tough Love Int'l
PO Box 1069
Doylestown, PA 18901
Tel. 800 333-1069

Of course, there is more to being a member of a family than raising kids or even helping out as a loving aunt, uncle, or grandparent. Other family responsibilities can serve as nearby windows of opportunity for volunteering. For example, people are living longer as adults and are increasingly responsible for the care of their parents as they age. The expression "sandwich generation" is used to describe today's 40- and 50-year-olds who are trying to support both their college-age children and their aging parents. If you are providing support for older relatives, you may want to join one of the many groups that deal with the older segment of the population. Such organizations include:

Arthritis Foundation
1330 W. Peachtree Street
Atlanta, GA 30309
Tel. 800 283-7800
http://www.arthritis.org

Alzheimer's Disease and Related Disorders Association
919 N. Michigan Ave. #1000
Chicago, IL 60611-1676
Tel. 800 272-3900
http://www.alz.org

Children of Aging Parents (CAPS)
1609 Woodbourne Ave., Suite 302A
Levittown, PA 19057
Tel. 800 227-7294

National Family Caregivers Association
10400 Connecticut Ave., Suite 500
Kensington, MD 20895
Tel. 800 896-3650
http://www.nfcacares.org

Support groups are also open to people whose family members have serious health problems and addictions. The number and variety of these groups are impressive. They illustrate the power of the family as a source of strength and development for the Genuine Do-Gooder. They almost always start with the drive of a few who are faced with a strong personal need to do something to deal with their own family problem. If the groups work for them, they usually work for increasingly larger circles of people affected by the same problem.

This is true for John Walsh, host of "America's Most Wanted," who became involved because his son, Adam, was abducted and killed. It is also true of Patricia Wetterling of St. Joseph, Minnesota, the recipient of the March 2, 1998, Points of Light Award, profiled on the next page.

Patricia Wetterling: Helping other parents

In 1989, Patricia Wetterling's son, Jacob, was abducted near home. She and her husband established a foundation of more than 120 active volunteers to educate parents and children and also to search for abducted children. Wetterling has become active throughout the state and country. She has served on the board of the National Center for Missing and Exploited Children, and she trains U.S. Department of Justice's law enforcement officials. She also speaks all over the country raising awareness about the risks our children face.

The progression from small support groups to large and complex institutions is not always warranted and is sometimes counterproductive, as we will see in subsequent chapters. Sometimes the support group that tries to grow may neglect the family problem that stimulated their development in the first place. However, those who join support groups to deal with a family problem or crisis frequently become those who give the most in helping others.

QUIZ RESULTS

1. Trying to improve conditions for your child leads to opportunities to do good for society.
Answer: Yes. This chapter illustrates that by working to improve programs for your child, you are also helping to improve conditions for others and are serving as a role model who will encourage your child to be a Genuine Do-Gooder.

2. Volunteering to improve conditions for your child is a win-win situation.
Answer: Not Sure. The triple effect of helping to improve your child's environment, improving conditions for other children, and improving society, as well as being a positive role model for your child are the benefits of such volunteerism. Therefore, this type of doing good presents a win-win situation.

However, the normal tensions associated with working with others also carries many risks that can have negative results. Recognizing such risks is the key to minimizing them.

3. Making a huge commitment to support groups that help you deal with family challenges can be a direct path to making a major impact on society. Answer: Yes. Almost every major organization was born from the act of a single person, and different coalitions of people that form these support groups can emerge if the mission and leadership are right.

^{9} Neighbors

QUIZ

1. Neighbors need to tear down the moats that surround their homes.

Circle one: Yes   No   Not Sure

2. It is always preferable to work with neighbors on a common problem rather than to work individually.

Circle one: Yes   No   Not Sure

3. The not-in-my-backyard syndrome is a major challenge to progress in improving society.

Circle one: Yes   No   Not Sure

INTRODUCTION

The Dunwoody Homeowners Association, which currently has 15,000 members, is located outside of Atlanta, Georgia, in an unincorporated area in DeKalb County. It is one of the largest and most successful associations in the country. The profile below describes the evolution of this association into a positive community resource.

Numbers build clout

The Dunwoody Homeowners Association was initially formed in the late 1960s when about 20 people successfully stopped the building of condominiums in an area adjacent to large single-family homes. The association then disappeared until the middle 1970s when seven residents banded together to convince a shopping mall developer to adopt a "Williamsburg" look instead of a Mexican adobe theme.

Homeowners associations are frequently viewed as antidevelopment factions, and sometimes they are, although Dunwoody is not. Dunwoody represents a large

number of people who have differences of opinion, participating in community decisions in a variety of ways.
Some of its actions include*:

- Undertaking a reforestation program to compen-
sate for damage from a tornado that went through
the area in the spring of 1998. Dunwoody financed
the purchase of trees and assisted the county in
planting them.
- Stopping the demolition of a historic house and
then purchasing the site and building a town hall
for public meetings.
- Supporting the conversion of an elementary
school into a library and art center.
- Being a source of support for the county planning
and development departments by working with
developers.
- Sending a representative to a regional commission set up to improve the flow of traffic through
the Atlanta metropolitan area.

The Dunwoody Homeowners Association shows how neighbors in
a community can problem-solve together. Neighbors help each other
solve all kinds of problems, from watching the house of another
neighbor who is on vacation to forming a coalition to maintain zoning standards. Forming communal bonds generates power that is
much greater than the sum of the efforts of individual neighbors. To
become part of this source of power, you can work at being a neighborly do-gooder.

Principle 9.1: Build bridges across your moat

Most people see their home as a refuge where they can pursue their family obligations and their personal pleasures, as well as,
for some, a place for their vocational activities. Whether it is a house
or a small apartment, their home is their castle.

However, this metaphor can be taken too seriously when
neighbors build figurative moats around their homes. Over the last
50 years, trends in residential and commercial areas have contributed
to moats that are increasingly difficult to cross. This is true for housing developments as well as for modern apartment buildings.
Sometimes this makes sense, such as when your neighbors are
involved with illegal drugs or are dangerous, but in most cases, it does
not.

*Based on notes from an interview with an early leader of Dunwoody Homeowners, Herb Sprague.

Unfortunately, the moat mentality is characteristic of far too many neighborhoods.

It is possible, however, to build bridges over the moat around your home and in your neighborhood.

There is a nationwide movement, usually termed "New Urbanism," that has been working to develop concrete alternatives to the moat mentality. Below is a list of the features of what a community might look like when community problem solving follows the New Urbanism philosophy. Additional information on the New Urbanism movement can be obtained from Robert Steuteville, editor and publisher of *New Urban News*, PO Box 6515, Ithaca, NY 14851, tel. 607 275-3087.

What a New Urban Community Might Look Like*

1. The neighborhood has a discernible center. This is often a square of green, and is sometimes a busy or memorable street corner. A transit stop would be located at this center.
2. Most of the dwellings are within a five-minute walk of the center, an average of roughly 2,000 feet.
3. There are a variety of dwelling types—usually houses, rowhouses, and apartments—so that younger and older people, singles and families, the poor and the wealthy may find places to live.
4. There are a variety of shops and offices at the edge of the neighborhood that supply the weekly needs of a household.
5. An elementary school is close enough so that most children can walk to it from their homes.
6. There are small playgrounds near every dwelling—not more than a tenth of a mile away.
7. The streets within the neighborhood are a connected network, providing a variety of pedestrian and vehicular routes to any destination, which disperses traffic.
8. The streets are relatively narrow and shaded by rows of trees. This slows traffic, creating an environment suitable for pedestrians and bicycles.
9. Buildings in the neighborhood center are placed close to the street, creating a strong sense of place.

*Adapted from an article by Robert Steuteville, "The New Urbanism Challenges Modern Automobile-Oriented Planning and Development," *In Business,* Aug. 1998.

10. Parking lots and garage doors rarely front the street. Parking is relegated to the rear of the buildings, usually accessed by alleys.
11. Certain prominent sites at the termination of street vistas or in the neighborhood center are reserved for civic buildings. They provide sites for community meetings, education, religion, and cultural activities.
12. The neighborhood is organized to be self-governing. A for mal association debates and decides matters of maintenance, security, and physical change. Taxation is the responsibility of the larger community.

One surefire way to build bridges is to cooperate on specific things. You can collect mail and newspapers when someone is going on vacation. The same is true for dog sitting and cat feeding, not to mention creating a safe haven for children who arrive home before their parents. Cooperation on these specific things will allow you to gather a group of neighbors together when a serious problem needs to be addressed.

Bridge building does not just happen. It requires courage. The biggest threat to people building bridges is the fear that they might be rejected or perceived as pushy. Courage means taking risks, but the opportunities provided by the creation of these bridges far outweigh the risks. A Genuine Do-Gooder will ask a neighbor to feed his cat, for example, before that neighbor asks him. Asking for help may seem to be the opposite of doing good, especially if you believe such obviously flawed universal statements as it is better to give than to receive. On the contrary, making the first move to ask for a favor is a very courageous act that can have the effect of placing the foundation for the bridge that will tie you and your neighbor together. This is true, unless, of course, you are always asking for favors and never returning them.

The test on the following page has two purposes: to determine your good-neighbor potential and, by implication, to show you how to set the stage for neighborly cooperation when neighborhood power is needed.

The Genuine Do-Gooder Neighborhood

Unless you answer yes to all 10 statements, you have some work to do. They are listed in the order of difficulty.

1. I say hello every time I see my neighbor.
   Yes   No
2. I cooperate in watching my neighbors' children.
   Yes   No
3. I offer assistance if I see my neighbor having a problem.
   Yes   No
4. I donate to neighbors who collect for good causes.
   Yes   No
5. I know the names of my 10 closest neighbors.
   Yes   No
6. I would not hesitate to ask my neighbor for help.
   Yes   No
7. I do one neighborhood charity collection myself.*
   Yes   No
8. I participate in welcoming committees for new neighbors.
   Yes   No
9. I try to mobilize neighbors to deal with common problems.
   Yes   No
10. I would participate in and help create a neighborhood phone tree.
    Yes   No

Principle 9.2:   Start small and stay focused

Having many bridges across the moats surrounding the homes of those living in your neighborhood creates a basis for the real work of the Genuine Do-Gooder: working to solve problems that threaten life, liberty, and the pursuit of happiness. A drug house on the block, a mad dog loose on the street, an apartment complex in disrepair, a dangerous corner for driving, or any number of problems that threaten the interest of neighbors are opportunities for cooperative problem solving.

The most common example of how neighbors can mobilize around a problem is in the creation of Neighborhood Watch groups. In response to a growing crime rate, neighbors are working together

*This will count as double do-gooding since you will be collecting money for charities *and* building bridges!

with support groups from local police. The idea first developed in the late 1960s in Los Angeles and received support from the federal government in the 1970s. Today Neighborhood Watch groups exist in more than 9,000 communities throughout the United States. For more information, contact the National Sheriff's Association, 1450 Duke Street, Alexandria, VA 22314-3490, tel. 703 836-7827, http://www.sheriffs.org. While the groups were originally started to provide assistance to police in dealing with crime, many of them have broadened their activities, particularly in highly stressed areas. For example, they may improve the quality of life by providing after-school tutoring programs or by lobbying politicians.

Listed below are three reasons why cooperative efforts to solve community problems are greater than the efforts of a single individual:

1. There is always strength in numbers. Six neighbors have more clout than one. Six neighbors calling a government official, whether it be the police, or a local politician, will get more results than will one person acting alone.

2. As more people become involved in problem solving, it becomes more likely that one of them might know somebody who knows somebody who can say something to the person who is responsible for the problem.

3. As more people are involved, it is more likely that a full and accurate picture of the problem will emerge and a set of possible policies be generated.

There is a tendency for people involved in community problem solving to lose focus. They mistakenly see the goal as building a strong organization rather than solving the problem that created the opportunity in the first place. Those starting neighborhood groups can spend too much time on membership drives and not enough on cooperating to solve the problem.

This discussion raises the question of how much organization is necessary. The answer, like all of the answers in this book, depends upon the context and the persistence of the problem. If a couple of phone calls to the police twice a year can take care of the beer-drinking neighbors who party loudly all night, perhaps a Neighborhood Watch group is not necessary for that problem. In contrast, persistent criminal activity calls for a more formal group.

Many people faced with a problem jump too readily to create

a formal group, when in most cases it is better to form a small committee. Form a committee with two neighbors, get another 10 neighbors to say they are members, give the committee a name and have a telephone list. When you need to get the troops out, you can easily do so by using this approach without the hassle of having monthly meetings. In fact an annual meeting might be sufficient until there is a crisis, at which time frequent meetings would take place.

My general advice is to start small, keep focused on the problem, and grow slowly in size and sophistication. This advice applies in most neighborhoods facing a broad range of traffic, zoning, environmental, and minor criminal problems. Some neighborhoods, particularly in low-income areas, need to take a more systemic approach toward solving the problems that negatively affect their quality of life. High levels of criminal activity, poor service from the government, inadequate low-income housing, poorly performing schools, and lack of local employment opportunities, for example, require a much more organized effort. Such organizations require strong local leadership and a significant effort. Fortunately, you can get help building a grassroots organization. The organizations below provide publications, training, and consultation to help you develop a powerful grassroots group that can coordinate volunteer efforts, obtain grants from government and nonprofits, and lobby government officials.

Association of Community Organizations for Reform Now
(ACORN)
88 Third Street, 3rd floor
Brooklyn, NY 11217
Tel. 718 246-7900   Fax 718 246-7939
http://www.acorn.org

Center for Community Change
1000 Wisconsin Ave., NW
Washington, DC 20007
Tel. 202 342-0567
http://www.communitychange.org

National Training and Information Center (NTIC)
810 N. Milwaukee Ave.
Chicago, Il 60622
Tel. 312 243-3035   Fax 312 243-3038

Principle 9.3:   **NIMBY is not a bad word**

NIMBY is an acronym for "Not in My Backyard," often used negatively to refer to people who object to changing the use of land nearby. It is used by politicians, real estate developers, builders, and homeowners to discredit and demean those who protest the development of an unwanted project in their community. It is a slur tactic that is used indiscriminately. People who participate in neighborhood groups to protect their property values and their standard of living are often watching out for more than just themselves.

On one hand, it is easy to discredit groups that pursue their own self-interest. For example, a group in Englishtown, New Jersey, tried to stop New Horizons in Autism from buying a group home that would house five developmentally disabled teenagers who would be monitored 24 hours a day. The group initially offered New Horizons $10,000 to look elsewhere for the home, and eventually went to extreme legal lengths to stop the agency.* Such behavior is an example of the irresponsible pursuit of self-interest and may deserve the negative connotation the NIMBY word usually carries. However, it is unfair to use the term to discredit a group with a responsible approach to protecting their property and their own safety, especially when the local officials want to rezone an area in a radical way that will have a negative impact on property values.

Many good NIMBY groups work with developers to make sure a new building does not create harmful traffic patterns, rather than just trying to stop development completely. The collaboration of NIMBY groups and developers can make efficient and significant changes in the community, as illustrated by the actions of the Dunwoody Homeowners Association. Developers and local politicians may have quarrels with NIMBY groups but over the long haul, they usually respect and work with them.

In short, both good NIMBYs and bad NIMBYs exist. Some NIMBYs accept the need for economic development for the sake of the community, and others want to hang on to the status quo forever. Building permits and zoning issues occupy enormous blocks of time for government officials and can set off very heated debates within communities. However, if a town board is going to allow some builder to pave over vast areas of the local wetlands or create another million square feet of retail space six blocks away from a dead mall, it may be time to lie down in front of the bulldozer.

*Evelyn Nieves, "Sure Things: Taxes, NIMBY and Waving," *New York Times*, Aug. 23, 1998, p. 29.

QUIZ RESULTS

1. Neighbors need to tear down the moats that surround their homes.

Answer: No. Moats are necessary to protect our privacy and our security. Neighbors need to build bridges across the moats so that they can help each other when problems arise. Block parties and frequent conversations serve as the foundation for those bridges, not sand to fill in the moats.

2. It is always preferable to work with neighbors on a common problem than it is to work individually.

Answer: Yes. Neighborhood problems are always better solved by a group.

3. The not-in-my-backyard syndrome is a major challenge to progress in improving society.

Answer: No. Most NIMBYs exist because community members are working together on behalf of their shared interests. When they become too narrow and selfish, they threaten life, liberty, and the pursuit of happiness for others. In most cases, though, they are representing the interest of the people, and that is the nature of democracy.

10 Employees

QUIZ

1. It is so difficult to develop and apply clear criteria for corporate social responsibility that little progress can be made in shaping the behavior of corporations.
Circle one: Yes   No   Not Sure

2. The business of business is to make a profit, which ultimately is incompatible with corporate social responsibility.
Circle one: Yes   No   Not Sure

3. Working to increase the social responsibility of your corporation's policies can hurt you and your company.
Circle one: Yes   No   Not Sure

INTRODUCTION

Whatever collar you wear as a paid employee, you are part of the organization you work for. This chapter looks at your place of work as something more than a contractual obligation in which you exchange your time and effort for a paycheck. It is certainly not that way for Judy Hamby.

Judy Hamby: Creating philanthropists

Judy Hamby's job title, senior managing director, general manager, and U.S. creative director for Hill & Knowlton, one of the world's biggest international public relations firms, provides some indication of the major role she plays at work. While some of her activities include direct marketing and public relations consultation services for a wide variety of traditional business clients, she also plays a major role in encouraging and focusing the philanthropic activities of her clients.

She is the chair of Hill & Knowlton's Corporate Philanthropic Asset Group, which provides services to clients who want to improve society as part of their corporate mission. She, personally, has a long record of doing good, including serving on boards of several charities and giving more than 500 speeches nationally for the American Cancer Society. Not only is she working for a profit-making company and earning a living by doing so, she is also helping her client companies to do well by doing good.

Hamby is also a driving force in the corporate world for creating nearby windows of opportunity for the employees of her clients. Like her, you need to see the place where you work as your "home away from home" and, therefore, a nearby window of opportunity for doing good.

Principle 10.1: **Take your principles to work**

The former CEO of the Coca-Cola Company, Robert C. Goizeuta (1931–1997), said, "The exercise of what is commonly referred to as 'corporate responsibility' is a supremely rational, logical corollary of a company's essential responsibility to the long-term interests of its shareholders." In short, he suggests that doing good in a purposeful and reasonable way is a good business practice.

"Corporate social responsibility" is the practice of weighing the long-term consequences for society in each business decision and taking positive actions to improve society rather than going for a profit at whatever the cost to society. There is plenty of room for interpretation over what the criteria of corporate social responsibility should be and even more over whether or not a given decision is responsible. Ultimately, like all other acts of the Genuine Do-Gooder, you as an individual have to make your own decisions.

Fortunately, we can rely on the work of the Council of

Economic Priorities (CEP) to evaluate "corporate social responsibility, with the goal of encouraging and expanding good corporate citizenship worldwide." CEP, which operates primarily as a research and recognition organization, is one of several very influential nonprofits that rate corporations on a variety of standards, or "screens."

CEP has developed a rating system to grade corporations from A to F that gives a pretty good idea of whether or not they are socially responsible. It rates hundreds of corporations to inform consumer and investor decisions (more on this in chapters 11 and 12). CEP rates corporations in the following eight areas:

1. Environment
2. Women's advancement
3. Minority advancement
4. Charitable giving
5. Community outreach
6. Family benefits
7. Workplace issues
8. Disclosure of information

Of the eight areas identified by CEP, five—environment, women's advancement, minority advancement, family benefits, and workplace issues—relate to everyday business practices within a company. As an employee you can encourage company policies that correspond to the standards contained in the CEP screens. You can suggest ways of improving the company's recycling efforts or, when participating in hiring decisions, make sure that women and minorities are treated fairly. You can make formal suggestions on corporate benefit programs or on how to reduce injuries on the job. Although your own position in the company will partially define the influence you might or might not have over company policies, you should seek to influence these policies through your day-to-day actions and specific initiatives when warranted.

Three of the eight CEP screens—charitable giving, community outreach, and disclosure of information—relate to external works. The first two need little explanation—the more corporate giving and involvement in the community, the more the corporation has taken a socially responsible role. However, disclosure of information requires some discussion.

Disclosure of information as measured by CEP is the degree

to which corporations provide complete and current material on social programs and policies either to CEP or in public reports. Willingness to admit to social responsibility is itself a measure of social responsibility, although as imperfect as most other measures. First, a company that is unwilling to do so can be presumed to be less than proud of its record. Second, a company that has its information organized enough to provide it is probably one in which top management has some commitment to corporate social responsibility, even if it is only for PR purposes. Third, the herd instinct is extremely important in building attitudes—good and bad. Given the competitiveness and the monkey-see-monkey-do pattern of behavior for people and business organizations, in particular, the more social responsibility comes out of the corporate closet by public disclosure, the more we will have of it.

Although these eight screens are relatively comprehensive, you may want to add others, such as protecting animal rights or refusing to use labor in countries that have abusive child labor practices. You can select those causes that are of high priority to you and work to change the practices of your company with respect to those causes. For further information on CEP and other sources of screens, consult any of the following:

> Coalition for Environmentally Responsible Economics (CERES)
> 11 Arlington Street
> Boston, MA 02116
> Tel. 617 247-0700   Fax 617 267-5400

> Co-op America
> 1612 K Street, NW, Suite 600
> Washington, DC 20006
> Tel. 800 58-GREEN   Fax 202 331-8166
> http://www.coopamerica.org

> Council on Economic Priorities
> 30 Irving Place, 9th floor
> New York, NY 10003
> Tel. 212 420-1133
> http://www.cepnyc.org

> Kinder, Lydenburg, Domini & Co., Inc.
> 129 Mount Auburn Street

Cambridge, MA 02138
Tel. 617 547-7479   Fax 617 354-5353

Socialfunds.com
http://www.socialinvest.org

Do not assume that social responsibility screens can be used only for what appears to be center and left-of-center issues of the political spectrum. The origins of the movement, as we will see in chapter 12, developed out of the anti-apartheid, civil rights, and environment protection movements of the 1960s and 1970s. However, the idea of corporate social responsibility is politically neutral. It permits you to support any company activity that you believe moves America closer to the principles of the Declaration of Independence. That may include company policies that contribute to a strong military or seek to raise standards of morality in the entertainment industry through advertising guidelines.

Given the general applicability of the idea, you should conduct your own "audit" of your company using the screens that make the most sense to you. You should include both positive policies (what your company should do) and negative policies (what it should not do). The checklist below is just a start. Revise it as you wish and then study where your company stands.

How Socially Responsible Is Your Company?

Rate where you work by circling the appropriate letter.
Exceptional: E   Satisfactory: S   Needs Work: NW   Horrible: H
Don't Know: DK
My company or organization . . .
   1. Follows all environmental regulations in disposing its waste.
      E S NW H DK
   2. Implements policies to reduce excessive waste.
      E S NW H DK
   3. Maintains an environment that supports the advancement
      of women and minorities.
      E S NW H DK
   4. Creates an environment safe from physical and
      emotional harm.
      E S NW H DK

5. Makes cash contributions equal to or more than 1.1 percent of the company's annual pre-tax profits—the current national average for corporate giving.
   E S NW H DK
6. Encourages its employees to take part in community service.
   E S NW H DK
7. Implements family-friendly policies (e.g., flex time).
   E S NW H DK
8. Practices a fair and open hiring process.
   E S NW H DK
9. Discloses answers regarding social responsibility questions.
   E S NW H DK
10. Avoids racial, gender, and class stereotypes in its advertising.
    E S NW H DK

Principle 10.2:   Duties don't end at bottom line

By now you may be saying to yourself, "I've got enough trouble pleasing my boss, working with my colleagues to increase profits, and helping my organization survive in the mean world out there. Now you want me to make sure my organization is a good citizen? Give me a break."

If you did say this to yourself, you are a slave to the viewpoint that doing good is incompatible with doing business. This viewpoint is embodied in a mean-spirited little article written by Milton Friedman,* the economist whose book *Free to Choose* argues that economic freedom is an end in and of itself and claims the social responsibility of business is to increase its profits.

Putting aside ideological arguments, which you, as a potential Genuine Do-Gooder, should have already done, you have every right to worry about the inherent conflict between getting your corporation to be a good citizen and keeping your wallet full. As an employee, you are taking a risk if you are perceived by some to be motivated by anything but the bottom line. At the corporate level, top managers would face a challenge if they proposed action that is not intended to increase profits, at least in the long run.

There is considerable truth to this. The bottom line, whether it is after-tax profits for Microsoft or the volume of service hours provided by the Salvation Army, should never be ignored. You should not miss a production deadline because you were busy organizing a

*Milton Friedman, "The Social Responsibility of Business Is to Increase Its Profits," *Case and Readings in Markets, Ethics and Law* (Ginn Press, 1997), p. 122.

walk-a-thon. Your company's management should not increase its corporate cash donations if its sales are plummeting. Doing good cannot get in the way of necessary business operations.

However, working to improve your company's treatment of its employees and the outside world can increase productivity and profits. For example, look at the following examples of doing good in the workplace.

Employees who do good tend to do well

As an employee doing your job well, you can act ethically when completing your job duties and be a model employee who cooperates with other members of the organization. Volunteering to work on committees that organize special events such as parties or internal awards is a way to build a stronger corporate community. Participating as much as possible in training programs and enrichment activities provided by your company also helps build the corporate community. Taking the time to demonstrate genuine caring for your colleagues is also critical. Being a good company citizen is likely to lead to higher salaries and career advancement while contributing to the general good.

Moreover, studies show that employees who work for companies that have good records of corporate responsibility are likely to have higher morale and to have better career advancement than those who do not.* Within reason, doing good has its direct payoffs to employees.

Companies can be generous and prosper

Organizations that are good citizens are likely to prosper more than those that are not. As we will discuss in the next two chapters, consumers and investors are increasingly interested in buying from organizations like Toyota, Colgate-Palmolive Co., The Body Shop, Tom's of Maine, and Levi Strauss, which have high ratings according to most of the eight CEP screens. Worker productivity tends to be higher as well, according to a survey of corporate managers in a 1992 study by the Conference Board.

To underscore this point, Curt Weeden has written a book entitled *Corporate Social Investing*. He suggests that we call the corporate acts of doing good "corporate social investing" because, if done

*Studies by David Lewis, UCLA. Portion of study available at http://www.usaweekend. com/diffday/ guide_employer.html.

right, doing good can help the bottom line. A former Johnson & Johnson vice president who directed his company's huge philanthropy program of close to $150 million a year, Weeden has plenty of experience in the world of corporate social investing. He suggests first that corporations change the way they think about giving from "philanthropy" to "corporate social investing." He also advises corporations to "identify significant business reasons for every corporate social investment and obtain as much business value from social investments as is allowable and practical."*

The point of these two recommendations is that corporations have a stake in the society in which they operate. In most cases, rising standards of living and social stability will help the business grow. Moreover, companies can use social responsibility as a marketing device like the Coca-Cola 10-year, $60 million deal with the Boys and Girls Club to get its name associated with a high-quality feel-good agency.** Johnson & Johnson's Community Health Care Crystal Award Program, where the award has the effect of associating the Johnson & Johnson name with an outstanding health service organization, encourages the award winner to invite its congressional representative to the ceremony. This markets the company's name not just to future consumers but to those in Washington who will be lobbied in the future.

Louise Arnett of Villa Hills, Kentucky, provides an example of what you can do as a volunteer who works for a business. This August 7, 1998, Daily Point of Light Award winner has played a key role in promoting community service by the employees at Federated Department Stores.

Louise Arnett: Bringing co-workers along

Louise Arnett has volunteered for the past 20 years at a variety of nonprofits, including the Boy Scouts of America and the Franciscans at St. Johns. She has perhaps had the biggest impact encouraging volunteerism at her place of work. Arnett is a founding member of her company's Partners in Time program, where she leads more than 50 employee participants in the annual United Way Community Care Week. She currently serves on the steering committee of the organization, which runs nearly 30

* Curt Weeden, *Corporate Social Responsibility* (San Francisco: Berrett-Koehler Publishers, 1998), p. 11.
** Ibid., p. 155.

projects each year. She also volunteers by regularly serving meals to children who are at risk of hunger in northern Kentucky.

If you want to enhance social responsibility at your own workplace, you can choose from a variety of activities that includes both rowing and steering. There are an infinite number of ways you can provide one or more services through your company. Here are a few rowing suggestions:

1. Community outreach: Clean up an at-risk local playground.
2. Tutoring of employees: Participate in a tutoring program for employees who want to improve such skills as reading, word processing, and writing.
3. Car pooling: Use e-mail and bulletin boards to help people find out about the possibility of traveling together.
4. Beautification projects: Plant trees and flowers outside the office building and in the neighborhood.
5. Local school outreach: Visit a local school and offer tutoring during lunch time or after school.

If you want to motivate your company and its employees to do more, you can take on a steering role. Here are some suggestions on how you might do that:

1. Set up formal programs: Each of the individual efforts listed above could lead you to develop a more formal company-wide commitment and thereby greatly expand the impact of your efforts. Be sure to coordinate your efforts through corporate managers who are assigned the task of encouraging community service.
2. Contact the National Association of Partners in Education (NAPE): With more than 400,000 partnerships between businesses and public schools nationwide, NAPE will put you in touch with local school officials and businesses that will help you sell a project to top management. Concern about our public schools is so deep in the business community that you should be able to get the attention of company officials.

   National Association of Partners in Education
   901 N. Pitt Street, Suite 320
   Alexandria, VA 22314
   Tel. 703 836-4880

3. Encourage your company to join Business for Social Responsibility (BSR). Founded in 1992, BSR reports that it has more than 1,200 members, including some of the world's largest corporations, such as AT&T and Time Warner, and small companies like the Bagelry and Patagonia. Dues are pro-rated by size of annual revenues. BSR provides assistance in the form of meetings, workshops, and publications. It serves to network with those in different corporations who can share their experience and expertise on pursuing socially responsible policies. For more information, contact:

   Business for Social Responsibility
   609 Mission Street, 2nd floor
   San Francisco, CA 94105-3506
   Tel. 415 537-0888   Fax 415 537-0889
   http://www.bsr.org

4. Contact the National Retiree Volunteer Center (NRVC): This nonprofit's goal is to convince companies to set up a program to involve retirees in volunteer activities. They will help you if you contact them at:

   NRVC
   4915 W. Thirty-fifth Street
   Minneapolis, MN 55416
   Tel. 612 920-7788

5. Encourage your company to brag about its corporate social responsibility. Apply for the various local (e.g., the Chamber of Commerce) and national awards programs, including the Points of Light Foundation Awards for Excellence in Corporate Community Service and the President's Service Awards (visit the Web site at http://www.points of light.org). Even if your corporation does not win, it will create future expectations. Suggest that your company include a social report section in its annual report.

6. Give a copy of Curt Weeden's *Corporate Social Investing*, or a similar socially conscious investment guide, to someone in top management. He or she might in turn invite Weeden or someone like him to give a talk.

Principle 10.3:   Social responsibility may hurt profits

The idea that corporate social responsibility is always positive for the company is an example of the naiveté that sometimes gives do-gooders a bad name. Like all individual acts of doing good, corporate acts require some sacrifice. The experience of Ben and Jerry's is very instructive on this point.

Started by two individuals who wanted to make good ice cream, create a sustainable and profitable business, and follow a set of corporate social responsibility principles, the company has prospered, but not without difficulty and much soul-searching. The annual report contains a "social report" section which describes not only what the company is doing but what difficulties it faces in keeping true to its mission. For example, when it decided to reduce waste generated by selling its Peace Pops in boxes, it put them in more environmentally friendly bags and saw a decline in sales. Similar tradeoffs between profit and social responsibility present themselves in every facet of business from raw material purchase to the salary of top management.

The Ben and Jerry's example does not mean that Milton Friedman and his profit-is-everything viewpoint is correct. Instead, it signifies that corporate leaders who try to behave responsibly must make choices that result in sacrifices.

Recognizing and integrating the role of corporate responsibility can be found in the mission statements of many companies. Johnson & Johnson has done an admirable job in its statement labeled "Our Credo," which is printed below. A version of the statement, which was written by General Robert Wood Johnson, who guided Johnson & Johnson from a small, family-owned business to a worldwide enterprise, details how the company should serve its customers, employees, the community, and the stockholder. The statement demonstrates how corporate responsibility can permeate the entire philosophy of a company and contribute to a healthy business.

Our Credo

We believe our first responsibility is to the doctors, nurses and patients, to mothers and fathers and all others who use our products and services. In meeting their needs everything we do must be of high quality. We must constantly strive to reduce our costs in order to maintain reasonable prices. Customers' orders must be serviced promptly and accurately. Our suppliers and distributors must have an opportunity to make a fair profit.

We are responsible to our employees, the men and women who work with us throughout the world. Everyone must be considered as an individual. We must respect their dignity and their merit. They must have a sense of security in their jobs. Compensation must be fair and adequate, and working conditions clean, orderly and safe. We must be mindful of ways to help our employees fulfill family responsibilities. Employees must feel free to make suggestions and complaints. There must be equal opportunity for employment, development and advancement for those qualified. We must provide competent management, and their actions must be just and ethical.

We are responsible to the communities in which we live and work and to the world community as well. We must be good citizens— support good works and charities and bear our fair share of taxes. We must encourage civic improvements and better health and education. We must maintain in good order the property we are privileged to use, protecting the environment and natural resources. Our final responsibility is to our stockholders. Business must make a sound profit. We must experiment with new ideas. Research must be carried on, innovative programs developed and mistakes paid for. New equipment must be purchased, new facilities provided and new products launched. Reserves must be created to provide for adverse times. When we operate according to these principles, the stockholders should realize a fair return.
—Johnson & Johnson

Q U I Z   R E S U L T S

1. It is so difficult to develop and apply clear criteria for corporate social responsibility that little progress can be made in shaping the behavior of corporations. Answer. No. There are several widely used methods to assess the corporate social responsibility of businesses. While there will always be some controversy over the criteria, especially when they are applied, there is clearly a basis to make judgments.

2. The business of business is to make a profit, which ultimately is incompatible with corporate social responsibility.
Answer: No. Short-sighted companies may view corporate social responsibility as a drag on earnings. Corporations that manage their corporate social responsibility activities properly can demonstrate that these expenses are actually investments that return benefits, enhancing the long-term prosperity of the corporation.

3. Working to increase the social responsibility of your corporation's policies can hurt you and your company.
Answer: Not sure. Unfortunately, there are always trade-offs, particularly for the Genuine Do-Gooder. People get fired or receive poor performance evaluations because they lobby for change. Corporations that admit wrongdoing can easily lose market share. Even those that are good corporate citizens may increase costs or lose markets because they adhere to socially responsible policies. However, the trade-off is not always negative. Many socially responsible policies can increase sales, lower costs, and provide great publicity for your company—which makes such choices a win-win situation.

11 Consumers

QUIZ

1. Small consumer purchases will have little impact on corporate policies.
Circle one: Yes No Not Sure

2. You can donate money through the products you buy if you choose the right company to buy from.
Circle one: Yes No Not Sure

3. Your buying decisions are the only thing you can do as a consumer to influence the social responsibility of a corporation.
Circle one: Yes No Not Sure

INTRODUCTION

A book published by the Council on Economic Priorities (CEP), *Shopping for a Better World*, suggests that you are what you consume. This suggestion is part of a campaign by the council to get consumers to vote with their dollars for socially responsible companies.

CEP is the brainchild of Alice Tepper Marlin. She started CEP in 1969, and is currently its executive director. She has been a major force in the field of corporate social responsibility for many years, as her profile below indicates. She has worked diligently to exert pressure on corporations to "do the right thing." Much of this chapter is based on my work with her over the years in raising the awareness of the buying public to corporate social responsibility.

Alice Tepper Marlin: Reforming standards globally

As a volunteer working on civil rights and anti-poverty issues in Harlem in the 1960s, Marlin transformed her daytime job as a securities analyst on Wall Street into a full-time do-gooding career. She knew that some investors had deep social concerns, especially involving the continued war efforts in Vietnam, and knew that there was a demand for information on corporations other than just the financial picture. She founded the Council on Economic Priorities in 1969 and has been its leader ever since.

The range of topics covered by CEP research and publications is immense. In addition to the eight screens described in the last chapter, CEP publications have touched on South Africa, child labor, nuclear power, and product liability. The publications include a monthly newsletter, individual company reports, and an endless stream of books including the flagship consumer publication, *Shopping for a Better World.* For more information on this publication or CEP, write, call, or visit CEP's Web site:

30 Irving Place, 9th floor
New York, NY 10003
Tel. 800 729-4237 or 212 420-1133
http://www.cepnyc.org

Always searching for points of leverage, Marlin has embarked over the past few years on a community problem-solving effort with key business, government, and union leaders from across the globe to establish labor standards worldwide. In its October 20, 1997, issue, *Business Week* reported that the effort was "a potential break-through not just on sweatshops, but on common labor standards for the global economy as a whole." Marlin has worked to create a certification process called SA8000 that can be thought of as something like a "good housekeeping seal of approval" for a product.

Whether or not this latest endeavor has the impact that Marlin hopes will not be known for some time. However, it is one more example of the way she has worked to improve society.

Principle 11.1: **Purchases can send a powerful message**

Buying decisions will not make or break you as a Genuine Do-Gooder, but though small and seemingly inconsequential, they can be part of a pattern that changes the behavior of corporations. Businesses live and die by competition, which is the source of the strength in the capitalist system as well as the source of much of the harm it generates. Many corporate leaders might ignore the fact that a small number of people are going to purchase their competitors' product because their competitor is more socially responsible, but don't bet on it. The slightest hint that their competitor might have the upper hand because it does more good can lead to a change in corporate behavior.

In fact, studies show that an increasing number of consumers are conscious of the citizenship qualities of the companies from which they buy. When price and quality are the same, more will opt for the good guy. "More than 60 percent of Americans said they switch brands or stores to purchase from companies that support particular social causes," according to a 1993 Cone/Roper Benchmark Survey on Cause-Related Marketing.*

Given the sensitivity of corporate managers to the preferences of consumers, you can join the growing chorus of consumers who want the companies they patronize to do good. If the trend continues, management will get nervous and do the right thing. This will happen not just because the bigwigs see doing good as a source of increased sales, but also because they most likely prefer to do the right thing anyway. The chorus of consumers will give them a "practical" reason for doing good and not expose them to the ridicule still, unfortunately, associated with being a do-gooder. These closet do-gooders would jump at the opportunity to show they are shrewd marketers who happen to be pleasing the social responsibility trend among consumers.

If you are convinced that you need to exercise your own consumer power to show corporations the way, CEP provides help. Its most recent publication, *The Corporate Report Card*, was published in May 1998, and rates 250 of America's largest corporations. It is an excellent source to help you to fully understand the range and complexity of corporate social responsibility and encourage you to think about the purchases you make. By having some idea about the best and the worst of specified products, you can pay more atten-

*Council on Economic Priorities, *Shopping for a Better World* (New York: Ballantine Books, 1994), p. 2.

tion to the products of the best and less to the products of the worst. You will also see that price and quality do not suffer if your producer and service provider are good citizens.

Companies That Made the CEP Honor Roll 1998*

These companies have met the criteria of the Council of Economic Priorities as good corporate citizens. None of the companies has perfect records, but all perform well in most areas.

- Adolph Coors Company
- Anheuser-Busch
- Applied Materials
- Avon Products, Inc.
- BankAmerica Corporation
- BankBoston Corporation
- Baxter International
- Ben & Jerry's Homemade
- Bristol-Myers Squibb Company
- Brooklyn Union
- Chevron Corporation
- Citicorp
- The Coca-Cola Company
- Colgate-Palmolive
- Deluxe Corporation
- Dole Food Company
- Gannett, Inc.
- Healthy Planet Products, Inc.
- Herman Miller, Inc.
- Hewlett-Packard
- International Business Machines
- Johnson & Johnson
- Kellogg Company
- The McGraw-Hill Companies
- Merck & Company, Inc.
- Pacificare Health Systems, Inc.
- PepsiCo, Inc.
- Pfizer, Inc.
- Polaroid
- Piper Jaffray Corporation
- Seventh Generation, Inc.
- Starbucks Corporation
- Sun Company
- Tennant Company
- UNUM Corporation

Principle 11.2: Buy from companies that give

As a consumer, you can buy from companies that send part of your money to charities. Some companies, like Newman's Own and Ben and Jerry's, build philanthropy into their business plan. All profits from Newman's Own go to selected charities. Ben and Jerry's donates 7.5 percent of its profits through grants and contributions to various organizations. Working Assets is a long-distance, credit card, and online service company that gives a portion of its customers' monthly payments to organizations that customers help select. For more information, contact

*Council on Economic Priorities, *CEP's Honor Roll List*, private fax transmittal from CEP, Jan. 28, 1999.

Working Assets
701 Montgomery Street, 4th floor
San Francisco, CA 94111
Tel. 800 788-0898
http://www.workingassets.com

Many more use donations as a marketing device. For example, each fall Wendy's sells a book of discount tickets that people can give to trick-or-treaters during Halloween. The proceeds go to the Special Olympics. The American Express Hunger Program donates a small percentage of credit card payments to support food pantries.

You can also exercise your consumer power by purchasing from the nonprofits themselves. You can buy cookies from the Girl Scouts or checkbooks from any number of organizations like the Audubon Society. These purchases help support organizations that do good and in some cases, like the Girl Scouts, are critical to their financial health.

The Internet also provides a way to contribute to charities. The two sites listed below say they will send a portion of the sales price to your favorite charity if you buy the product through their site. This development is new, like everything else on the Web, so it is too early to recommend their use. The spring 1999 issue of the "Wise Giving Guide," which is published by the National Charities Information Bureau, described in chapter 5, states that it has "an optimistic stance toward these sites," but has not had an opportunity to investigate how they might affect contributors. The sites themselves provide a wide variety of products and provide safeguards for the privacy of the user and a commitment to deliver from 3 to 25 percent of the sales price to your favorite charity. The average appears to be 8 percent. 4charity.com, which recently joined forces with SocialGoods.com, describes itself on its Web site in the following way:

> 4charity.com is run completely by volunteers in the Silicon Valley, allowing us to pass 100% of the revenues raised from our site directly to the chosen charities. The idea was originally conceived at the Stanford University MBA program in October 1977, when a few classmates built a site that allowed their fellow students to buy textbooks online while raising money for the Special Olympics. We have since expanded to include over twenty charities and nearly thirty shopping sites.

Its contact information along with that of another well-developed site is listed below:

4charity.com
457-13 Sierra Vista Ave.
Mountain View, CA 94043
Tel. 650 496-2457   Fax 650 496-2431
E-mail sdunlop@4charity.com
http://www.igive.com

IGive, Inc.
1890 Maple Ave., Suite 120
Evanston, Illinois 60201
Tel. 847 328-5293   Fax 847 328-5789
http://www.igive.com

Principle 11.3:   Consumers can be pro-active

As a consumer, you can do more than make purchases from those corporations that follow the policies you support or boycott those who do things you do not like. You can also:

1. Mail back empty junk mail return envelopes you receive from those corporations you believe show no signs of doing good and have invaded your privacy using the mail system that subsidizes their efforts. Mail the stamped return envelopes back empty. If there is no postage paid, throw it in the mailbox anyway; just don't put your return address on it. This act of protest will double their cost and lower their return on investment. (This idea came from H. L. Mencken, who apparently was bothered by junk mail in the 1930s.)

2. Support those companies that reach out to consumers for suggestions about their products and services. Such customer-oriented companies are likely to provide better products and service in any case; by working with them you are building a culture within the company to care not only about the customer but also about the community at large.

3. Send contributions to and provide support for the major public interest organizations that attempt to protect the rights as well as the health and safety of consumers. These organizations lobby for consumer protection legislation and also

perform watchdog functions. The major organizations are
listed below:

Center for Auto Safety
2001 S Street, NW, Suite 410
Washington, DC 20009
Tel. 202 328-7700
http://www.autosafety.org

Center for Science in the Public Interest
1875 Connecticut Ave., NW, Suite 300
Washington, DC 20009
Tel. 202 332-9110
http://www.cspinet.org

Center for Study of Responsive Law
PO Box 19367
Washington, DC 20036
Tel. 234-5176
http://www.csrl.org

Consumer Alert
1001 Connecticut Ave., NW, Suite 1128
Washington, DC 20036
Tel. 202 467-5809
http://www.consumeralert.org

Consumer Federation of America
1424 Sixteenth Street, NW, Suite 310
Washington, DC 20036
Tel. 202 265-7989
http://www.consumerfed.org

Consumers Union of the US, Inc.
1666 Connecticut Ave., NW, Suite 310
Washington, DC 20009
Tel. 202 362-6262
http://www.consunion.org

Co-op America
1612 K Street, NW, Suite 600
Washington, DC 20006
Tel. 202 331-8166

National Center for Tobacco-Free Kids
1707 L Street, NW, Suite 800
Washington, DC 20036
Tel. 202 296-5469
http://www.tobaccofreekids.org

National Consumers League
1701 K Street, NW, Suite 1200
Washington, DC 20006
Tel. 202 835-0747
http://www.natlconsumersleague.org

Public Voice for Food and Health Policy
1012 Fourteenth Street, NW
Washington, DC 20005
Tel. 202 347-6200

4. Write positive and negative letters to companies. If you spot a company that is doing bad things in your local community or elsewhere, write letters, get your kids to write letters, or better yet, get your kids to get their friends to write letters. Ask for a personal response. For companies doing good things, write constructive letters. Encourage the company to brag about what they do.

5. Write letters to the editor at your local paper to support local businesses who are doing good or denounce those that need to do good. This will give free publicity to a company that helps others or might change the actions of a company not interested in the welfare of others.

6. Other forms of communication such as the telephone and e-mail can also be used to register both support and opposition, but I believe that paper from the public is still the most powerful medium.

Writing letters is an excellent way to show your support for corporate responsibility. This shows corporations that you care about society and that you think that responsible corporate policies can make a big difference. The sample letters below are merely suggestive. If you are like me, you need something to get you started and then you will probably write something completely different. Go for it!

Consumer letter to irresponsible corporation

Dear Mr./Ms. (contact person):

As a consumer, I do not want my dollars to go to corporations that harm society. Unfortunately, I have learned that your policy on_____does just that. I consider this policy to be detrimental because it_____.

      If I am mistaken, please send me information that will help me reassess my views. In the meantime, I am discontinuing use of all of your products.

Sincerely,

name

Consumer letter to responsible corporation

Dear Mr./Ms. (contact person):

As a consumer I want my dollars to go to corporations that improve society. For that reason, I was very happy to learn about your policy on_____. I am pleased to see that your company has a deep concern for_____ specifically, and the need to be a socially responsible corporation in general.
I encourage you to keep up the good work and also to publicize your contribution to society more broadly. There are a lot more people like me out there than you might think.

Sincerely,

name

General letter to the editor

To the editor:

It is very important that companies seek to improve society or at least not harm it. Corporations are the lifeblood of our society and can influence what happens over the long term. For that reason I wish to commend_____company for its policy of_____. That policy can help us remedy a major problem facing our society.

Or:

For that reason I want to encourage_____ company to revise its policy on_____ I believe that this policy will do serious damage to our society.

Sincerely,

name

QUIZ RESULTS

1. Small consumer purchases will have little impact on corporate policies.
Answer: Not Sure. You can never be sure if your single purchase of Tom's of Maine over your former brand encourages a less responsible toothpaste maker to become more community conscious. Consumer decisions are like votes: they have a cumulative effect.

2. You can donate money through the products you buy if you choose the right company to buy from.
Answer: Yes. Several corporations make donations based on revenues or profits.

3. Your buying decisions are the only thing you can do as a consumer to influence the social responsibility of a corporation.
Answer: No. As a consumer, your letter, e-mail, or telephone call can have a significant impact. Politicians assume that every letter they get represents the views of hundreds who didn't send one.

12 Investors

1. Investing is another way to send a message to corporations about their behavior.
Circle one: Yes   No   Not Sure
2. On the whole, restricting your investment choices to those companies that have good records of corporate social responsibility will result in lower returns.
Circle one: Yes   No   Not Sure
3. As a stockholder, you can bring pressure on management to act in a socially responsible manner.
Circle one: Yes   No   Not Sure

I N T R O D U C T I O N

Saul Alinsky would be having a great time watching the corporate social responsibility movement gain the power that he thought it would have. In the five years preceding his death in 1972, he turned much of his attention from organizing the poor to pressure for more economic opportunity to encouraging the middle class to "persuade" corporate America to do the right thing. His efforts help to set the stage for the increasingly important role investors now play in the corporate social responsibility movement.

Saul Alinsky: Tapping the "Have-a-Littles"

Born in Chicago in 1909, Saul Alinsky set the standards for community organizing in the 1930s by helping the poor to get more access to economic opportunity. His tactics and his writings are confrontational because he saw a constant battle between the Haves and the Have-Nots and spent his time organizing the Have-Nots. Alinsky was a radical; he was arrested and jailed on several occasions. Alinsky used foul language frequently and was well known for outrageous publicity stunts. He once threatened the leaders of Chicago, who would not meet with an organization he supported, by contriving to send supporters to O'Hare airport to tie up all of the restrooms for a day. When word of this plan was "leaked" (Alinsky's words), a meeting was held and progress on negotiations resulted. The Alinsky method was characteristic of a period in which America was undergoing upheaval over Vietnam, civil rights, and poverty. His antics were the only thing he could do to bring organization and the power of publicity to the poor.

However, he eventually came to see that it made more sense to organize the middle class or, as he called them, the Have-a-Little, Want Mores. He writes in his classic and still popular book, *Rules for Radicals: A Pragmatic Primer for Realistic Radicals*, "Out of this class have come, with few exceptions, the great world leaders of change of the past centuries: Moses, Thomas Jefferson, Mahatma Gandhi. . . ."*

This new orientation led him to the idea that stockholder activism could be a powerful force for changing society. He stumbled onto the idea when trying to get Eastman-Kodak of Rochester, New York, to hire local minorities and poor whites. After getting nowhere through his traditional tactics of public ranting, private cajoling, and threatening economic boycotts and public demonstrations, he came up with the idea of gaining entrance to the annual stockholder meeting for purposes of, in his words, "harassment and publicity."

But how would he gain access? He knew he had to be a stockholder to get in. At that time, Alinsky had scheduled numerous speaking engagements at universities and conventions of religious and other do-good organizations. At each engagement he asked that proxies for Eastman Kodak stock be signed over or that the stockholders themselves would attend and make noise. It worked. Organizations from across the country signed over their proxies.

Alinsky started out with the idea that causing trouble at a stockholder meeting would embarrass the management into giving the disadvantaged blacks and whites in Rochester some jobs. As he moved on this idea, he saw the full potential of actually getting resolutions passed and, more important, in mobilizing millions of people to form a powerful bloc that was in effect the "boss" of corporate management. When the business community became aware of the tactic, they attacked Alinsky so vociferously

*Saul Alinsky, *Rules for Radicals: A Pragmatic Primer for Realistic Radicals* (New York: Vintage Books, 1971), p. 19.

that he suspected he was on the right track. When Eastman-Kodak stock dropped after the May 1967 stockholder meeting, he was sure of it.

Alinsky had visions of massive grassroots nationwide proxy organizations and thousands of college students who would "convince" their universities to use their large holdings to vote for responsible corporate policies. Neither of these visions materialized fully. Universities were too resistant to change, and university students were uninterested once the Vietnam War disappeared. Some large, grassroots organizations developed, especially among religious institutions, but not as extensively as Alinsky envisioned. However, the movement that he helped start has become larger and more powerful in a different way than he anticipated. Alinsky would probably not have been surprised. His long experience as a Genuine Do-Gooder and community organizer taught him that accidental discovery by doing something beats armchair theorizing every time.

Principle 12.1: Make socially responsible investments

Investment dollars are even more powerful than consumer dollars if used strategically. Using the criteria, or, as we called them in the two previous chapters, "screens"—environmental practices, tobacco sales, family-friendly employment policies, and the like—to decide where to invest can send a message to corporate managers. This practice is called socially responsible investing or SRI. Because these managers measure their performance by the price of their stock, your investment decisions can have serious consequences if other socially responsible investors make similar ones.

You can tailor your investments to include corporate social responsibility concerns in the following three ways:

1. Use corporation ratings to help to decide which ones to invest in. Ratings of 250 corporations are provided by CEP in its latest book, *The Corporate Report Card*.* There are other rating systems that can be identified from sources provided below.
2. Ask your broker to screen for you. Most brokers are not really into this type of thing and may try to talk you out of it. However, they are sufficiently eager for the commission and

---

*Council on Economic Priorities, *The Corporate Report Card* (NAL/Dutton, 1998), p. 227.

therefore may be willing to accommodate you. They can turn to help from within their firm. A growing number of firms actually offer screening services. Contact numbers are provided in the sources listed below.

3. Invest in mutual funds that only buy into corporations that rank high on certain screens. You need to study the fund to make sure the screens it uses are the ones you like, but it is a lot less work than option number one. Some of the more well known funds are: Ariel Mutual Funds, Calvert Group, Domini Social Equity Fund, Dreyfus Third Century Fund, Neuberger Berman Socially Responsive Fund, Parnasus Fund, and PAX World Fund.

Hundreds of organizations and services provide investment advice using corporate responsibility screens. One source, *Co-op America's Financial Planning Handbook*, is particularly helpful and has distributed more than 440,000 copies. It provides general tips on what it calls "social investing" and contains the *Social Investment Forum Directory*, which lists most of the financial advisers, planners, and money managers who specialize in the field. You can obtain a copy by contacting Co-op America at 202 872-5307. It also lists the major mutual funds that screen for social responsibility. The following organizations and their Web sites may prove useful for your investment decisions:

Co-op America: http://www.coopamerica.org

Coalition for Environmentally Responsible Economics (CERES): http://www.ceres.org

Council on Economic Priorities: http://www.cepnyc.org

Good Money Publications: http://www.goodmoney.com

Green Money: http://www.greenmoney.com

The Impact Project: http://www.efn.org/~impact/

Kinder, Lydenburg, Domini & Co.: http://www.kld.com

Socialfunds.com: http://www.socialfunds.com

S-R-Invest: http://www.tbzweb.com/srinvest/

If you already have a broker whom you would like to keep, ask for help in screening your investments for values that are important to you. More and more brokers are following the lead of

Smith Barney Asset Management. Its Social Awareness Program provides profiles to potential investors. These profiles are compiled for companies that have enviable records. For example, in its 1997 review of American Express, it describes the company's "generous and innovative" charitable giving of $21.6 million in 1996 to several charities targeting education, inner-city youth, the arts, and AIDS research. The profile provides a list of publications in which American Express is cited by books such as *The Best Companies for Minorities* and magazines such as *Working Mother* in which the company made the list of 100 best workplaces for women. The report also describes American Express's environmental policy, which included an environmental audit by Arthur D. Little, a highly respected consulting firm. Such a positive endorsement of American Express suggests that they are a model of corporate social responsibility and would make a great investment.

Your broker will send you this kind of information after a few requests.

If you choose the mutual fund route, you'll have more than 100 from which to select. You can obtain up-to-date information for the majority of them by using the service provided by the Social Investment Forum (SIF). It reports only on funds that are members of SIF, but most are included. Information is available on what the funds screen for as well as performance and size.

The mutual fund route is by far the best way to send a message. If you plunk money down on a socially responsible mutual fund, the message is loud and clear. Regardless of which of the three approaches you choose, you should develop your own list of screens to guide your investments. Advisers recommend that you think about two types of screens: avoidance and supportive. The list below provides suggestions by one of the investment advisory services. You can add or subtract from this list when developing your own personal screens.

People can now really make a difference and make profitable investments by including their personal, moral, and ethical issues and concerns in their investment decisions. By checking the social screens applied by the SRI mutual funds, investments in these funds and using the extensive research now available, one can have an investment portfolio that closely matches who they are and be assured of good financial results.

Screens You Might Use to Guide Investment*

Possible screens to tell you which stocks to avoid:
- Tobacco sales
- Alcohol sales
- Gambling
- Nuclear power
- Animal testing
- Pornography
- Human rights violations
- Environmental offenses
- Ongoing record of discrimination
- Controversies and/or fines

Possible screens to tell you which stocks to support:
- Community involvement and charitable giving
- Environmental problem solving
- Innovative employee benefits and programs
- Commitment to promoting diversity throughout worldwide operations
- Upholding global human rights in all operations worldwide

Investors can supply their individual account brokers with their own screens, using those employed by various groups, as well as some less common ones. One investor requested that any company having anything to do with Michael Jackson be off his investment list. Just as Genuine Do-Gooders can be working from any ideology as long as they respect the rights of others to express their views, social investing can represent radically different viewpoints.

For example, if you are particularly concerned with deteriorating conditions in poverty-stricken areas, you might want to examine the role of community investing. Banks are required by law to provide loans and grants to poverty areas. Some banks like the Bank of Newport in Portland, Oregon, the Elk Horn Bank in Little Rock, Arkansas, and the South Shore Bank of Chicago are dedicated to renewing communities. Investment in these banks as well as in funds

---

*Smith Barney, Inc., *Concert Social Awareness Fund—Smith Barney Mutual Funds*, brochure, 1998.

that support such banks is a way to earn income and support community development.

The big question for most investors is how screening impacts the rate of return of the investment. Critics of SRI suggest that using screens limits investors' options and will thereby reduce the rate of return on investments. However, this logic ignores the fact that the application of screens still leaves thousands of stocks, bonds, and mutual funds. Remember that all government bonds and funds are by definition contributing to broad social improvement. According to the authors of *Investing with Your Values: Making Money and Making a Difference,* "Solid statistical evidence shows that investments chosen with social, environmental, or ethical criteria perform as well or better than those chosen with financial criteria alone. In 1990, the Domini 400 Social Index was launched, modeled after the Standard and Poor 500; it includes socially screened companies in a similar range of sizes and industries as the unscreened S&P 500. From its inception in 1990 through July 1998, the Domini 400 has outpaced the S&P 500 with a total return of 376% compared to 321%. . . . It is only one of many studies that show a positive correlation between corporate responsibility and corporate profitability. So much for the myth that 'good guys finish last.' "* Of course, as the broker advertisers say in small print, "past performances are no indication of future performance."

Those who ignore the corporate social responsibility screens may be at a financial disadvantage in the future. As Paul S. Hilton, portfolio manager of the Dreyfus Third Century Fund and the Dreyfus Socially Responsible Growth Fund notes with respect to areas of social and environment concern, "Social research may even uncover some problematic aspects of companies not discovered through traditional financial analysis and actually save investors money." In other words, companies providing services that improve or do not harm society may have a business advantage over those that do not. Investors may eventually favor socially responsible companies, and that preference will contribute to better performances on the stock market.

An ad campaign used by one of the brokerage houses for many years featured a very high-class actor, John Houseman, saying, "We make our money the old-fashioned way, we earn it." An increas-

*Hal Brill, Jack Brill, and Cliff Feigenbaum, *Investing with Your Values: Making Money and Making a Difference* (Bloomberg Press, 1999).

ing number of brokers today are saying, "We make money the old-fashioned way *and* the good way." One of them is Jack Brill of San Diego, California, who has been featured quarterly since July 1993 in the *New York Times* special study on mutual funds. In the January 10, 1999, issue, Brill was tied for first place among the five mutual funds advisers that participated in an exercise where hypothetical retirement savings are invested. The other four did not use SRI screens. Brill's career path to SRI is described in the profile below and shows that you can make a difference and make money.

Jack Brill: High-mindedness makes money

Trained as a mechanical engineer, Jack Brill took a job in 1967 to feed his family by working for the U.S. Navy overseeing hundreds of millions of dollars annually in Navy contracts. By 1985, he decided he could no longer stay in the job. While he did some good by blowing the whistle on unscrupulous contractors, several of whom were convicted, he objected to repeated interference by high-level government officials.

Fortunately, he had started to develop his investing skills. After he quit the Navy, he decided to try the investment business. However, he did not know anything about SRI. He was approached by someone selling SRI mutual funds and was very happy to see that he could make money for his clients in a way that could have positive social effects. He has co-authored two books, *Investing From the Heart: The Guide to Socially Responsible Investments and Money Management* (Crown Publishers, 1993) and *Investing with Your Values: Making Money and Making a Difference* (Bloomberg Press, 1999). Brill is very bullish on socially responsible investing.

Principle 12.2:   Become a shareholder activist

If Saul Alinsky's vision led indirectly to the corporate social responsibility investment trend that has taken hold in the 1990s, his fight against Eastman-Kodak led directly to shareholder activism. This activism ranges from letter writing to meetings with management and sponsoring shareholder resolutions. Shareholders can take action individually, but groups are more effective.

Help for the Would-Be Stockholder Activist

Co-op America
1612 K Street, NW, Suite 600
Washington, DC 20006
Tel. 800 58-GREEN or 202 872-5307   Fax 202 331-8166
http://www.coopamerica.org

Interfaith Center on Corporate Responsibility
475 Riverside Drive
New York, NY 10115
Tel. 212 870-2295   Fax 212 870-2023

Investor Responsibility Research Center
1350 Connecticut Ave., NW, Suite 700
Washington, DC 20036-1701
Tel. 202 833-0700   Fax 202 833-3555
http://www.irrc.org

Kinder, Lydenberg, Domini & Co., Inc.
129 Mount Auburn Street
Cambridge, MA 02138
Tel. 617 547-7479   Fax 617 354-5353

The Shareholder Activism Handbook Online
http://www.bath.ac.uk/centres/Ethical/Share/Ohome.html

One of the most visible and powerful organizers of shareholders is the Interfaith Center on Corporate Responsibility (ICCR) which grew out of the 1971 efforts by the Episcopal Church when it filed a shareholder resolution calling for General Motors to withdraw its investments from South Africa. Eventually 160 U.S. corporations sold their South African assets. Today, the ICCR is an association of nearly 275 Protestant, Roman Catholic, and Jewish institutional investors, including denominations, religious communities, pension funds, foundations, dioceses, and health care corporations. The ICCR coalition has more than $90 billion in stocks, and $473 billion is "controlled by investors who either sponsor shareholder resolutions or vote their proxies," according to *Co-op America's Financial Planning Handbook.*

Shareholder resolutions are proposals that shareholders vote on in either an annual meeting or a special meeting of stockholders.

These proposals can be on any number of topics. In 1996, the ICCR listed the following issues often considered:

- Tobacco sales
- Environment and energy
- Board diversity
- Equal employment
- Workplace issues
- Human rights

A relatively new approach has been to get resolutions passed that ask companies like EXXON to link executive compensation to the social and environmental performance of the company. CEO compensation has also caught the eye of shareholder activists who are seeking to put salary caps on the pay of CEOs by suggesting that the cap be determined as a multiple of the pay of the lowest workers. A century ago, J. P. Morgan established a policy for all the companies he owned that the CEO would not and could not earn more than 20 times the wages earned by any worker in the company. Today, the average U.S. CEO paycheck is more than twice what it is for CEOs in the industrialized countries of the world.

The biggest obstacle to getting your resolution on the voting slate is understanding the process and getting the support of thousands of stockholders. For that reason, it is best to consult with one of the organizations previously listed or consultants mentioned in *Co-op America's Financial Planning Handbook*. Remember that shareholders may proxy; that is, sign over the voting rights of the shares to another individual. While you still own the stock and collect dividends, someone else is voting on company issues for you. Since companies have thousands of shareholders, most vote by proxy instead of attending the meetings. Therefore, proxies are quite common in investing and can be a valuable tool in gaining enough investor support to propose shareholder resolutions within a company.

Marty Nathan, an adviser in Atlanta, says, "The board of directors would rather hear from the IRS than a shareholder threatening a resolution." While shareholder resolutions rarely result in company policy changes, a large vote in favor of the resolution, from 5 to 10 percent, is a clear signal to the company's board of directors that investors are displeased with certain business practices the company currently employs. Business leaders react to even the slightest hint of investor dissatisfaction if only because of fear of what that might mean to the price of the stock. For that reason, company officials will often address proposed shareholder resolutions before annual meetings. In the past, companies such as Wal-Mart and Intel have met with the filers of shareholder resolutions over access to environmental and safety information before a vote was taken. The result in both cases was the withdrawal of the resolution after each company pledged greater access to the desired information.

If you want to be active as a shareholder, first try writing a letter. You never know where the path will lead. Your letter may be simply a request for information in which you ask for the corporate reports on its environmental, community giving, diversity, or labor code of conduct. Or, you could argue about the need for policies in the areas of your concern. Personal letters that are well argued and constructive in tone can help convince the corporate management and the board of directors that they should look more closely at their policies that affect the community. The letter provided below should help get you started.

Investor letter to urge social responsibility

Dear Mr./Ms. (contact person):

As an investor (of ____shares) in your company, I am interested in your policies toward _____.

Could you please send me information that will help me understand where your company stands on these questions? If you do not report these activities in your annual report, I would strongly urge that you do so in the future. In the meantime, I would appreciate either that section of your annual report that addresses my concerns or a detailed letter describing what your company is now doing.

I strongly believe that companies that combine the drive for return on investment with the need to keep America responsive to its citizens are the ones that will be the most successful in the stock market over the long run. Please send me the information requested as soon as possible so I can guide my investment decisions.

Sincerely,

name

QUIZ RESULTS

1. Investing is another way to send a message to corporations about their behavior.
Answer: Yes. Corporations are extremely sensitive to any fluctuation in their stock prices and will be susceptible to the idea that their actions outside of normal business will play a role. That is one reason why they spend so much money on public relations.

2. On the whole, restricting your investment choices to those companies that have good records of corporate social responsibility will result in lower returns.
Answer: No. There is at least as much evidence that investors who screen get higher returns than those who do not. The trend may in fact be going in favor of screened investments.

3. As a stockholder, you can bring pressure on management to act in a socially responsible manner.
Answer: Yes. It happens all the time. Even if proxy votes result in the defeat of a resolution that would be viewed as being more socially responsible, the fear of a vote and the cost of the battle over a vote will have a positive effect in many instances.

13 Social Organizations, a.k.a. Packs

QUIZ

1. Social organizations are not appropriate organizations for doing good.
Circle one: Yes   No   Not Sure
2. Working with other do-gooders is important, but not imperative.
Circle one: Yes   No   Not Sure
3. The decline in traditional social organizations should be a major source of concern for the Genuine Do-Gooder.
Circle one: Yes   No   Not Sure

INTRODUCTION

"I have a special dream: to help those children who have no hope for a promising future," wrote James L. Lacy, president of the Rotary International in the September 1998 edition of *The Rotarian*. The rest of his 500-word message details the many planned activities of Rotary organizations around the world, including a $20 million Children's Opportunities Grant program through the Rotary Foundation of Rhode Island. The profile below describes arguably the world's biggest social organization.

Rotary International Foundation

The Rotary International Club was founded in the United States in 1905 as the first service organization in the country. Since then, it has grown to encompass 30,000 clubs with more than 1.2 million members in 159 countries worldwide.

Each month, Rotary publishes a magazine that highlights activities of its branches across the world. One program that was spotlighted in the magazine is the Life Club. Rotary members adopt a club of 11th- and 12th-graders that works to provide drug-free programs within the school. After the club carries out one drug-free activity on its own, the members commit to helping the club plan one additional activity for each quarter in the school year. The Rotarians furnish start-up money, chaperone events, and provide students with rides to events.

Rotarians in 50 countries have committed to starting such programs. They are able to do this, in part, because of their large membership. Rotarians hold meetings each week with a reported attendance rate of 76 percent of their total membership. The high number of active Rotarians allow the association to commit to projects worldwide.

Other service organizations similar to the Rotary exist. There are large organizations like the Lions, the Kiwanis, and the Junior League, and small local service clubs as well. The existence of these clubs, large and small, provides evidence that do-gooders like to work in packs.

The term "pack" is not to be confused with political action committees (PACs). PACs are legal constructs designed for the purpose of feeding and influencing the political process. The term "pack" is used throughout this chapter in place of the more cumbersome phrase "social organization." The term fits because it refers to groups of people who meet for the common purposes of playing, working, and doing good, just like wolf packs meet to play and protect themselves and their futures. Like wolf packs, our packs are complex social organizations. An alpha wolf that depends on cooperation from the rest of the pack leads the organization and there is almost always an occasional "lone wolf." We will get back to the alpha and lone wolves later in the chapter.

On the next page is a list of the types of packs you can join. This is by no means an exhaustive list, but it should give you an idea of where to start.

Types of Social Organizations

CIVIC OR SERVICE
- Lions
- Kiwanis
- Rotary
- Junior League
- Jaycees

CULTURAL, EDUCATIONAL
- Association for Family Living
- Literary club
- Symphony orchestra association
- Museum board
- Lecture club
- College alumni association

ECONOMIC, OCCUPATIONAL, PROFESSIONAL
- Truck Drivers Association
- Law Enforcement Officers' Association
- American Bar Association
- Retail Grocers Association
- Civil Engineering Association
- Farm Bureau

HEALTH
- Hospital Board
- Nurses aide club
- Retail Druggists Association
- Registered Nurses Foundation
- Sister Kenny Foundation
- County medical society
- Lupus Foundation of America

HOBBY, RECREATIONAL, SOCIAL, SPORTS
- Country club
- Bridge club
- Newcomers club
- Singing club
- Garden club
- Travel club
- Homemakers club
- Little League

- Scuba club
- National Ski Patrol
- Historical society

LODGES, FRATERNAL, SECRET SOCIETIES
- Masons
- Knights of Columbus
- Knights of Pythias
- Elks (Lady Elks)
- Loyal Order of the Moose
- Daughters (Sons) of the American Revolution
- College fraternities/sororities
- Nationality or ethnic club
- Sons of Italy
- Sons of Poland
- Lithuanian Alliance of America
- Daughters (Sons) of Norway
- Ukrainian National Association

VETERANS, MILITARY, PATRIOTIC
- Vietnam Veterans of America
- American Legion
- Veterans of Foreign Wars

Principle 13.1: Blend work, play, and doing good

You might make the mistake of thinking that social organizations such as those based on hobbies are all play. Scuba clubs, for example, lobby to protect coral reefs, and each local club cleans up lake and ocean sites in their localities on Clean up the World Day, which is sponsored by the United Nations Environment Program. Packs are organizations where people meet to pursue common interests whether in doing good, playing, or working. The motivation for those who join packs is usually a mixture of the three interests, with the emphasis shifting throughout the length of their participation. You may join the Rotary for "playful" reasons. You may want to discuss the issues of the day, learn about the local community and the world, or want the prestige of being a Rotarian. You might also see membership as a way of networking to help yourself in business or in finding a new job. However, as a Rotarian, you may find yourself doing a great deal of charity and community service work that you enjoy and that keeps you committed to the organization.

We can look at any specific social organization and classify it in terms of the doing good, work, and play continuum. Professional and labor associations like the local Bar Association or unions have a clear focus on work, but there is plenty of play and occasional doing good. Civic and service organizations exist primarily for doing good, but the glue that holds them together may be play or work. Primarily playful organizations like your local bridge club or golf club serve to cement business relationships and may occasionally take on a community service dimension. Religious organizations that primarily give to charity and seek spirituality also provide opportunities for play and business. The point is that these organizations offer nearby windows of opportunity because they are multifaceted and provide an efficient way of contributing to society.

Packs are important nearby windows of opportunity for doing good because they are able to blend work, play, and doing good. Consequently, they provide a setting for your desire to do good.

Principle 13.2: **Packs have the power of numbers**

Not only does working in packs provide a window through which you might blend work, play, and doing good, it also gives you power through collective action and mutual reinforcement. People like to do things in groups. In most cases, they would never think of doing alone the things they would readily tackle in a group.

Doing good with friends provides us with a level of energy that most of us could not generate on our own. You might find that you give more time and money when you work with those you enjoy spending time with. If this is the case, you are probably already in one or more social organizations. If not, think about joining one. Try it, you might like it.

Group activities can range from college students traveling 1,000 miles during spring break to build houses for Habitat for Humanity to the United Way's Days of Caring, when teams of employees do home improvement projects for a day. Formal service organizations—like the Rotary, Lions, Kiwanis, and Junior League—generate hundreds of millions of dollars and work for good causes year-in and year-out.

If you are in an organization that has play or work as its primary purpose, you might suggest that the club take on a service project. For example, your bridge club or bowling league might work in a soup kitchen for one day once a year. Or, if you are a doctor and belong to the local medical society, you might convince the group to conduct health seminars. Many clubs exist not only because people have a similar interest, but also because members like each other, and they may enjoy working with each other on a service project. For example, if you are able to mobilize your antique car association to take on a fundraising event, you could energize the association and attract new members while also generating cash for a good cause. The key to this activity, and to the other activities described in this chapter, is that your interests bring you to a nearby window where you can work with others to make the world better.

This notion of pack power raises, as we have already noted, two related concepts: the lone wolf and the alpha wolf. You will need to do some self-assessment to determine if you have either of these tendencies.

Some do-gooders have serious lone wolf inclinations. In some ways, you may be a lone wolf yourself. An example of this would be if you are a doctor who sets up a free clinic on a Saturday afternoon in a housing project. You may be very successful and continue this indefinitely. While this is commendable, you need to realize that you have limitations. Very few can sustain such efforts over long periods of time without the emotional support of others. Most of us need to be in a pack to maintain interest and enthusiasm and to improve our skills at doing good. Genuine Do-Gooders who have lone wolf tendencies can make a difference, but in most cases it is better to join or form a pack to enhance the scope and performance of your effort.

Some do-gooders seek to lead; that is, to become the alpha wolf. All packs need leaders, so having such desires is not bad. However, you must first earn the respect of other members of the pack through deep commitment, hard work, and demonstrated skill. This is true whether you join an existing pack or start out as a lone wolf seeking to create a new pack.

Principle 13.3: **Packs multiply like rabbits**

A major concern among researchers and pundits in this country is what Robert Putnam calls "bowling alone." His article, "Bowling Alone: America's Declining Social Capital," makes the point that the kinds of social organizations we have just discussed are losing members. He supports his point with the astonishing statistic that "between 1980 and 1993 the total number of bowlers in America increased by 10 percent while league bowling decreased by 40 percent." Fewer people are joining traditional groups. He cites the following trends:

- Religious organization membership has declined about 12 percent since 1960.
- Labor union membership went down by 50 percent between 1953 and 1992.
- PTA membership went down 40 percent between 1964 and 1994.
- Membership in women's clubs went down 59 percent between 1964 and 1994.
- Boy Scouts membership has declined by 26 percent since 1970.
- Red Cross membership has declined by 62 percent since 1970.
- Most fraternal groups' membership has declined by more than 10 percent since the late 1970s.

However, do not fret about the decline in the traditional packs. Most of the traditional groups are still big and powerful, and some of them could resurge. In addition, Putnam and the National Commission on Civic Renewal point out that new forms of social organizations are developing that could, in part, replace the declining traditional organizations. Genuine Do-Gooders will be able to find plenty of nearby windows for companionship and for doing good. Five sources of these "new" packs are briefly described below, and there are plenty of other sources that will be discussed in subsequent chapters.

1. Support groups

The first alternative to traditional service organizations is the development of support groups. These groups usually come about when individuals who find it difficult to deal with a problem discover that there are others in the same boat. They form an informal self-help group at the local level that, in many cases, can become permanent and eventually evolve into a worldwide federation. The most well known and successful of such groups is Alcoholics Anonymous (AA),

which started in 1935 and now has over 97,000 chapters worldwide.*
While addiction groups are perhaps the most numerous, groups exist
that deal with almost every conceivable medical and social problem.
These specialized groups are likely to grow through the use of online
connections and may help to reverse the decline in the broad social
organizations that were important over the last two centuries.

We have already discussed the role that support groups play
in family matters. They are also important for the individuals who
face social, psychological, and health problems. A full list of support
groups is available in Barbara J. White and Edward J. Madara's *Self-Help
Sourcebook* (Denville: Northwest Covenant Medical Center, 1998) and
the *Self-Help Sourcebook* Web page, http://www.mentalhelp.
net/selfhelp.

Probably, the largest single type of support groups are health
related, in which individuals with diseases as well as their friends and
family work together. These groups are numerous and specialized;
The *Self-Help Sourcebook* lists 15 different cancer support groups
for different kinds of cancers and there are 243 health-related support groups in all. For example, one health concern, breast cancer, has
generated a variety of local support groups and national efforts. The
local support groups have been augmented by Web efforts like
http://www.letlive.com, which puts people in touch with Leigh
Moorhouse, a breast cancer survivor who paddled a kayak solo from
Florida to Maine to raise awareness.

The interesting thing about self-help groups is that, by definition, they combine the ordinary person's drive for self-improve-
ment with the Genuine Do-Gooder's drive to help others. You cannot benefit from a support group by being only a taker. In this sense,
"self-help" is not the operative word; it is "group-help," since you help
yourself through a collective effort.

2. Vacation groups and other fun groups

A second new source of packs for doing good resulted from
the idea of providing volunteers with possible vacation opportunities. Bill McMillon's book *Volunteer Vacations*, now in its sixth edition,
lists 271 organizations you can call to work anywhere in the world.

---

*Alcoholics Anonymous home page: http://www.alcoholics-anonymous.org.

Some projects include building railroads in western England, renovating houses in rural Canada, planting trees in Antigua, doing community development work in Kenya, and working in national parks in the United States. The cost can range from under $500 to more than $2,000 and the vacation can last anywhere from one weekend to six weeks. These opportunities provide hands-on help and a good time, just like traditional organizations.*

When it comes to doing good, the fun does not have to end when the vacation ends. All hobby groups, like the scuba clubs, book clubs, and hiking clubs, can do good. Then, there is the clever idea of Single Volunteers, first developed by Anne Lusk in Stow, Vermont, to help single people find dates. Single Volunteers of Washington, DC, began in March 1997, and reports that it has 3,500 members. Members must be over 21, and the average age is early 30s. They are placed at a variety of nonprofits like the Food Bank and government organizations like the local zoo. The power of the idea behind the organization comes from the interaction between doing good and playing, and it certainly helps people who have common interests and values find each other. It's also cheaper and safer than a singles bar.** For more information, visit the organization's Web site at http://singlevolunteers.org/dc/.

3. Marathons and days

A third "new" source of working together to do good comes from the many "marathons" springing up all over America. Douglas M. Lawson, in his book, *Volunteering: 101 Ways You Can Improve the World and Your Life*, writes about the practice of raising money by asking donors to pledge money for the solicitors promise of undertaking some activity. He writes:

> Because of the walkathons' extreme success, charities have
> extended the walkathon theme to include jog-athons
> for runners, hike-athons for nature lovers, bowl-athons
> for bowlers, drive-athons for golfers, dance-athons
> for dancers, swim-athons for swimmers, jump-athons
> for trampoline enthusiasts, ride-athons for horse lovers.

Marathons are a modern approach to doing good made possible by instant communication and easy transportation. They require a very

---

*Bill McMillon, *Volunteer Vacations* (Chicago: Chicago Review Press, 1997).
**Alex Witchel, "Romance at the Soup Ktchen," *New York Times*, Dec. 6, 1998, Sec. 9, p. 1.

small organizing group, but draw large numbers of people in a very short period of time. These events enable you to earn large amounts of money for valuable missions and to feel good at the same time. You can then disband the pack until the next cause comes around.

Closely related to the marathon phenomenon is the day phenomenon. Earth Day, when people join together to clean up roads, streams, and parks, is an example, as are the many days of caring, where charities like the United Way organize for a broad set of activities. By far the biggest and most varied "day" is the Make a Difference Day, sponsored by *USA Weekend* magazine and more than 500 carrier newspapers in partnership with the Points of Light Foundation. Held the last Saturday in October for the past eight years, the day's activities drew more than 1.3 million people in 1998. More than $2.5 million in awards and grants were given that day. For more information, see the Web site at http://www.usaweekend.com/diffday/, or call 800 416-3824.

City Cares of America in more than 24 cities provides the kinds of brief and focused packs that engage 100,000 people each year on specific day-long projects. The Care units in each city maintain databases with individuals who have signed up and who are given the opportunity to participate as events take place. Many of the volunteer events take place on a single day. For more information, see the national site to see if there is a Care organization near you.

City Cares of America
Po Box 7866
Atlanta, GA 30357
Tel. 404 875-7334
http://www.citycares.org

Like the marathons, the days serve to create transitory packs that bring people together for a specific purpose and a specific time. They are a critical source of volunteer activity, and they frequently lead to more long-term projects and relationships.

4. Celebrity-led groups

Another phenomenon is the role celebrities play in forming both permanent and temporary packs. They usually take the form of concerts and benefits to raise both money and awareness. For example, the Indigo Girls started the Honor the Earth Campaign in 1991 to raise money for Native American organizations to support land rights claims. The efforts of Oprah Winfrey, described in the profile below, are well known, but hundreds of sports and entertainment figures have created less ambitious pack activities. They are successful in raising money, awareness, and volunteer efforts precisely because their fans see them as a leader.

Oprah Winfrey: Pack leader for doing good

Oprah Winfrey's Angel Network was a year-long campaign to encourage people to open their hearts and see the world in a different way. On a September 1997 Oprah Winfrey show, she outlined five specific things you could do to make a difference, in other words, to use your time, talents, and heart to improve the quality of life for others:

1. Contribute to the world's largest piggy bank. To show that small change makes a difference, she asked you to start collecting spare pennies, nickels, dimes, and quarters. More than $1 million was collected and distributed to 50 high school seniors. Each state's Boys and Girls Club award winner received $25,000 to help pay for college.

2. Build an Oprah house. Winfrey asked the residents of the 205 cities with TV stations carrying her show to build a Habitat for Humanity house. Furthermore, business owners were asked to donate money, materials, and supplies. In May 1998, a group of volunteers broke ground on the first house, in Omaha, Nebraska.

3. Do your job for free. Oprah asked you to volunteer your special skills to help someone else. Once a week or once a month you could provide your services for those who wouldn't normally have access to them. For instance, an "Angel" mechanic in Los Angeles offers free repairs and advice to single moms with car trouble. Once a month you can find him in a church parking lot doing routine inspections and repairs for those with fixed incomes.

4. Help at your child's school. Oprah told you to go to your child's school and ask how you can help. People are still participating in restorations, tutoring, and special projects.

5. Create your own mini-miracle. Finally, Oprah told you to take a look at your own life and find ways to help the people in your community. For more information on Oprah's good deeds, check out her Web site at http://www.oprah.com.

5. The Internet

We have saved the most explosive for last. As already noted in chapter 4, there are thousands of organizations looking for volunteers to work from their homes via the Internet. Just looking at the Virtual Volunteering page of Volunteer Match, at http://www.volunteermatch.org, will provide you with unlimited activities that might fit your skills and provide causes that might pique your interest. Most of these opportunities are interactive, allowing you to exchange ideas with both the rowers and the steerers of the organization. Although you may never physically meet these people, you will establish a relationship that will help you realize your dream of doing good

QUIZ RESULTS

1. Social organizations are not appropriate organizations for doing good.
Answer: No. These groups are an ideal outlet for easily organizing groups of people to help improve society. Their existence provides a nearby window of opportunity to do good.

2. Working with other do-gooders is important, but not imperative.
Answer: Yes. Although I strongly suggest that you not be a lone wolf, the choice is yours to make. If it works for you, do it. However, think about joining or even starting a pack to enhance the power of your efforts through community problem solving. Perhaps your lone wolf tendencies are a cover for your alpha wolf desires.

3. The decline in traditional social organizations is a major source of concern for the Genuine Do-Gooder.
Answer: Not Sure. Although I have argued that there is more than enough capacity to generate leaner and meaner packs of do-gooders, you may not be persuaded, so "not sure" is the right answer.

14 Retirees

QUIZ

1. There are so many retirees looking for volunteer opportunities that good positions are hard to find.
Circle one: Yes   No   Not Sure

2. Retirees will have difficulty competing with younger, more educated, and more energetic volunteers.
Circle one: Yes   No   Not Sure

3. Volunteering can be a low-cost and highly rewarding, playful pastime for retirees.
Circle one: Yes   No   Not Sure

INTRODUCTION

Susan Anderson, a retiree who is a reading tutor for Literacy Volunteers of America—Chippewa Valley in Eau Claire, Wisconsin, found volunteering to be a key to her health and happiness. Her story illustrates the healing power that volunteer work can bring to those whose activities and state of mind are limited by illness or age.

Susan Anderson: Volunteering as a lifeline

At the age of 15 months, Susan Anderson was stricken with polio. Her case gradually worsened until, at the age of three, she left the hospital in order to die at home. Though many expected the worst for her, her community came to the aid of her family and together helped her to make a miraculous recovery. Despite the fact that she could walk only with heavy leg braces, she went through college, earned a master's degree, and began a career as a teacher. But in the midst of her active teaching career, a number of changes affected the direction of Anderson's life. By the late 1980s, her physical disability proved to be too much of a challenge to her career, and she retired. This, along with the death of her mother, she says, left her "almost reclusive." Fortunately she decided to volunteer some of her time at the Literacy Volunteers of America (LVA). Her work with LVA, beginning in 1990, was not only a way for Anderson to fulfill her desire to teach, but it was also "a lifeline" to another world, and her experiences changed her life.

As it turns out, the work of LVA was also a lifeline for Howard Hayden, a Vietnam War veteran who hardly ever smiled, according to Anderson. Hayden could not read and was educated only through the eighth grade, but in order to keep his job he needed to earn a commercial driver's license—something that would require the ability to read. In 1991, Hayden was connected to Anderson through the LVA office. Anderson determined through testing that Hayden had dyslexia, and she developed a program that taught him how to read. Because Hayden made such excellent progress in learning to read, Anderson began to encourage him to write. "Like a dog with a bone who would not give it up," as Hayden says. Anderson felt that writing about his Vietnam experiences would both help Hayden learn to write and also deal with the nightmare of his war experience. Anderson also helped him file the paperwork required to receive the four Purple Hearts and the Bronze Star he had earned but never received. Ultimately, Hayden became a published writer with stories appearing in military magazines and a book of war stories published by the State Historical Society of Wisconsin. For their joint efforts, Anderson and Hayden are the recipients of the 1998 Tic Tac R.E.A.C.H. Award (Reading Enables Adults to Climb Higher).

Anderson reports that "our ability to share painful memories was something that made Howard and me a unique team. Working through post-traumatic stress was something I understood, having struggled with asthma and polio for my whole life. . . . I knew about pain and bitterness. Besides, helping Howard was also good for me. It kept me from self-pity. I was so proud of him, and he smiles so much more."

Retirees should take a serious look at the opportunities for doing good that retirement brings. If you are retired, or plan to retire soon or know someone who is, you should be aware of the powerful nearby windows of opportunity for helping society that await retirees.

Principle 14.1:   **Retirees are a tremendous resource**

As a broad generalization, this principle risks stereotyping both the younger generation and retirees, but the powerful impact that retirees can have on improving our society needs to be highlighted. In a society that tends to diminish the powerful gifts that the older generation can provide, a principle that suggests that retirees can do things better than the rest of us is in order.

Giving back to society completes the circle for those retirees who recognize the many gifts provided by others outside their immediate family. For Anderson, her success with Hayden was only part of the reward. The other part was giving back to a community that had rallied behind her with monetary and moral support when she contracted polio as an infant. Whether giving their time and money to nonprofits or becoming more active citizens, doing good usually has great meaning to those who have reached a stage in their life where they do not have to work full time to earn a living. The important thing is to keep that circle unbroken.

The most significant source of information on volunteer opportunity outside of the government is the American Association of Retired Persons (AARP). The AARP also encourages volunteerism for its own programs offered through its 4,000 local chapters. The descriptions below are of several of the programs offered by AARP.

• 55 Alive/Mature Driving provides education to increase awareness of aging as it affects driving, and provides tips on coping with the effects of aging. Volunteer instructor opportunities are available by contacting AARP 55 ALIVE State Coordinators through field offices.

• Connections for Independent Living helps individuals remain in their homes or in their communities by connecting AARP members as volunteers with human service organizations in those communities, to perform a variety of services.

• Tax Preparation Assistance provides counselors, coordinators, and instructors to help low- and moderate-income older persons with their federal and state tax returns. Tax-Aide, AARP's largest volunteer program, was started in 1968 and received the Presidential Award for Private Sector Initiatives in 1986. Beginning in 1996, the AARP Foundation administered the program.

• Widowed Persons Service works with religious, social services, and mental health agencies and others to develop support programs for the newly widowed of all ages.

• AARP/VOTE helps inform the electorate about issues of concern to older persons through candidate forums, workshops, and voter guides.

• Minority Affairs Specialist stimulates a climate of change in the thinking and actions of mid-life and older minorities and the population at large, to improve economic, physical, and social well-being.

• Women's Issues Specialist finds solutions to the economic, health, and other concerns of midlife and older women in their communities and states. Through public speaking, workshops, panels, and the media, they draw attention to the contributions women have made to society.

AARP seeks volunteers to provide the counseling and professional services that each of these programs provides. To contact AARP, write or call:

AARP
601 E Street, NW
Washington, DC 20049
AARP Volunteer Talent Bank
Tel. 202 434-3219
http://www.AARP.org

For readers in Canada, contact:

Canadian Association of Retired Persons
Suite 1304, 27 Queen St. E
Toronto, ON, M5C 2M6, Canada
Tel. 416 363-5562   Fax 416 363-7394

AARP, along with the Gray Panthers and the Older Women's League, are advocates for the interests of older people. If you are concerned about policies and problems that specifically affect the elderly, you may want to work on lobbying efforts. These groups seek to shape policies with respect to Social Security, health care, and the protection of the elderly against fraud (which according to the FBI is the primary base of illegal telemarketing).

Thanks to the work of the National Retiree Volunteer Council (NRVC), discussed in chapter 10, more corporations are developing special programs for their retirees. Check to see if the organization you retired from is one of them. If not, encourage your former company to join.

A final source of help for retirees to find meaningful volunteer activities are the numerous organizations, or "packs" as we called them in chapter 10, that have a retiree focus. Such packs grow out of hobby groups such as bridge clubs or professional organizations such as associations of retired teachers. Because these organizations have a base in your past experiences, they can provide a receptive home for future volunteer efforts.

While their major impact is in volunteering, they also can have an impact as donors and citizens far beyond their numbers. As donors, retirees often have more disposable income, although there are a large number living at or below poverty levels. Many choose to leave their money to charities as an integrated part of their estate planning. As citizens, retirees have the time to run for office, work for candidates, and serve on civic committees in areas like economic development, master planning, or library boards. They can afford to run for offices that pay very little for the time commitment required. In addition, they have the networks and experience to deal with the difficult challenges of making and administering government policies.

Principle 14.2: Doing good can make retirement fulfilling

If you are a retiree you are, in a sense, free to pursue what you want to do. Some retirees donate hours of their time to help young children, others serve on boards vital to their community, and many work in homeless shelters and soup kitchens. The point is that the choice is yours.

Robert Keeling: Resident grandfather

Robert "Papaw" Keeling is a retired engineer who has been a resident grandfather at Katy Elementary in Katy, Texas, since 1983. Volunteering more than 30 hours each week as a mentor for at-risk students, a tutor for custodians preparing for their GED, an interpreter for front office staff, and a composer and in-house musician, Keeling has made a significant difference.

Why would you make the decision to serve others when you could be playing golf or bridge, traveling the world, or just hanging out with your friends and family? Who says you have to make such a choice? With unlimited time, you can have it all. Sheila Dineen is a retired schoolteacher who works on the Town of Manlius Coalition, a community group that I currently chair in a suburb outside of Syracuse, New York. She makes me gasp for breath when I listen to her current activities. In addition to typing, editing, manufacturing, and managing the mailing of the coalition's newsletter, she maintains a mailing list for the local senior center, attends local government meetings, works on dog rescues, gets petitions signed for candidates, designs brochures for candidates and other groups, maintains daily contact with her mother (whom she also takes on cruises), plays tennis and golf, and has time to raise a black lab puppy. She uses her professional skills as an English teacher for some of her volunteer activities, but she has also moved into other areas, learning all the time.

To give you one final example of what retirees can do, let's take a look at Jimmy Carter.

Jimmy Carter: Astonishing in Retirement

He is perhaps the most active of all ex-presidents and, quite possibly, the most active of all retirees. Once he was free from the burdens of his presidency, he was able to accomplish astonishing things. These accomplishments, some of which are listed below, illustrate that retirees can achieve great things.

- 1982—Founds the Carter Center, a nonpartisan and nonprofit center that addresses national and international public policy issues.
- 1984—Becomes involved with Habitat for Humanity and leads a group of workers in New York City that creates 19 new homes. The Jimmy Carter Work Project becomes an annual event.
- 1989—Meets with heads of African states and works with them on center's Global 2000 agriculture and health projects.
- 1991—Starts the Atlanta Project, a major domestic

initiative to address inner-city social problems in Atlanta, Georgia.
- 1991—Leads an international delegation observing elections in Zambia and Liberia.
- 1993—Hosts peace summit with members of the Sudan People's Liberation Army-United.
- 1994—Testifies before Congress advocating mental health and substance abuse benefits in the national health care reform plan.
- 1994—Heads a diplomacy team to Haiti that negotiates the terms of departure for the de facto government and helps avoid a U.S. military strike.
- 1995—Launches the America Project to share strategies on urban revitalization with other cities.
- 1995—Convenes the Great Lakes peace summit in Egypt to discuss the end of violence in Rwanda and Burundi.
- 1997—Meets with Palestinian President Yassir Arafat to discuss peace efforts in the Middle East.
- 1998—Establishes the Jimmy Carter Work Project for Habitat for Humanity and builds 100 new homes in Houston, Texas.

Retirees can truly have it all when doing good is a small but important part of their lives, like Susan Anderson, or they can dedicate most of their time to doing good, like Jimmy Carter. The point is that blending doing good, play, and work is a lot easier when you have the time to do what you want. Some of the reasons that you might want to blend doing good into your retired life are:

1. Some retirees find that community service helps fill a void that they may face if they no longer spend most of their time at the office.
2. Being a volunteer or active citizen can be an important source of self-esteem.
3. Service can reduce feelings of isolation because you will become a member of one or more do-gooding packs.
4. Participation as a volunteer, active donor, or citizen can improve your physical health and mental well-being.
5. Retirees who volunteer will meet more people and maybe even Mr. or Ms. Right if they happen to be single.
6. Volunteering is relatively inexpensive compared to cruises and other retiree pastimes—and can be just as much fun!

Retirees are likely to make better volunteers for several reasons:

1. The large supply of retirees allows for better matches because both the volunteer and the agency can be choosier. In 1980, there were more than 23 million retired workers in the United States. Today that number is more than 30 million and by the year 2030 is expected to double.

2. Retirees are likely to have more patience in general because heavy family commitments and the need to earn a living do not pressure them.

3. Retirees are more experienced than those in younger age groups. Experience brings more skill and more knowledge that should enable a retiree to work more effectively.

4. Retirees have more networks, which means they can recruit more volunteers and community resources to help the agency.

5. Retirees have the experiences required to meet the critical need to provide support to children, the sick, and the elderly.

Susan Anderson, profiled at the beginning of this chapter, provides the following keen insight in a letter written to me. "It just occurred to me that that's maybe an advantage of age—what you call retirees who volunteer. We've fought our personal battles. We are perhaps more secure, more relaxed. We've won our place in the sun, and it may be easier to think of ourselves less and other people's needs more."

This sense of self and place is ultimately what makes retirees pound for pound the most powerful of all volunteers.

Penny Poe: Help for needy children

Penny Poe, a retired schoolteacher from Oklahoma City, started the Putman City Care Share program to benefit needy children and their families in her community. The Share program includes entities such as the Kids Kloset, which provides free clothing to children; Hands Against Hunger, where high school students transport food to needy children; and Holiday Share activities. As an active retiree, Poe supervises these programs and provides ongoing support for the children of Oklahoma City.

Locating volunteer opportunities for retirees

Realizing the availability of high-quality volunteers from the pool of those who are retired, the federal government has developed a series of programs that are especially designed for retirees. They include:

National Executive Service Corps (NESC)
257 Park Ave. South
New York, NY 10010-7304
Tel. 212 529-6660

Retired Senior Volunteer Program (RSVP)
1110 Vermont Ave., NW
Washington, DC 20525
Tel. 800 634-0245

Senior Companions Program (SCP)
409 Third Street, SW, 6th floor
Washington, DC 20024
Tel. 800 634-0245

Service Corps of Retired Executives (SCORE)
409 Third Street, SW, 6th floor
Washington, DC 20024
Tel. 800 634-0245

Foster Grandparent Program
1201 New York Ave., NW
Washington, DC 20005
Tel. 202 606-5000

For those retirees who are busy, volunteering can be an important part of the mix. For those who are faced with illness and a desire to withdraw, like Susan Anderson, it can provide, in her words, a "true sense of accomplishment knowing I am doing something that really matters."

QUIZ RESULTS

1. There are so many retirees looking for volunteer opportunities that good positions are hard to find.
Answer: No. There are thousands of agencies working to recruit retirees who want to help. Supply does not exceed demand.

2. Retires will have difficulty competing with younger, more educated, and more energetic volunteers.
Answer: No. In general, retirees are better because they have more time, can select their spots more carefully, and have more experience and better networks than younger people.
3. Volunteering can be a low-cost and highly rewarding, playful pastime for retirees.
Answer: Yes. Retirees and, in fact, all do-gooders, are likely to find their volunteer activities are fun.

15 Students

QUIZ

1. Students should be good citizens at school.
Circle one: Yes   No   Not Sure

2. Students should see themselves as consumers of educational services.
Circle one: Yes   No   Not Sure

3. Students should work with other students to improve the learning environment at school.
Circle one: Yes   No   Not Sure

INTRODUCTION

So many young people do so much to help the world. So much natural energy to improve society comes from students of all ages. Once they learn about new ideas, they see new possibilities for the world around them. Perhaps the most spectacular example of the power of students to do good can be found in the impressive efforts of Craig Kielburger, who is profiled on the next page.

Craig Kielburger: Defending children

Craig Kielburger was 12 years old when he read about Iqbal Masih, a four-year-old child who was sold into slavery by his parents. He was shackled to a carpet loom and forced to make carpets. Iqbal was killed in 1995 when he was 12 years old. Organizing his friends and classmates in his hometown outside of Toronto, Craig started an organization now called Free the Children (FTC), which by the end of 1998 had offices in 20 countries and more than 5,000 youth members. "Free the Children is a group of children speaking in defense of children," according to Craig. The organization has four main goals:

- Create greater awareness of issues of child labor and exploitation.
- Convince world leaders to make the education and protection of children a priority in their decisions.
- Raise money to create alternatives for children who are being abused and exploited.
- Act in collaboration with children around the world to help bring about change.

Since 1995, Craig Kielburger has met with children and with the powerful business, labor, nonprofit, and government organizations that shape the future of children in Africa, South America, and Asia. He has written a book entitled *Free the Children* to encourage other children to join him. He has given speeches and has raised more than $1 million from organizations like the Canadian government and the Ontario Federation of Labour. His lobbying has also caused changes in Reebok's production methods. In 1998, he received the Franklin and Eleanor Roosevelt Freedom Award. All previous winners were adults like Desmond Tutu, Vaclav Havel, and Harry S. Truman. Craig has demonstrated by word and action the reservoir of idealism and energy that exists in our youth. His success in no small measure is a result of his ability to mobilize youth around the globe.

For more information on Craig's remarkable effort contact:

Free the Children International
1750 Steeles Ave., West, Suite 218
Concord, ON, Canada L4K2L7
Tel. 905 760-9382   Fax 905 760-9157
http://www.freethechildren.org

Craig's success is part of the growing activity by youth to work as volunteers and citizens to improve society. Thousands of teachers throughout the world have encouraged and led their students to make a difference. One of the most important pioneers in this field is Barbara Lewis of Salt Lake City, who is an elementary school teacher whose students have done wonderful things. Lewis has written a book entitled *The Kid's Guide to Social Action*, which Ralph Nader aptly says is the "liveliest practical civics book for young students in print." The book, which can be obtained from the sources listed at the end of this chapter, contains many examples of student power not just in Utah but throughout the nation. They include:

- A fifth-grade class in Salt Lake City that conducted a door-to-door voter registration campaign.
- The Earth Angels in St. Louis, who got petitions signed on national, state, and local environmental issues. They were instrumental in saving a popular park in the city from real estate development.
- The Conflict Busters, a conflict resolution program created by an elementary school in Franklin, Nebraska, that stop fights on the playground using conflict resolution skills.

These examples underscore the positive role that students can play in improving both our schools and the world outside of the schools. This chapter will provide additional examples and some guidelines for students as Genuine Do-Gooders. While the chapter is addressed to the general reader, it is intended to mobilize those who influence educational institutions to become Genuine Do-Gooders by encouraging students to see themselves as active citizens within the school and community. For those readers who are students, you need to take the challenge to play an enhanced role in your school and your community.

Principle 15.1:   Students must become watchdogs

Students have many nearby windows of opportunity in and around their schools. They can work to improve their schools by acting as responsible "clients." This means doing more than their homework, being prepared for class, acing their tests, and staying out of trouble. It means working with the faculty and staff on physical conditions within the school building and on problems such as high dropout rates. It also means holding teachers and administrators accountable for the education they provide, and requires taking action when teachers perform poorly or when their curriculum does not meet the students' needs. It also means holding their classmates responsible for the learning environment. Whether in middle school, high school, or college, students should both praise and criticize teachers and administrators on a regular basis, just as clients do to their service providers.

The school is the primary community for students outside the family, and students must act toward the authorities in their schools as citizens act toward their government. Obviously, this principle becomes more relevant as students move into high school and college. High school students and college students must see themselves as clients, their teachers as service providers, and school administrators as managers. Once they make that adjustment, they can take on the watchdog role required of the Genuine Do-Gooder as a citizen.

Students have a right to demand that teachers and administrators lead them to drinkable water, that is, an education that will serve their basic needs. They also have a right to demand that the job be done with some minimum level of competence. Patients are clients of doctors and, in general, they accept their authority, but good doctors see their role as working *with* their patients, not *on* their patients. Teachers and administrators need to have the same attitude with their students. Students need to exercise the right to be treated as clients, rather than as objects. Fortunately, the work of Wendy Schaetzel Lesko and her Activism 2000 Project, described in the profile below, provides models and guideline that will help students play the role they should in shaping school policies.

Wendy Schaetzel Lesko: Empowering youths

A former community organizer and journalist, Lesko is so dedicated to the idea that young people need to be given more responsibility for shaping their own environment that she spends most of her hours awake in preparing materials and spreading the word through meetings, training sessions, and consultation. Her latest book, *Youth: The 26% Solution*, says it all with the title. Youth constitute 26 percent of our population, and they need to be made part of the solution, in the words of the 1960s. She has helped students all over the country take actions to improve their schools. These include:

- A sophomore, Detra Warfield, who convinced the school board in Louisville, Kentucky, to include African-American history in the school curriculum.
- Middle school students in Geneseo, New York, who gained enough public support to ensure community approval of the school budget for the first time in three years.

• A freshman at Hempstead High School in Dubuque,
Iowa, who got 650 signatures on a petition to put
doors on individual stalls in the bathrooms, which the
school board agreed to.
  Contact information for Lesko and information
on her publications appear at the end of this chapter.

The previous examples show how students can create change one
step at a time within the framework of existing policies. However, students can also become an ongoing part of the policy-making process.
They can work with the teachers and administrators to shape general
policies. To illustrate, I will briefly describe two examples I have
been personally involved with, one at high school and one at
college. In the fall of 1997, I helped start a project at the Jamesville-
Dewitt High School located in a suburb outside of Syracuse, New York.
Seniors working in a classroom setting conducted focus groups with
hundreds of people including students, teachers, administrators, and
members of the community. They also collected and displayed data
and prepared reports in order to determine the goals of the high
school and assess progress toward those goals. One of the findings
in the first study completed by the students startled observers when
it concluded that most people participating in the focus groups
saw too much of an emphasis on college prep and not enough on
career preparation, financial management, and citizenship. The teachers and administrators used these findings to help them revise the
curriculum.

    The key to the success at JD is that those in power viewed the
students as clients who needed to be listened to. This does not necessarily mean losing control to the students; companies who do customer surveys do not turn their company over to the customer. What
it does mean is that students are viewed as human beings that have
a stake in what happens. It presumes that students are ready to act in a
responsible way when given a legitimate opportunity.

    Students also need to be incorporated into the policy process
at the college level. One way to create a base for mutual cooperation
is for students themselves to form a lobby group that earns the respect
of the administration and at least some faculty. This is what has happened at Syracuse University when a group of students formed
Undergraduates for a Better Education (UBE). UBE has established its

authority by carefully studying problems and making suggestions to faculty and administration.

Undergraduates for a Better Education

UBE was formed in the fall of 1987 when a group of students asked me to conduct an extra weekly discussion session for my freshman course. Being the dedicated teacher that I am, I agreed, but only on the condition that the discussion lead to action and that they deal with something on campus. Out of this discussion group emerged a student organization that is one of the most powerful on campus in the eyes of the administration and faculty.

The group of five students undertook a survey of 400 students and 50 faculty members to find factors that reduced the quality of undergraduate education at Syracuse University. They came up with the usual list of problems at a research university, such as inadequate contact with faculty, too much emphasis on research and not enough on good teaching, and teaching assistants who had inadequate command of the English language.

This report led to a campaign during parents' weekend that year, when the group rose at 5 A.M. to put up hundreds of posters all over the campus that asked in very big type, "Are you getting what you paid for?" Physical plant employees were still removing the posters as parents were milling about the campus.

Another survey followed, and activity continued as student interest and commitment grew. In the fall of 1989, the group published a book for students to steer them through everything from registration to getting around the library. UBE garnered national publicity by holding two national conventions for would-be UBE groups around the country and was written about in the *New York Times* and other national papers. The president of UBE appeared on the "Today Show" in 1990 and made negative remarks that got the full attention of the university administration.

Since that first project, UBE has been a strong lobbying force on the SU campus, getting the attention of faculty and administration all the way to the chancellor. Though their stance has been labeled extreme by some, UBE has pushed undergraduates to reject the status quo and to demand more from the administration. Among its accomplishments have been to convince the administration to:

- Open computer clusters 24 hours a day.
- Extend library hours.
- Establish explicit policies within each college on handling student grievances.

- Place students on key policy-making committees, including tenure and promotions.

UBE was able to do this through the use of its own studies, private conversations, and clever publicity. Here are some of the activities it has undertaken:

- Publishing a book of advice to undergraduates, including a review of liberal arts core courses.
- Conducting and privately reporting a study on how well faculty members kept office hours.
- Holding two national conferences in its early years and bringing in Charles Sykes, who wrote a book called *Profscam*, for a lecture to raise awareness and bring legitimacy to the conference.

The ultimate evidence of its success is that the slogan of Syracuse University is now "a leading student-centered research university," and there is enough of a reality in that slogan that the university was awarded the Theodore M. Hesburgh Award for Faculty Development to Enhance Undergraduate Learning. This award recognized that the University had made great strides in encouraging faculty to better serve its undergraduates and that other universities needed to follow in its footsteps. Although much work needs to be done, the university and its students have benefited greatly from UBE's work.

Students who seek to cooperatively problem solve in their school are likely to become active citizens. They see problems, and rather than whine or act out in some other way, they find a way to remedy the problem. If you are a student, here are some suggestions on what you might do to play a more active role as a citizen within your high school or college:

- Work with teachers and administrators on your concerns.
- Lobby for student evaluations of teachers. If the administration won't do it, conduct and publish the results of your own surveys.
- Strengthen your student government. You must organize to be strong advocates for *all* students. If your student government is weak, set up your own lobby group.
- Conduct and publish studies like the JD benchmarking study or the UBE study.

Principle 15.2: Communities are classrooms

According to the Independent Sector report entitled *America's Volunteers*, 59 percent of all youth (under the age of 18) and 38 percent of those between 18 and 24 volunteered at least once in 1995 (the latest date for which trustworthy information is available). The experiences can range from students working as rowers in the Rescue Mission where they might spend the day preparing food to the kinds of activist projects suggested by Barbara Lewis and described at the beginning of this chapter. This extension of student activism into the community is a natural progression from activism in the schools.

Particularly important at the K–12 level are the kinds of projects that Barbara Lewis and Wendy Schaetzel Lesko have pioneered. Consider encouraging your school to get their students involved in one or more of the types of actions listed below:

• Conduct and publicize environmental studies that show such conditions as dangerous waste sites; deteriorating buildings, roads, and sidewalks; and abandoned buildings.

• Conduct and publicize opinion surveys and focus group studies to demonstrate that a problem exists.

• Write letters to the editor and to public officials about problems in the community and possible solutions.

• Use faxes, e-mails, and Web sites to inform others about existing problems.

Common Cents New York, described in the profile below, demonstrates how powerful community-based learning can be. In chapter 8, we described the origins of the idea when Ted Gross's three-year-old daughter raised his consciousness about homelessness. This nonprofit reached an agreement in 1998 with the Dallas School District to provide technical support for creating a similar program. Many districts throughout the United States have adopted some aspects of this path-breaking program.

Powerful learning from Common Cents

Established in 1991 by Ted Gross, Common Cents New York established a partnership with the New York City Board of Education in 1994. It conducts the annual fall Penny Harvest where students in each school attempt to fill at least 25 sacks with 30 pounds of pennies each. A half-million students in 500 schools participate. Since 1991, more than $1 million worth of pennies have been collected. The activity is incorporated into the math, history, geography, social studies, and literature curricula through a set of materials developed by the organization. Students in all grade levels decide how to allocate the Penny Harvest in the form of grants to charitable organizations and youth-run pro-

grams. They do this through processes that ensure they
have done their homework before making the decisions. For
further information contact:

    Common Cents
    104 W. Eighty-Eighth Street
    New York, NY 100024
    Tel. 212 PENNIES   Fax 212 579-3488

Considerable support for community-based learning exists at the
K–12 and college levels, and has grown in recent years. At the K–12
levels, many school systems and the state of Maryland, have made serving the community a graduation requirement. Even more have encouraged it as an extracurricular activity and as part of career development.
At the college level, most institutions of higher education provide
administrative support to help place students in community service
positions. A few have community service as a graduation requirement,
but more have it integrated as fieldwork into regular classes. Campus
Compact is a coalition of university and college presidents who work
with students, faculty, and staff to develop the community service
experience for college students. Campus Compact organizations are
found in more than 20 states, and each year college students from
these campuses dedicate more than 22 million hours to community
service.*

A decision to commit resources to community-based learning by schools and colleges is only part of the puzzle. The key, ultimately, is the motivation of students to take some responsibility for
the future of their society by giving their time to specific projects.
Students themselves must be willing to participate responsibly if they
are to learn something from the experience, just like any other form
of learning.

To help promote student activism to improve schools and
community-based learning, contact the following sources:

At the K–12 level:

    Activism 2000 Project
    PO Box E
    Kensington, MD 20895
    Tel. 800 KID POWER   Fax 301 929-8907
    http://www.youthactivism.com

*Campus Compact home page: http://compact.org.

Close Up Foundation, *Active Citizenship Today*
(Close Up Foundation, 1994)

The Giraffe Project
PO Box 759
Langley, WA 98260
Tel. 360 221-7989   Fax 360 221-7817
e-mail: office@giraffe.org
http://www.giraffe.org/

International Student Activism Alliance (ISAA)
32 Grand Street
Hartford, CT 06106
Tel. 860 232-8452   Fax 860 728-0287
http://www.avonct.com/ISAA

Wendy Schaetzel Lesko, *No Kidding Around! America's
Young Activists Are Changing Our World and You Can Too.*
(Kensington: Information USA, 1992)
Wendy Schaetzel Lesko, *Youth: The 26% Solution*
(Kensington: Information USA, 1998)

Barbara Lewis, *The Kid's Guide to Service Projects*
(Minneapolis: Free Spirit Publishing, 1995)
Barbara Lewis, *The Kid's Guide to Social Action*
(Minneapolis: Free Spirit Publishing, 1998)

National Society for Experiential Education
3509 Haworth Drive, Suite 207
Raleigh, NC 27609-7229
Tel. 919 787-3263   Fax 919 787-3381
http://www.nsee.org

Teen Empowerment
48 Rutland Street,
Boston, MA 02118
Tel. 617 536-4266

Youth Volunteer Corps of Canada
#720, 640 Eighth Ave., SW
Calgary, AB, Canada, T2P 1G7
Tel. 403 266-5448   Fax 403 264-0266

At the college level:
Campus Compact
Box 1975, Brown University

Providence, RI 02912-1975
Tel. 401 863-1119   Fax 401 863-3779
http://www.compact.org

Campus Outreach Opportunity League (COOL)
Tel. 202 265-1200

QUIZ RESULTS

1. Students should be good citizens at school.
Answer: Yes. Students should generally accept the
authority of the faculty and the administration, but
they should seek to be treated as clients when their
interests are seriously challenged. Students are citizens
within their schools and therefore must take on
the role of watchdog.

2. Students should see themselves as consumers of
educational services.
Answer: No. The word *client* is better. There is actually
a continuum between consumer, someone who uses
products and services, and client, someone who
works with a service provider to meet his or her
needs. Students should see themselves as needing the
expertise of teachers to help them decide what to
learn and to find out if they learned it. This requires
mutual respect on both sides.

3. Students should work with other students to
improve the learning environment at school.
Answer: Yes. Equally as important if not more important to the learning of students is the attitude and
behavior of peers. Peers who act out or reject the
rights of the entire learning community prevent
students from learning despite the best efforts of
teachers and administrators. The student as Genuine
Do-Gooder must recognize and deal with this reality.

16 Alumni

QUIZ

1. Your K–12 school probably needs more of your help than your college or university.
Circle one: Yes No Not Sure

2. To help your alma mater, it is more important to give money than your time.
Circle one: Yes No Not Sure

3. Never give money to institutions of higher education without attempting to steer.
Circle one: Yes No Not Sure

4. Alumni organizations should give most of their time and money directly to their college or university.
Circle one: Yes No Not Sure

INTRODUCTION

Being an alumnus, whether from an elementary school, high school, or college, gives you an enormous window of opportunity to do some good. School is the place where you got your start, a place where you found connections with other peers, and it can be a place where you reinvigorate relationships. It is a place that was your "home" for a significant period of your life. To give back to it is almost like giving to your family. As the profile below of Eugene Lang shows us, it is also a place where dreams can come true.

Eugene Lang: Keeping the dream alive

When Eugene Lang visited his old elementary school, Public School 121 in East Harlem, NY, to give a graduation address, he'd planned to give the ordinary speech about the great opportunities that lay ahead for those who do well in school. As he looked into the audience of children from this poverty-ridden area, he realized that the message assumed that the students would have the means to take advantage of those opportunities and, specifically, to go to college. He realized that this might not be so; many might not have the resources for a college education. Lang made a bold offer. He would pay for the college education of each child in the room.

Eugene Lang did not want the children he faced to know that their dreams of the future were to be deferred because of their poverty. They had dreams; he would help to realize them. Although on paper only about 25 percent of those students should have ever graduated from high school, 90 percent of the students he spoke to actually graduated. In addition, 60 percent went on to college.

His success and drive stimulated the creation of the I Have a Dream Foundation in 1986. Through his experience with the first Dreamers, Lang recognized that financial assistance alone was not enough so he added services from tutors, mentors, and a full-time social worker. IHAD now encompasses 160 projects in 63 cities and serves more than 13,000 students. The different projects are locally funded and run, and each project follows disadvantaged students from elementary school through high school graduation. The projects pledge college scholarships for students who choose to pursue higher education. Lang's efforts show how commitment and nearby windows can lead to the spread of a good idea nationwide. More important, his accomplishment highlights an opportunity that not enough of us take—giving back to the K–12 schools that gave us our start.

Principle 16.1:   Give back to your K–12 schools

If you are looking for a place to spend your time or money, look at the elementary, junior high, or high school you attended. If it is already well financed, you should think about giving your time rather than your money. Even well-endowed prep schools could be greatly helped by their graduates coming back and telling their current students about life after high school. If your school lacks resources, giving your time and your money could make a critical difference, as it did for P.S. 121. You may not have the resources to start your own IHAD program, but you could make a major difference in helping your school do a better job for its students. It would be best to request that monetary gifts be directed at a specific program. The ones that would have the most leverage are:

- Improving computer training for students;
- Supporting the implementation of a proven program such as Junior Achievement into the curriculum;
- Supporting a mentoring program; and
- Offering well-run competitions where prizes such as field trips are provided to the winners.

If you do have these resources or the network of donors to develop a program such as IHAD at your school, join that existing network. Contact IHAD through their Web site at http://www.ihad.org, or by phone at 212 293-5480, and they will provide you with technical support and advice from those who have mounted successful programs.

Unfortunately, the alumni who do give back to their K–12 schools are in short supply. They would prefer to give back to their college if they give back at all. While such gifts are welcomed and beneficial to colleges and universities, who are ever searching for more money, the leverage point is clearly at the K–12 level. We know this from the widespread practice of college admissions committees, which consider the quality of a high school as one of the most important criteria in their decisions. So give back to your K–12 schools, many of which may not even have a checking account to receive such gifts. If you give money, ask for a report on how it was spent even if you do not specify its use.

Principle 16.2: **Designate your college gifts**

Higher education consumes huge resources in this country, with respect to operating expenses and the time and energy students spend on it. In its consumption of these resources, higher education leaves millions of students with significant levels of debt and millions of parents with depleted assets. Despite consuming huge resources, less than 50 percent of all full-time freshmen graduate within five years, and many never graduate at all. As a whole, higher education may be performing even more poorly than many of our K–12 schools.

Colleges and universities can and do contribute greatly toward improving society. They fulfill the educational needs of some of their students and the creative needs of society in such ways as developing new scientific findings, new art forms, and new ways to apply knowledge to everyday life. Alternatively, they can waste financial and human resources if they fail to educate and do little more than provide a playful pastime for different faculty groups. Alumni can provide the positive pressure needed to make our institutions of higher education the resource for moving toward the good society that they claim to be.

Most colleges and universities, no matter how wealthy, could benefit from the direction of their alumni. This direction should be attached to the money if you are a substantial donor. Alumni who make unrestricted donations may actually be contributing less to their alma mater than they hope. To avoid this, you should ask hard questions about how your money will be spent and the degree to which students will be helped by your donation. If you give scholarship money, find out whether the money will be used for scholarships that are merit-based (awarded on academic potential) or need-based (awarded on the financial circumstances of the applicant), and choose whether the one they approve is for you (either is acceptable based on the giver's viewpoint).

We described in chapter 5 how difficult it is for donors to shape what recipients do with their cash in the case of most charities. This is not as true when giving to colleges and universities. Development officers would prefer a blank check, but they will offer you some program choices. Use your money for a program you support. If you promise enough money, you may actually be able to start a new program or even significantly change an existing one.

Beyond the money, as an alumnus you can play a very important role. You can:

- Mentor students;
- Offer career advice;
- Invite students to shadow you at your job;
- Give lectures;
- Write letters suggesting how to improve programs;
- Serve as an admissions recruiter; or
- Become active in your alumni association.

Principle 16.3:   Alumni should tackle civic tasks

College alumni are a potentially powerful resource for improving society beyond the walls of the academy. Like the packs discussed in chapter 13, their strength grows out of the group solidarity that comes from playing and doing good. Fortunately, we have some very good examples of alumni groups that have formed to work directly at solving problems of society. The two discussed below represent models that you can follow in working with your fellow alumni from your college or university.

Establish a mentor program

The first example comes from my own experience in working with a dedicated set of Syracuse University alumni located in New York City. Syracuse University began collaboration with the High School for Leadership and Public Service at the suggestion of an alumnus in 1993. That collaboration continues today at several levels, but the most successful component by far has been a mentoring program called Syracuse University Mentor-Mentee Alliance (SUMMA). The program is designed, implemented, and funded by a group of New York alumni and operates as a nonprofit corporation. More than 50 mentor-mentee relationships exist in a school that has about 500 students, a large percent that signifies a major commitment of both time and money by the alumni. If you are a graduate of a college or university that has large clusters of alumni within a specific geographic area where there is also a distressed school system, consider setting up a similar program. For advice, contact Jane Present, who is president of the SUMMA at the New York City offices of Syracuse University, tel. 212 826-0320.

Establish a program that incubates new initiatives

Princeton Project 55 Inc. (PP55) was started in 1989 when Ralph Nader challenged his fellow classmates "to form an alumni organization that would provide civic leadership in addressing critical national and global problems." PP55 has no official tie to Princeton since it is a nonprofit corporation, but it works closely with the university community. One of its leaders, Chet Safian, writes, "We are simply trying to be good citizens" and recognize that "it is our enlightened self-interest to address the problems which we all know exist." The program has supported several initiatives, including:

1. The Public Interest Program, which places qualified students and recent graduates in internships (summer and full time for one year after graduation) at nonprofits dedicated to systemic change around the country.

2. Experiential Education Initiative, a group of PP55 members, students, administrators, and faculty, generated a working paper that advocates the use of more experiential education at Princeton and elsewhere.

3. An outreach program that has directly stimulated similar efforts by alumni at Harvard, Dartmouth, Smith, Amherst, and Williams.

4. Challenge '97, a mentoring program for an inner-city middle school in Trenton started by Princeton students in the class of '97 and supported by PP55. The class of 2,000 has taken over the project and provided future Princeton undergraduates with the opportunity to serve in one of their nearby windows.

5. A PP55 tuberculosis initiative that arouses and organizes the public to support global policies to prevent or treat tuberculosis, which kills 3 million people each year.

PP55 starts these efforts using an annual budget that it raises from members of the Class of '55, but it requires that the programs themselves become self-funding so that new initiatives can be started. If you are interested in mobilizing your alumni to follow this path contact Chet Safian through PP55 offices in Princeton, tel. 609 921-8808, or e-mail: pp55@aol.com.

To illustrate the potential power of this idea even further, read about the Appleseed Foundation in the profile below. That program was also started at the urging of Ralph Nader to his 1958 Harvard Law

class. There were several other members in that class from the
Princeton class of 1955. The foundation received technical assistance
from PP55. As of 1998, the Appleseed Foundation had established 12
state public interest law centers around the country. Imagine how
many more nonprofit organizations alumni throughout the country
from other universities could generate. They might have any one of
the following missions that the alumni could support through their
own activities or a nonprofit they establish:

- With help from Appleseed they could provide legal advocacy
to the disadvantaged;
- Medical and nursing schools could establish free clinics
or provide educational programs;
- Management schools could provide tax advisory services
to the poor;
- Journalism schools could create newsletters for community
organizations.

From small (apple) seeds . . .

The Appleseed Foundation established 12 public interest
law centers in 12 states, each with an average budget
under $300,000. The program was set up to offer an alter-
native to law school graduates who wanted to work in the
public interest sector, and it has established local organizations to promote a more level playing field all over the
country. The South Carolina center has gotten increased
funding for subsidized legal services for the poor.
Massachusetts Appleseed has taken action to protect the
elderly from financial scams. Nebraska Appleseed has
helped the working poor keep some of their benefits and
published a study on a "living wage" that highlights their
plight. People in New Jersey have benefited from the
action of Appleseed's Public Interest Law Center of New
Jersey, which has forced disclosure of agreements among
gigantic HMOs in that state. These are just some of the
activities of the centers. For more information on this program, contact:

The Appleseed Foundation
910 Seventeenth Street
Washington, DC 20006
http://www.appleseed.org

As an alumnus who wants to mobilize others to do good, you need not take on ambitious projects like PP55 has. You can start small by working on projects that have a more direct impact on the students at their university, just as PP55 did with its internship program. Or, you can adopt a distressed school in your area similar to the efforts of SUMMA. These types of activities will not only help to improve society; they will also enhance the educational experience for those undergraduates who will inevitably become a part of these efforts. In addition, you will be providing a model of the Genuine Do-Gooder that can only persuade this generation of students to follow in your footsteps.

QUIZ RESULTS

1. Your K–12 school probably needs more of your help than your college or university.
Answer: Yes. Colleges and universities are funded at approximately twice the per-pupil level as K–12 schools, and there is clear evidence that early schooling is more important than later schooling. You can have more leverage by giving your money and your time to your K–12 school.

2. To help your alma mater, it is more important to give money than time.
Answer: Not Sure. It depends on your alma mater. The wealthy schools could benefit more from your time to better link their classroom education with life after college. In any case, it is important that you use your money to help steer the institution in the direction you think it should be heading.

3. Never give money to institutions of higher education without attempting to steer.
Answer: Yes. Even if you give a small sum, direct it to the place where you think it is needed the most. Universities and colleges need more direction from their alumni, and you can help them get that direction.

4. Alumni organizations should give most of their time and money directly to their college or university.

Answer: No. Some alumni should develop projects that serve to improve society. They should seek to organize their graduating class into a group that takes on these projects. In doing so, they would be tapping the potential power of alumni organizations and could help to restore the guidance, direction, and energy needed to improve society.

IV

The Power to Create Change

17 Cooperative Problem Solving

QUIZ

1. Good problem solving will result in effective solutions.
Circle One: Yes   No   Not Sure

2. All individuals who influence or are impacted by a policy are players.
Circle One: Yes   No   Not Sure

3. You must always be nice to people even when faced with opposition.
Circle One: Yes   No   Not Sure

INTRODUCTION

How can you create change? How can you solve the problems in your community? The traffic light that never works, the playground that's unsafe, the high school with elevated dropout rates, drug and alcohol abuse among teenagers, and local businesses that pollute the air and water. Most communities face these problems. You probably have been troubled by at least one such problem. Maybe you've thought about how to fix the problem. Perhaps you've even taken action. But, if you're like most of us, you've probably only complained and wished the situation would change. Well, as you know by now, wishing a problem away isn't the way of the Genuine Do-Gooder. You need to take action. But how?

This chapter and the subsequent chapters will show you how you can create change. In this chapter we'll go over a few of the basic principles you need to keep in mind when first evaluating a problem. By following a few simple steps you'll be able to clearly identify the true nature of the problem, understand who you will need to contact in order to fix it, and develop the skills to cooperatively problem solve. We'll begin with the story of Ida Siegal.

Ida Siegal: Resourceful problem solver

During her sophomore year of college, Siegal started tutoring young children at an after-school program offered by a local community center. Though she has worked with several children, one, whom we will call Ron, stands out in her mind. The problem was Ron's poor reading skills. Though some of the other students at the center also had difficulty reading, Ron's skills were especially poor. Siegal could have easily said, "Oh well, I'm doing the best I can." Instead, she searched for causes and solutions. Since her brother is dyslexic she was aware of the common signs a child might display if he or she had a learning disorder. She spoke to people at the community center and to Ron's grandmother on a number of occasions. Unfortunately, his grandmother refused to consider the possibility that Ron had a learning disorder. Like many grandmothers (and parents), she seemed overprotective of her grandchild and feared that he might be labeled as needing special education. Siegal was unable to talk to Ron's teacher about his reading skills because his grandmother would not provide the necessary permission, nor would she allow Ron to be tested for a learning disorder.

What was Siegal to do? She decided to research learning disorders, particularly dyslexia. She read books, spoke with experts, and talked to her mother and brother about the disorder. After much research and observation of Ron's reading and writing, she concluded that in all likelihood Ron was dyslexic. She created lesson plans based on her research and her mother's advice in dealing with the reading problems of her brother. In the end, Siegal and Ron got results: Ron's reading improved.

Genuine Do-Gooders are problem solvers like Siegal. She saw a problem, Ron's poor reading, and figured out a way to help improve his skills. Siegal had to be creative in finding the right solution and she had to go to other resources, books and experts, to help her determine the true nature of the problem and the best solution.

Principle 17.1: Always think problem solving

If you want to create change and help others, you must approach the issues and dilemmas you face with a problem-solving mind-set. The triangle pictured below contains the three steps that must be completed when problem solving.

The Problem-Solving Triangle

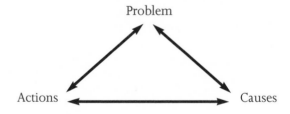

As you might guess, the steps are represented in a triangle, rather than a straight line or ladder, to suggest that you can start anywhere as long as you complete all steps. It also suggests that you go through the steps on a continuous basis. Thinking about causes may force you to change your definition of the problem, and thinking about the actions may cause you to rethink your definitions of the problem and its causes. What appears to be a straight line march to reducing problems is really a waltz where you repeat the steps in your mind over and over again to come up with a reasonable analysis. Briefly, here's what you need to do:

1. Identify the problem

Siegal studied Ron's reading performance and his grades and concluded that he had difficulty reading because his reading level was below that of the other children his age.

Decide what the problem is. For example, at the individual level, the problem might be one student reading below grade level. At an organizational level, the problem might be the poor reading test performance of an entire school. At a societal level, the problem might be high dropout rates by students living in poverty.

After you have identified the problem, you need to take one more step. You need to define a benchmark for your problem. A benchmark is a meaningful goal that can be measured. For example, Siegal might set as her benchmark that Ron read at an age-appropriate level; a literacy organization might use as a benchmark that 100 percent of all Americans read at the 9th grade level or higher. Benchmarks consist of two parts: indicators that measure some condition, and a goal for that condition. The benefits of benchmarks are:

1. What gets benchmarked gets done.
2. If you benchmark results, success becomes more visible.
3. Being able to see success enables you to learn from it.
4. Using benchmarks to gauge results allows you to see what works and what doesn't.
5. If you can demonstrate results, you can win public support.

Benchmarking provides a powerful way to identify problems. It helps you make sure you have clearly defined a problem and have provided a specific goal to mobilize others who may be important to remedying the problem. Although the term sounds somewhat exotic, it is really quite easy to think about and use. Just think of it as taking your temperature so you can measure when you are getting better.

2. Identify the causes

By talking with experts and researching the problem, Siegal was able to determine that Ron was dyslexic.

Once the problem is identified, think about the factors that created it in the first place. This is the "why" question that children will keep asking until parents are ready to ask themselves why they decided to have children in the first place. Like most of what children do, asking why is a reasonable and important exercise.

Careful study of the problem and serious discussion with people involved at all levels of the problem help you identify its causes. Identifying causes can help you think of possible solutions as it did for Siegal with Ron.

3. Identify the action

Siegal decided to treat Ron as dyslexic and use available tools in tutoring him.

With the problem and causes listed, you are ready to explore actions. Siegal concluded that exercises to deal with Ron's presumed learning disability would be the proper course of action. Some leaders concerned with reducing drug abuse in this country think that actions aimed at cutting the supply of drugs will work while others think that policies aimed at cutting the demand will be more effective.

Thinking of actions to meet the problem must be tentative for two obvious reasons. First, because most problems are caused by many factors, no single action is likely to work. Second, because the action will require the cooperation of others, getting their agreement on the best way to deal with the problem is never easy. The best way to get the agreement is to let those directly concerned adopt an action themselves. You may have a good idea of what needs to be done, but you must remain flexible so that others can decide for themselves.

In searching for viable actions, you need to be aware of the danger of the "law of the hammer": Those who have a hammer will use it regardless of the problem. For example, the chairperson of a fundraising committee at a nonprofit may suggest that a new four-color brochure be created to raise more money. Unless she demonstrates that funds will increase by producing a more effective brochure, she has rushed to an action that may make no sense.

You may advocate a solution because you have found it worked elsewhere or because you may have some expertise in its application. Siegal may have too hastily concluded that Ron had dyslexia because her brother had that problem. Be on guard against firm solutions to poorly defined and misunderstood problems.

Principle 17.2: **Identify key players and stakeholders**

Genuine Do-Gooders can never problem solve alone. Even reading to the elderly in a nursing home requires the cooperation of the person you are reading to as well as the administrator of the facility. Societal problems like air pollution, juvenile crime, or heart disease can be reduced only if many individuals and organizations work together.

Therefore, it is clear that a remedy to any serious problem requires cooperation. What is far from clear, however, is who must do the cooperating. There is no single easy answer to this question because the answer depends on the specific problem you are addressing. Unfortunately, no computer software will allow you to type in a problem and receive a list of relevant people and organizations. You will have to identify the people and organizations yourself.

In order to develop your own specific list of people and organizations, which is at the heart of building a cooperative solution to a problem, you must first understand the basic distinction between "players" and "stakeholders." Players are individuals and groups who have power over the policies of an organization. Stakeholders are individuals and groups who are affected by the activities of the organization and therefore have a stake in them. All players are stakeholders because what happens in their organization affects their power. The converse, however, is not true for societal problems. Not all stakeholders are players, because ordinary stakeholders have little or no power over the policies of an organization. In the feudal system, serfs were stakeholders but not players, while nobles were both. High school students are stakeholders, but in most schools they are not players. For individual problems, like Ron's poor reading, the stakeholders are also usually players (Ron controls whether or not he will cooperate with Siegal to improve his reading).

Before we provide tips on how to find players and stakeholders of a given societal problem, we need to talk about the relationship between the two. Players have a more integral part in the problem-solving process than stakeholders because they have the capacity to change the direction of organizations. They choose whether to satisfy the needs of the stakeholders since by definition stakeholders have little power over the problem. If the players refuse to address the needs of stakeholders, the stakeholders will have to become players themselves to resolve the problem. Cooperative problem solving is the process through which players work together to solve the problems that impact the life, liberty, and the pursuit of happiness of stakeholders. Good players are sensitive to the needs and suggestions of stakeholders. Bad players ignore all or all but a few of the stakeholders.

Searching for the key players requires considerable knowledge on your part. If you are trying to make a change in an organization in which you are already involved, you will have much less difficulty in identifying the players and stakeholders and in obtaining the information you need about their attitudes toward, and power over, the problem. If you are working on changing something in an institution to which you do not belong, such as a piece of legislation at the state or federal level or the policy of a large corporation, you need to do extensive research to decide what you can do to make a difference. Brief guidelines provided in this section will help you identify players and stakeholders.

The four guidelines below require you to obtain specific information that will help you determine who the key players are for the problem you want to address. In using these guidelines, remember to make sure the players you identify have some power over, and interest in, the problem.

Guidelines for identifying players

1. Start by looking at the official position of the players who have some responsibility for the problem.

Do not make the common mistake of going too high upin the organization. The top officials in the organization are critical players for only major problems. Sometimes the people at the top have neither the knowledge nor interest to do anything about the problem.

2. Study networks, the group of people whom the individual or group can call upon for support and favors.

Players who are influential because of networks are sometimes very hard to identify, especially if you are outside the loop. You would not know the relative influence of two different senators on employment issues, for example, unless you knew which one had the closer ties to labor unions. Knowing specifics about players, especially their ties to key stakeholder groups, will help you identify players you might otherwise miss.

3. Find out which groups and individuals have expertise on the problem.

Lobby groups have power because their staffs know more about policy issues than the staffs of the legislators to whom they lobby. Key players are often people who have detailed knowledge of a specific issue, particularly those who have many years of experience as leaders in a specific field.

4. Remember that money is a major source of power.

The outcry over campaign financing and the role of rich lobbyists in controlling our government is on target. Money talks when influencing players, especially if the money is backed by a large number of stakeholders who are presumed to vote. However, money is not just what lobbyists use. In every organization, those who have financial responsibility play a role in major policy decisions of the organization. The people in organizations who manage the money, or in some cases bring the money in, are likely to be players on any problem area that might require financial resources or otherwise impact the bottom line. If you don't follow the money, you may miss some really important players.

First, ask who is officially in charge of the organization's divisions that are likely to impact the problem. Then, ask who has key networks, who has important and valued expertise, and who has enough money or enough control over the organization's money to be a player

Guidelines for identifying stakeholders

Any organization, big or small and operating locally or globally, will have four types of stakeholders (other than players): workers, customers, supporters, communities. In looking at these four categories, keep asking yourself if the individuals or groups are affected by the problem.

1. Workers

By definition, workers are stakeholders because what happens to the organization affects them. In most cases, we are talking about paid workers, but this also applies to volunteers who are stakeholders also.

2. Customers

The quality and quantity of the goods and services offered by businesses, government, and nonprofits affect customers. In most cases, customers are not players because they are not organized. Occasionally, they may be represented by players such as the Consumer Protection Agency, Consumers Unions, and other groups.

3. Supporters

Varying according to the type of organization, supporters include investors, citizens, volunteers, and funders.

4. Communities in which the organizations operate

For businesses, government, and nonprofit organizations, the immediate community in which they are physically located is a stakeholder. How these organizations care for the physical property, how they deal with traffic and waste, and where they find their employees will have a major effect on the local community. Other broader communities may also be viewed as stakeholders. Large businesses also have state, federal, and even global communities as stakeholders since their economic performance, their contribution to the tax base, and their environmental policies affect large numbers of people in each of these communities.

These four categories should serve as a checklist when you search for stakeholders. Never ignore the stakeholders of the business, governmental, or nonprofit organization you are trying to change. They can be vital to your success or failure.

Principle 17.3:   Lay the groundwork for teamwork

In the remaining three chapters, we will discuss how you can work specifically to get key players to implement solutions to a problem you feel strongly about. However, the base for such cooperation does not develop overnight, and the Genuine Do-Gooder must work all the time to build that base. It is a lot like sales. Building your reputation and network in your daily activities will determine your success in getting players to work together to solve problems. You may not wine and dine these players like big-ticket salespeople do, but you should make sure that you develop cordial relations with as many as possible.

Fortunately, we have a great teacher in building such a basis of support under whom we can study: Dale Carnegie. We can benefit from his wisdom by reading and applying the principles in his convincing and successful book, *How to Win Friends and Influence People*. First published in 1937, the book has sold, according to the book's jacket, "over 15 million copies" and been translated into "virtually every language." The book has many competitors that aim to improve your skills as a politician, negotiator, mediator, salesperson, or leader, but there's a reason why Carnegie's book has probably sold more copies than all of the others combined: it's excellent. I strongly recommend you purchase a copy of Carnegie's masterpiece and read it frequently. If you apply the 30 principles it provides, you will build the coalitions of players needed to reduce the problems you are attacking.

The essence of Carnegie's advice is to be nice as a person, to act as someone to be trusted, as someone trying to get people to think differently, and as a leader. Here are four of his principles to help you get started:

1. **"Don't criticize, condemn or complain."**
   Or, as Carnegie aptly entitles the chapter supporting this principle, "If you want to gather honey, don't kick over the beehive."

2. **"Smile."**
   People want to know that you have their interests at heart, and there is no better way to do that than to smile and mean it when talking to them.

3. **"The only way to get the best of an argument is to avoid it."**
   This is difficult advice to follow for do-gooders who feel passionate about things. Try to be a steerer on a course toward agreement, rather than someone who tries to force everyone to see the true path.

4. **"Make the other person happy about doing the things you suggest."**
   This usually means getting the person to see your concerns and ideas as theirs, even if you don't get the credit for solving the problem.

Even looking at this small sample of principles, you can see how Carnegie's advice can be effective in building connections with people who will help you develop solutions to the problems you and they think are important.

The career of Louis L. Goldstein demonstrates that Carnegie was right. The profile below describes how he won friends and influenced people throughout Maryland for 56 years, first as a member of the state general assembly for 16 years and then as comptroller for the next 40 years. Goldstein passed away in 1998, but left a legacy of his integrity, his desire to listen to people, and his ability to make decisions that benefited most of the people, most of the time.

Louis Goldstein: "Beloved Tax Collector"

"And besides, you have to be a very special person to be a beloved tax collector." That's how William Donald Schaefer, governor of Maryland, ended his statements about Goldstein upon his death. Schaefer described him as a "velvet glove over a hand of steel . . . on the surface, all smiles, a charmer. But certainly no pushover, nobody to try to pull one over on. He fiercely guarded the state's triple-A bond rating like it was his own. People were in for a rough time if they came before the board of public works and didn't have the right answer." Goldstein was described as a campaigner who never stopped. A lover of parades, he knew and listened to everybody that he met. A four-minute walk to lunch usually ended up in a 20-minute procession of greeting people, most of whom he knew by name. He would frequently end his talks, big or small, with the statement, "God bless you real good."

The key to remember is that good relationships will assist you in identifying and researching problems. You will have good access to the stakeholders whose interests you are trying to enhance to make sure that you are truly doing what they value. You will also develop good relationships with players and people who in a few years will become players.

Cooperative problem solving and the "be nice" principle do not mean that you will avoid all confrontations or that you will not take actions or speak your mind when you are actually working to put together a particular cooperative solution. Conflict is frequently the path to cooperation, and that may require you to at least threaten to kick over the beehive at a strategic moment. However, as we will see in chapter 19, departing from the principle should be done cautiously and very rarely.

QUIZ RESULTS

1. Good problem solving will result in effective solutions.

Answer: No. The application of the Problem-Solving Triangle for planning purposes will lead to solid ideas for solutions, but getting those ideas to be implemented is equally crucial. Therefore, while you need to start out thinking problem solving, you must quickly move to cooperative problem solving.

2. All individuals who influence or are impacted by a policy are players.

Answer: No. The problem area in this statement is "impacted by a policy." Stakeholders are individuals who may have no influence over the policy. They can become players if they organize or join forces with existing players, but until they do they are not players.

3. You must always be nice to people even when faced with opposition.

Answer: Not Sure. No matter how much opposition initially comes from someone, you need to show respect, avoid trying to win the argument. However, once you enter the stage of actually developing a group of players that need to cooperate to solve a problem, you may have to get tough.

18 Getting on the Agenda of Players

QUIZ

1. If you cannot get your issue on the agenda of key players, you might as well forget about it.
Circle one: Yes   No   Not Sure

2. Getting key players to put your problem on their agenda is usually very difficult.
Circle one: Yes   No   Not Sure

3. Getting the attention of key players to consider your problem is half the battle.
Circle one: Yes   No   Not Sure

INTRODUCTION

General Colin Powell retired from the military and immediately took on what he considered to be America's most serious domestic problem: the growing number of at-risk youth. Powell developed an organization called America's Promise—The Alliance for Youth. His background and that program are described in the profile below. The objective he sought was to get his problem squarely on the agenda of every corporation, nonprofit organization, and governmental agency in America.

Colin Powell: Master agenda builder

What do VH1, the University of Southern California, Miss Teen Maryland 1998, B'nai B'rith, Janet Jackson, every living president, and a float in the 1997 Macy's Thanksgiving Day Parade have in common? They are all helping General Colin Powell get children on the agenda of every business, government, and nonprofit organization in America.

As Chairman of America's Promise—The Alliance for Youth, Powell uses his energy, resources, and star power to mobilize corporate, government, and nonprofit leaders across the country to help America's youth. The organization aims to improve the lives of 15 million at-risk youth. Recognizing this formidable task, Powell, the unpaid leader of America's Promise, has enlisted the help of many prominent organizations and public figures. The retired Army general understands the value of allies.

Hundreds of corporations, nonprofits, philanthropic foundations, service providers, communities, and governments at all levels have joined America's Promise. The alliance hopes to win the war against the problems confronting young people, by keeping promises to provide them with:

- An ongoing relationship with a caring adult—parent, mentor, tutor, or coach;
- A safe place to be with structured activities during non-school hours;
- A healthy start;
- A marketable skill through effective education; and
- A chance to give back through community service.

Specifically, the organization aims to provide all five developmental resources to 2 million young people and at least one resource to 5 million young people by the year 2000. The organization uses these benchmarks to show how many people have yet to be reached and how large an effort it will require.

Powell and his allies have pulled this simple message into communities across the United States by way of a Little Red Wagon. Powell offers the wagon, a symbol of youth, adventure, and responsibility, as a promise and challenge to America's youth. "In the beginning, we will pull you along, support you, nurture you. Soon you will support yourself, proudly, independently. And then, you will support others."

The simple message and symbol, the allies enlisted by Powell to motivate more people to get involved, and a clear goal (benchmark) are all helping to put at-risk youth on America's agenda. For more information on America's Promise, contact:

America's Promise—The Alliance for Youth
909 N. Washington Street, Suite 400
Alexandria, VA 22314-1556
Tel. 888 55-YOUTH   Fax 703 535-3900
http://www.americaspromise.org

Powell uses what he learned in his military career, especially his experience in the Vietnam and Gulf wars. From those experiences, he knows that a successful effort requires a clear purpose and overwhelming resources to achieve one's goals. He has a clear definition of his purpose. He uses all of the resources in his campaign, which include enormous popularity and public recognition, to achieve his primary mission—to get the problems facing disadvantaged youth on the agenda of those that can do something about it. His efforts are an example for every Genuine Do-Gooder.

Principle 18.1: Raising awareness is essential

Suppose you want your community center to create a program for children whose parents do not come home until late, or you want your company to provide more jobs for those living in a nearby neighborhood, or you want your local government to do something about the large number of business signs on Main Street. You must make the key players in those organizations realize there is a problem, otherwise you are not even at the starting gate. The graveyard of do-gooder ideas is filled with problems that never made the agendas of key players.

Powell does what Genuine Do-Gooders must do as the first and most crucial step in cooperative problem solving. He raises awareness and convinces the players who have the power that there is a problem. It is what we mean by "getting on the agenda of key players."

In some cases, getting on the agenda of key players is all that is needed. It appears to be working for Powell, who has compiled an impressive string of commitments from hundreds of different organizations to put more resources into helping at-risk youth. At the individual level, it can work if a volunteer to a bedridden senior can inform the administrators of the nursing home that her client needs more help walking or a volunteer tutor discovers that a student is weak on fundamental arithmetic and is able to pass along this information to the student's parents. It worked for AIDS activists who publicized the growing menace of the disease and eventually saw business, government, and nonprofits mobilize to fight the disease through a variety of initiatives.

Just getting a problem on the agenda of key players is the best and easiest path to cooperative problem solving. You do not have to reach an agreement on solutions by yourself because the players themselves decide what will be done. The only thing you have to do, as Powell demonstrates, is raise awareness of the problem and then keep score on how well everybody is doing.

Unfortunately, getting your problem on the agenda of key players does not always result in action. Sometimes other key players work to keep it off the agenda, which means there is disagreement over how serious the problem is. However, the more common obstacle is that no consensus among the key players develops on how to solve the problem cooperatively.

The next principle suggests how you can convince enough key players that a problem is serious enough to set the stage for action. Actually getting positive action requires more than just getting it on the agenda. It requires that you use the strategies discussed in the next chapters to promote cooperative problem solving.

Principle 18.2:   Use multiple approaches to get on agenda

Your awareness of a problem is no guarantee that the problem will even be recognized, let alone dealt with. Getting your problem on the agenda of an organization, whether it be a company, a nonprofit, or a government agency, means convincing at least one key player that the problem is important enough for the organization to take action. That key player could then work to get other key players to take action. If you fail, however, to get one key player to give a high priority to your problem, you will not be able to start a cooperative problem-solving process.

In order to formulate an effective strategy that demonstrates that your problem deserves the consideration of busy and powerful people who can make things happen, you need to understand the obstacles in your way. Recognizing and confronting these obstacles requires the persistence and resourcefulness demonstrated by millions of Genuine Do-Gooders, from Mother Teresa to your neighbor who gets the city to put a stop sign at a dangerous corner.

Obstacles can be formidable because key players may initially not want to put your problem on their agenda. There are several reasons for this reluctance. First, players who are influential in an organization share responsibility for what that organization does, and nobody wants to hear that they may share responsibility for a problem. This is true for managers of a manufacturing company who are ultimately responsible for the safety of their workers, the executive director of a nonprofit community center who is responsible for unknowingly allowing drug dealers on the premises, or local government officials whose police rough up suspects. Second, players are busy people who have to satisfy the demands of other players. Recognizing a problem will mean longer meetings and who knows what else. Finally, never underestimate the insecurity of key players when potential problems are raised. The existence of a problem could threaten their power and self-interest. Generally, influential players usually think it is better to deny that the problem exists than to take a chance on what might happen if the problem is placed on the agenda of the organization.

Given the circumstances that contribute to denial of a problem by players, be prepared for hard work throughout the long haul. The figure below suggests that there are four stages in getting your problem on the agenda of key players. First, expect to be ignored, then attacked, then acknowledged but not taken seriously, and finally to the stage where enough key players have it on their agendas to move toward cooperative problem solving. Do not get discouraged by the attacks. People get defensive when they fear they have done something wrong. The more you are attacked, the more progress you are making in getting on the agenda. Remember, however, to follow the suggestion of Carnegie. Your purpose is not to have a good fight, but to promote cooperative problem solving. Ignore attacks and never retaliate.

You may get to stage III or IV by doing very little. Sometimes outside forces help you. The agendas of key players sometimes change by themselves if the problem becomes increasingly serious over time. Enough traffic fatalities will lead to the consideration of lowering the speed limits; persistent unemployment will eventually force the government to start more public spending programs; and growing numbers of deaths from a disease like AIDS will lead government and nonprofits to consider education programs for risk groups.

Four Stages of Getting on the Agenda

I. Ignored
Silence from all players even when you approach them.

II. Attacked
You are called any one of the following: naysayer, someone who only sees the glass as half empty; dishonest, having ulterior motives; cracked; stupid; hot tempered; rude or otherwise mentally, intellectually, or socially impaired.

III. Grudgingly Acknowledged
Perhaps one or two players, who are not so key, place it on their agendas, lip service is paid but not formally placed on the agenda of meetings.

IV. Success
Several key players indicate their concern and initiate a process that is likely to lead to a serious consideration of action. They make public statements frequently, and they place the problem on the agenda of the organization.

However, as a Genuine Do-Gooder, you should not be waiting for fate to intervene. You need to develop plans to get to stages III and IV. Start by making a list of key players, and then ask what you can do to get each player sufficiently concerned about the problem to put it on their agendas. Once you have done that, you should use the five guidelines presented below to develop a workable strategy.

Guideline 1: Do your homework to build your case

Conduct research with an open mind so you have your facts straight. Consult experts and collect information to make your pitch that the organization faces a serious problem. Make sure the problem represents the viewpoints of a large number of stakeholders. For example, if you decide that the reading levels at your elementary school are low, be sure to go beyond your own experiences or even the experiences of a few friends. Talk to at least 10 different parents of children in the school to gather information that will allow you to evaluate your own views and provide a stronger base for stating the seriousness of the problem.

Guideline 2: Use horror stories, statistics, emotions

The KISS principle, or Keep It Simple Stupid, should be kept in mind at all times. Develop a brief statement that you make over and over again to drive home the seriousness of the problem. Simple ideas supporting your view need to be rehearsed and repeated ad nauseam to build an awareness of the problem. Key players are busy and have limited time; they become irritated with long-winded appeals. In this case (as in most cases), less is more.

Powerful arguments must be concrete. So, provide specific "horror stories" and specific statistics showing the seriousness of the problem. Horror stories and statistics must be designed to have an emotional appeal that makes the player take notice. The facts of the story and the statistics are only as good as the emotions they stir.

Once you have hit key players with the horror stories, move to the numbers. When set in context, numbers can stir emotions. If you want to show how widespread the problem is, use real numbers expressed through percentages—e.g., 80 percent of the students read below grade level. If you want to show that the problem is more serious in your community than in others, prepare a simple bar graph showing the number of students reading below grade level in your school and others.

Guideline 3: **Ask allies among players to advise you**

If you have laid the groundwork for cooperative problem solving, you will already be on good terms with the people you will need to help get your problem on the agenda of key players. Approach those players with whom you have the best rapport and ask for their advice on whom to approach and how. Maybe those players will take the hint and make the approach for you.

Stakeholders constitute a critical source of allies. Problems exist in the first place because stakeholders' interests, whether they be workers in the organization, customers of the organization, or the entire community, are threatened. Therefore, you need to consult them and win their support. You goal is to be able to convince key players that you speak legitimately on behalf of stakeholders.

Guideline 4: **Decide how public you want to be**

Saul Alinsky, who was discussed in chapter 12 as one of the fathers of stockholder activism, was fond of making a lot of noise. He did this on the grounds that because he was representing poor stakeholders, key players would ignore him unless he created public spectacles like his threat to tie up all the lavatories at O'Hare Airport. However, even Alinsky used behind-the-scenes conversations whenever possible. Genuine Do-Gooders should always think twice about going public because, given the resistance to change by most key players and their superior access to the media, going public can become confrontational and, if we follow the advice of Carnegie, nonproductive.

However, sometimes it is necessary to go public, particularly if you're stuck in stage I—Ignored. There are a variety of "places" where you can go public such as at formal meetings, through letters to the editor, private letters, or e-mails that will eventually become public, and media coverage of people and events. The basic idea behind going public is that once everyone hears about the problem, they will be convinced that it is important enough to do something about.

It is sometimes beneficial to get the media involved. Private letters, speeches at meetings, and even a letter to the editor suggest that you think the problem is important. Key players usually interpret media coverage to mean that people throughout society think the problem is important. If you cannot figure out how to get media coverage, perhaps you need to think about how you have phrased your problem.

Getting the media involved has benefits at a later stage. The primary benefit is to appeal to a large number of stakeholders who would be outraged if they heard the horror stories or saw the statistics. These reactions could convince some key players that something has to be done. A secondary benefit is that media coverage reduces the amount of time and stress required to talk to players one on one. Media coverage is particularly helpful if there is a lot of it. For example, politicians' staff keep files of news clippings of issues important to their constituents. The more clippings in a file, the more attention it will garner from the politician. You should find the following guidelines helpful:

1. Newspaper coverage is almost always better than TV coverage. You can distribute photocopies of the former much more easily than tapes of the latter, and reading is quicker than using the VCR.

2. Prepare a two-page fact sheet that gives statistics, expert testimony, and a couple of horror stories. This will help journalists write the story. Reporters will not copy verbatim in most cases, but they have short attention spans and even shorter deadlines, so they need all the help they can get. Much of Nader's success in attacking unsafe automobiles and in his other campaigns over the years came from his efforts to make sure that reporters had the information they needed to write the story.

3. Try to get journalists to interview stakeholders who are impacted by the problem. Here TV may be more effective than usual if you can get a convincing person on camera, but newspaper stories can also be powerful. A single in-depth story on someone hurt by the problem could be effective.

4. Get your supporters to write letters to the editor. This will allow you to cite it as evidence of the problem when you talk to others. It is better if several people write because it motivates the editor to assign a reporter to the story. Also, politicians are likely to respond to three or four letters on the same problem. In a best-case scenario, someone who disagrees that there is a problem will attack the letters supporting you, because this will encourage follow-up behavior by the newspapers,

and possibly the politicians.

5. Don't try to get coverage through public demonstrations
and other staged events unless you are desperate. Although
frequently attempted, these activities rarely work because they
can be dismissed by the players as being staged. They are also
dangerous because the people doing the demonstrating might
do something to put off key players. Public demonstrations
can backfire in other ways. You might ask the media to attend
a school board meeting where a large group of parents will be
complaining about the poor reading program, for example,
and only you, your spouse, and one neighbor show up.

Guideline 5:   Use outside events to mobilize

In thinking about how you can build a consensus, you need
to also consider the role of outside events. Frequently, outside events
can heighten awareness and sensitivity to the problem more effectively than anything you can do as an individual. For example,
President Ronald Reagan's relative indifference to the AIDS epidemic
early in his administration changed when a longtime friend of his,
Rock Hudson, became ill with AIDS. This may have had the effect of
raising Reagan's priority on the need to take action to stop the
spread of AIDS.

Changing conditions and visible events can be a catalyst for
community problem solving. They can help to get the problem on
the agenda of key players even when you have been stuck in Stage I
for a long period of time. You need to be prepared for such an event
by having your information ready for dissemination to key players and
the media at a moment's notice.

The hard work necessary to get on the agenda of key players
should not discourage you. If they are sure that they are attempting
to remedy a serious problem, they will persist until the problem is
taken seriously. They will follow the advice of Nader quoted earlier:
"You have to know not to be discouraged; to be resilient when things
don't work as you planned." Genuine Do-Gooders know how to balance their vision of what they would like to see happen with their
knowledge of the forces that are always working against change.

QUIZ RESULTS

1. If you cannot get your issue on the agenda of key players, you might as well forget about it.

Answer: Not Sure. Getting on the agenda is the first and most essential step. The good news is that once you get your problem on the agenda, cooperative problem solving may happen spontaneously. The bad news is that if you encounter trouble, you may find it necessary to give up. Failure to get on the players' agenda after a concerted effort will tell you how seriously other players and stakeholders are taking the problem and that perhaps you need to rethink your approach. However, sometimes fate can intervene even when it appears hopeless. Something can happen that suddenly puts one problem on everybody's front burner. Therefore, keep working and hoping.

2. Getting key players to put your problem on their agenda is usually very difficult.

Answer: Yes. Because problems are threatening, the reflex reaction of key players is to deny. You must work very hard, very long, and very smart to overcome that reflex.

3. Getting the attention of key players to consider your problem is half the battle.

Answer: No. Getting even the direct ear of the key player, no matter how loud and persuasive you are, is about 10 percent of the battle in most cases. You also must get them to think seriously about doing something about the problem or it is not firmly on the agenda. To do this, you must develop a multiple strategy campaign that requires you to do your homework, use horror stories and statistics, find allies, decide how public you want to be, and prepare for something to happen in order to drive your point home. All of these strategies must be carefully planned and executed.

19 Problem Solving through Existing Organizations

QUIZ

1. You can change an existing organization only if you have a clear and firm idea in your mind of what you want to change.
Circle one: Yes No Not Sure

2. It is impossible to forecast how successful your cooperative problem solving will be in getting the change you want.
Circle one: Yes No Not Sure

3. Conditions and events can dramatically alter your chances of success.
Circle one: Yes No Not Sure

4. Solid justifications are the most important way to increase your chances of success.
Circle one: Yes No Not Sure

INTRODUCTION

Nelson Mandela was the key player in what is arguably the most stunning and positive change of an organization in the 20th century. Unlike the Soviet Union, where change brought the collapse of the existing state, South Africa went from a country where only whites could vote and rule to one in which each individual could vote and leaders from every race played a role. The country of South Africa did not disintegrate; power was transferred to a political party that had been banned for decades until the early 1990s. Mandela did not save South Africa from a bloody civil war alone, but he was the central figure in this astonishing process of cooperative problem solving.

Nelson Mandela: Commitment to unity

Nelson Mandela is a major Genuine Do-Gooder. He dedicated most of his life, which included 27 years in prison, to the cause of creating a South Africa where no group was excluded from voting.

Born in 1918 in a remote village, Mandela was prophetically named Rolihlahla by his father. This name literally means "pulling the branch of a tree" but colloquially means "troublemaker." His father was a village chief who believed in education and made arrangements for Mandela to receive one. However, the troublemaker label proved prophetic because Mandela was thrown out of college after his sophomore year. He refused to take student office after being elected through what he considered to be an undemocratic election process.

The story of Mandela is the story of a troublemaker turned into a cooperative problem solver. He tells the story very well in his autobiography *Long Walk to Freedom.* He joined the African National Congress (ANC) in 1942, was jailed in 1963, was released in 1990, and became president in 1994.

Mandela succeeded through his commitment to and his genius for keeping things together. First, he worked effectively to keep the ANC from splintering for more than half a century. Then, he worked with the ruling National Party in 1990 to keep together a coalition of whites and nonwhites that led to the complex political solution that governs South Africa today. He shared the spotlight with President F. W. DeKlerk, the leader of the white ruling National Party. The new government and Mandela have their critics because many social and economic problems remain. But no one can deny that the problem of the political disenfranchisement of the nonwhite population has not been solved.

As a Genuine Do-Gooder, you can learn a great deal from Mandela's achievement. Even though your problem-solving missions are much less ambitious, your job is to orchestrate a solution that is supported by key players. Cooperative problem solving always requires getting key players to figure out how their existing organizations can remedy a problem. Whether it is the Boys and Girls Club opening an after-school computer laboratory to bring technology to disadvantaged youngsters, a business adopting more environment-friendly policies, or a government taking action to reduce the number of children bitten by roaming dogs, key players must work together on a solution. This chapter is about how to encourage a winning combination of key players to come up with viable solutions. It assumes that the players already have the problem on their agenda and that you can play some role in bringing them together.

Please do not be intimidated by the use of Mandela as our model for cooperative problem solving within organizations. Although his achievements are beyond what any of us can ever expect to do, the rules he followed are easy to understand. Take the strong self-discipline that characterizes the Genuine Do-Gooders we have discussed throughout this book, and that can be applied in any organization and for any purpose. Mandela's rules are the ones you need to follow in cooperative problem-solving activities, whether it is getting your school to have more resources for remedial reading programs, convincing your bridge club to hold a benefit for the new wing of a senior center, lobbying your state representative to lower the threshold of blood alcohol in drunken-driving cases, or convincing your company to invite the National Retiree Volunteer Coalition to set up a program that will encourage retirees to volunteer.

Principle 19.1: **Be a shepherd—lead from behind**

Mandela tells us that as a child of 10 he was sent to the court of a regent after his father died; he observed meetings that included both rowers and steerers, chiefs and their subjects, landowners and laborers. He was impressed with the way the regent would permit open discussion, including criticism of his own views. He writes:

As a leader, I have always followed the great principles I first saw demonstrated by the regent at the Great Palace. I have always endeavored to listen to what each and every person in a discussion had to say before venturing my opinion. Oftentimes, my own opinion will simply represent a consensus of what I heard in the discussion. I always remember the regent's axiom: A leader, he said, is like a shepherd; he stays behind the flock, letting the most nimble go out ahead, whereupon the others follow, not realizing that all along they are being directed from behind.

To work toward a cooperative solution to a problem, key players and their associated stakeholders need to be directed first by having the problem on their agenda and then by having some idea of a viable solution. Being a shepherd means that you will point the flock of key players in the direction you want the flock to take. Mandela was always clear that he wanted a constitution in which each adult member of South African society had one vote regardless of gender or ethnicity.

While Mandela never wavered from his goal, he was flexible. Many of his own supporters wanted a nonwhite state and wanted more state control over the economy. However, Mandela stayed committed to a multiracial government and a mixed economy along with one person, one vote. He knew that social and economic problems could not begin to be addressed unless the political solution was achieved.

This focus on one policy at a time is essential if you are trying to find a solution to your problem. It is hard enough to make a change in the face of those forces that are likely to oppose it. If you add more changes, you succeed only in increasing the number of enemies.

Principle 19.2: **Continually gauge your chances**

Everything you undertake in life requires at least an implicit forecast. Action without anticipating the consequences is foolish.

For someone like Mandela trying to bring about a huge political change, forecasting is an integral part of cooperative problem solving. He had to identify key players who would determine whether or not there would be a political system in which everyone had a vote. Then he had to ask three questions of all of them:

1. Do they support or oppose my policy?
2. How influential will they be in a community problem-solving process?
3. How important is the policy to them?

Those three questions will give you a rough idea of how likely you are to succeed. If most of the key players who have power and care about the policy are on your side, you are likely to succeed. If they are not, or even if they are equally divided, your chances of success are low.

This approach to forecasting assumes that the problem itself is on the players' agendas and different proposals are under consideration. This was not a problem for Mandela, especially in the 1980s. The problems associated with the dissatisfaction of the nonwhite members of South African society had been a top priority for most key players in South Africa for many years.

Principle 19.3: **Assess the potential impact of change**

Once you have a feel for your chances of success, the next step is to see whether or not changing conditions and existing pressures will have an impact and, if so, in what direction. These kinds of conditions and pressures can relate to players, internal conditions of the organization, and the organization's external environment.

1. A change in players can make a big difference. It did for Mandela when F. W. De Klerk replaced the more dogmatic P. W. Botha as president of South Africa.
2. Internal conditions within the organization can alter the influence and views of players. The growing imbalance between the white and nonwhite population in South Africa led to an increasing number of business and military leaders to push for a compromise solution.

3. The organization's external environment can aid or block desired changes. The international business community and many governments were calling for the end to the existing government. Economic boycotts and political sanctions, started in the 1980s, took a toll on the economy.

An analysis of possible internal and external conditions is crucial because you may discover time is on your side, just as Mandela did. That is, the longer you wait, the more conditions will bring players to your point of view, and you can then seize the moment.

Principle 19.4: Compromise is key to success

Mandela's chances of success were not very good in the mid-1980s when he was quoted in the *New York Times Magazine* that he knew there would be one person one vote within his lifetime. He was sure that he or someone else could shepherd the key players to a new constitution that gave everyone a voice in the government. We can learn several things from his example.

First, Mandela had enough support to command influence in the problem-solving process because of his stature as de facto leader of the African National Congress and as a leader with worldwide standing as a player. He made himself a player by his persistence and steady behavior. Even while in prison, he was open to talking with members of the regime, as long as they didn't make the talks conditional on his renouncing his party's position.

Mandela built a support network by laying the groundwork for cooperative problem solving. Although he got into plenty of arguments, and though sometimes his tendency to be very stubborn led him to "kick over the beehive," he followed most of Carnegie's principles. He has an enormous network of supporters who are attracted to him by his personality and his willingness to listen respectfully to others.

Whatever cooperative problem-solving activity you try to shepherd, your current network will be crucial. Establish cordial relations with all players and stakeholders in your organization so that they can work with you in a cooperative way to solve problems. This requirement means that you can only use cooperative problem solving in nearby windows since that is the only place in which you will have such a network. Do not attempt to shepherd the process as an outsider or a peripheral actor. It will not work.

There are four traditional tools used by people who are trying to get support for a specific action. They are: justification, bribery, threats, and compromise. The first three are not as important as the fourth.

The goal of justification is to get players to support your proposal through rational and emotional arguments. You will have to go beyond emotions in order to justify your proposal to key players. This will require two very different approaches. The "high road" is to provide justifications to appeal to players as if they were Genuine Do-Gooders. The "low road" is to create justifications that appeal to the different special interests of the players. Mandela used both, and so should you.

The second strategic tool, bribery, sounds immoral, so people use other terms like the Latin affectation "quid pro quo" or, the Americanized twin "scratching each other's back." However, offering to do something nice or actually doing something nice for a player to gain that player's support is a bribe. Offering support to players on other proposals they care about in exchange for support for your proposal is so accepted that it is called "log-rolling." Mandela promised De Klerk that he would encourage moderation within the ANC during the constitutional negotiations.

Threats are similar to bribes because you promise or actually do something in the hope that the players will act differently. The only difference is that while bribes offer something players would like, threats promise things that players would hate.

Mandela and the ANC leadership throughout its struggle threatened and used violence, strikes, public demonstrations, and economic boycotts when they felt they had no other options. Threats have their place in getting players to cooperate, but they are risky because they can create anger and eventually destroy the trust ultimately needed to problem solve cooperatively.

We have saved the best and most powerful strategic tool for last. Justifications have a limited role in gaining support, and do-gooders have little capacity to bribe and even less capacity and taste for threats. Your chances of ever getting your proposals implemented through cooperative problem solving would be close to nothing if these were the only three tools available to you.

Compromise is the tool of choice for the do-gooder because it embraces the spirit of cooperative problem solving. It shows your willingness to listen to and respect the needs of all players and stake-holders. It may require you to abandon part of your initial plan to solve the problem, but it could lead to an even stronger solution than you imagined in the first place. Mandela orchestrated a constitution that embodied one person one vote, but he allowed for the ruling National Party to protect its members and to share in the transition process even though the ANC had an overwhelming election victory.

Using compromise strategies, however, can have complica-tions. Any idea of compromise can weaken the cohesion of the play-ers who make them. It happened to Mandela several times, when he supported the principle that South Africa's white power elite should have a role in the future multiracial government. Many members of the ANC disagreed with his compromise position, and breakaway leaders and splinter groups emerged frequently. However, Mandela's ability to hold enough of his party together while accepting this middle road built trust with the governing elite, which in turn restored cohesion to his own party. He eventually met his ultimate goal: producing a radically different government, controlled by the nonwhite majority but still including the right of whites to vote and some protection for them as a powerful minority group.

Another related danger is that you might "give away the store." You may get approval for a watered-down proposal that would ultimately lead to defeat of the policy. Many initial supporters of President Bill Clinton felt that he gave up too much on welfare reform to reach agreement with Congress, and as a result he has lost their backing. The ability to keep your supporters when compromising with players is what separates successful leaders, like Mandela, from the rest of the pack.

The compromise strategy is a major problem for most do-gooders. People become do-gooders because they have a fire in their belly about societal problems. If not, they would be exercising their own self-interest with little care for its consequence to the commu-nity. People with such passion do not think half a loaf will feed the hungry, even if it represents real progress and the possibility of the whole loaf at a later date. This kind of thinking is called zero-sum thinking, and it can be counterproductive even as a ruse. So get rid of it; expunge it from your behavior; be calculating; be nice and take the long view. Compromise is the Genuine Do-Gooder's best friend.

1. You can change an existing organization only if you have a clear and firm idea in your mind of what change you want.

Answer: Not Sure. If you have no clear and firm objective, you are in the problem-defining and agenda-building stage and therefore are not ready to move to the next level. However, your position cannot be too firm because in most cases some basic compromises will be needed.

2. It is impossible to forecast how successful your cooperative problem solving will be in getting the change you want.

Answer: No. You can always make forecasts on anything, including whether or not your proposal will be implemented. The problem is that so many factors are operating that the forecast can only be an educated guess. However, you must make these forecasts continuously if you want to improve your chances of success.

3. Conditions and events can dramatically alter your chances of success.

Answer: Yes. Outside events as well as changes within the organization, especially personnel changes, can completely turn around the chances of success. Unfortunately, they can do so in either direction. However, if you have a low chance but a solid proposal, the best thing to do is wait because time will be on your side.

4. Solid justifications are the most important way to increase your chances of success.

Answer: No. Justifications are more like icing on the cake. The most powerful of all strategies is compromise. Threats and promises can easily backfire and cost you a great deal. Compromise can work but you have to be careful not to give away the store and lose your own base of support.

20 Creating New Organizations

QUIZ

1. It is better to start a new organization than to get an existing institution to help remedy a problem you have identified.
Circle one: Yes   No   Not Sure

2. A useful mission statement should lead to a list of doable and measurable objectives.
Circle one: Yes   No   Not Sure

3. Make sure that you build up a large membership and volunteer base before you begin to plan your short-term objectives.
Circle one: Yes   No   Not Sure

4. An organization has been institutionalized when it can survive and function effectively without the founding leadership.
Circle one: Yes   No   Not Sure

INTRODUCTION

In 1989, Wendy Kopp founded Teach for America (TFA) a nonprofit organization that in effect is a national teacher corps. It recruits and places new college graduates in disadvantaged areas where there are teacher shortages. The profile below describes the remarkable birth and survival of TFA. The major lesson of Kopp is not that she founded TFA, but that she steered TFA from a great idea that had a spectacular birth to a viable institution that has a good chance of long-term survival and high-quality performance.

Wendy Kopp: Tireless drive, steady focus

It was a conference she organized about the state of American education that ignited a spark in the then 21-year-old Princeton student. She was convinced that a teaching corps of bright, ambitious college graduates from all academic majors could help reduce the disparities in American education. The ember that came to life in the fall of 1988 is now a fire, the national organization Teach for America.

Kopp wrote her senior thesis, the start-up plan (complete with timeline and budget) for the national teacher corps, the semester after the conference. She decided that the time was ripe for her idea.

While most of her peers were sending letters and resumes to prospective employers, Kopp sent letters to Ross Perot and other top executives asking for help. After little response, she systematically wrote more letters to handpicked CEOs.

Rex Adams, then vice president of administration at the Mobil Corporation and director of the Mobil Foundation, was impressed by the letter and materials he received from Kopp. Mobil Oil called to congratulate her the day after she graduated. Adams had approved a $26,000 seed grant.

This was no time to celebrate or to relax. Kopp continued to write about 100 letters a week, many of those updating the companies that had declined to help her. "Teach for America became my entire life, but that was perfectly fine with me," she remembers. She and her staff worked around the clock, sleeping alternate nights. By the fall everyone was convinced they could get teachers in the schools by the next year.

The following spring, Kopp got the call she had once been waiting for. "The phone rang in our office, and the person who answered the phone said the call was from Ross Perot. I thought at first she was kidding. Apparently, he had taken an interest in one of the many letters I had sent him and was calling to invite me to meet with him in Dallas the following week to talk about what he could do to help us. The result was a $500,000 check."

By September 1990, when the first 500 teachers had made their way to their rural and inner-city place-ments, Kopp had assembled enough small grants (totaling more than $2.5 million) to help with the bills.

Today, almost 11 years and 4,000 placed teachers later, Teach for America can be called a success. It was the vision of a great leader, her undying faith, and her unyield-ing focus that made it all possible. For more information on this program, contact:

Teach for America
315 W. Thirty-Sixth Street, 6th floor
New York, NY 10018
Tel. 212 279-2080   Fax 212 279-2081
http://www.teachforamerica.org

The long-term survival of TFA was not preordained from the start, and its effectiveness and survival is not guaranteed for the future. Just because Kopp was able to raise millions of dollars and field a large number of teachers in the first few years did not mean that a viable institution had been created.

In fact, by 1994, the organization had nearly $800,000 in long-term debt and $1.2 million in an operating fund deficit. The financial crisis was part of a deeper crisis that plagues all start-up non-profits and many that have been around for a long time. The crush of daily events to serve clients and meet the payroll prevented both the long-term planning and the short-term decisions that are neces-sary in order to match resources to objectives.

TFA needed to develop more diverse sources of funding, and it needed to try to spend less by cooperating with existing organiza-tions and reducing peripheral programs. It reduced its budget from $8 million to $5 million in part by choosing to leverage help through collaborations with other educational organizations rather than by providing all the services directly. By 1996, TFA had a long-term plan, a stable fiscal position, a professional staff, and a future even if Kopp decided to leave.

In working toward this goal, Kopp passed the acid test for those who start a new organization. That test is guiding the transition from start-up organization that runs on the imagination and energy of its leaders to a stable institution that has a structure and a profes-sional staff.

According to Rick Love of the Knight Foundation, "It was Kopp's openness to change that convinced the Knight Foundation to continue supporting Teach for America . . . it has held on to its dream while managing to be practical and realizing adjustments need to be made along the way to make it a secure operation." While keeping her eye on the basic mission of TFA, Kopp was able to manage a restructuring of the organization.

This chapter is about starting informal organizations to remedy a problem. It can be a group to help neighborhood children stay out of trouble or a national organization like TFA. The chapter will provide some basic principles about what you should do at the beginning, and how you can develop the organization. Many resources are available to provide more detailed advice that you will need to consult if you embark on this path. Four of the best are:

Center for Community Change
1000 Wisconsin Ave., NW
Washington, DC 20007
Tel. 202 342-0567
http://www.communitychange.org

The Foundation Center
79 Fifth Ave.
New York, NY 10003
Tel. 212 620-4230
http://www.fdncenter.org

Independent Sector
1200 Eighteenth Street, NW, Suite 200
Washington, DC 20036
Tel. 202 467-6100   Fax 202 467-6101

Self-Help Sourcebook
Northwest Covenant Medical Center
25 Pocono Road
Denville, NJ 07834-2995
Tel. 973 625-3037
http://www.cmhc.com/selfhelp

Principle 20.1: Don't duplicate existing services

When they see a problem and want to remedy it, do-gooders have a tendency to be impatient. The inevitable frustrations of working with existing institutions can easily lead to a desire to create a new and better institution. For example, when parents complain about the lack of activities for teenagers in the community, someone usually gets the bright idea to set up a teen center. They may even defend the idea as a way to combat drug and alcohol use. The do-gooder who lacks commitment would rush to this solution without surveying what opportunities already exist, and whether or not teenagers are using those opportunities. They overlook the possibility of helping the existing community organizations to improve their programs or at least advertise them better.

This impatience is not just a result of the inherent fire-in-the-belly tendencies of do-gooders. It also results from the role that freedom plays in the structure of our society. On the positive side, that freedom has generated an economic system in which change comes from new enterprises. The entrepreneurial spirit is important in all types of business, nonprofits, and government activities because it leads to new ideas and facilities to help in implementing those ideas. On the negative side, the individualism implicit in the entrepreneurial spirit tends to encourage do-gooders to take too much responsibility on their shoulders and to ignore the reality that improving society requires a commitment to use existing community resources as well as to develop new ones.

Rushing to create a new organization is not the way of the Genuine Do-Gooder. Considerable open-minded research is required, and the first step should always be to explore improving the performance of existing institutions. The reasons for this are easy to understand.

1. **It takes a huge amount of energy and commitment to start a new organization.**
   Despite the success of Kopp, part of the lesson we can take from her is the difficulty inherent in setting up and sustaining a new organization. One gets exhausted even reading Kopp's profile.
2. **Some existing institutions will be highly critical of new efforts.**
   This was true for TFA. Traditional schools of education felt threatened by TFA because it placed teachers in classrooms after only six weeks of training rather than following two to four years of formal education training. The new organization may siphon off resources that could greatly improve existing organizations. This is likely to create a struggle between the old institutions and the new organization that is sometimes counterproductive.

3. **The leadership and commitment necessary to make a new organization is in short supply.**

   The kinds of people who are likely to be successful in establishing a new organization are usually involved in other projects. This means that you will tend to get help from either novices or those who are already over-committed.

4. **The transition from start-up organization to permanent institution is truly the difficult portion of the mission.**

   Rarely can the initial leadership change like TFA's leadership did. Frequently, a new leadership is required in order to make that transition, but often it is prevented from emerging because the original founders will not permit it. The result is that rather than helping to remedy the problem, the new organization can actually become part of the problem.

5. **There are so many organizations already that adding a new one increases the complexity of the solution.**

   It brings in more people with different interests and perspectives. It creates confusion among clients over which organization they should go to for help and among funders over which organization deserves their support.

For these reasons, it is crucial that you thoroughly evaluate the option of working within existing institutions. Kopp spent time studying alternative ways of increasing the supply of teachers. She could have tried to get the federal government to establish a national teaching corps, but she chose to go the independent non-profit route. Since the idea of a government-run corps had been discussed for years, she correctly concluded that it was not likely to happen anytime soon. You need to seriously study the alternatives, which may include volunteering with an organization that is most likely to be effective in dealing with the problem you have chosen. You need to see if working with an existing organization may yield better results before you embark on the time-consuming task of building yet another organization.

Creating a new organization to remedy a social problem is just like establishing a new business. It is a gamble, and serious study and planning can reduce the risk of failure. You must make sure you have both the resources and the clients who would benefit from your services, no matter who they may be. Since most of the new organizations that are likely to be established to improve society are nonprofit or governmental, whether or not you make a profit cannot ultimately determine whether or not you survive. You will have to pay close attention to whether or not you are achieving your mission and whether or not you continue to receive monetary and symbolic encouragement from your supporters.

Principle 20.2: Set five goals to meet in a year

Genuine Do-Gooders must make sure that the organization they plan has a clear mission statement that yields objectives that are clearly doable in the short run. A mission statement describes the long-run goals of the organization and indicates priorities among the goals. Even so, mission statements are not permanent; elements of the statement change as the organization changes and the environment within the organization changes.

For example, the core mission of TFA is to provide high-quality temporary teachers for school districts that need them. There were other significant spin-off goals like creating a political constituency to provide more support for disadvantaged school districts, increasing the supply of high-quality people who see teaching as a career, and developing innovative approaches to education. The spin-off goals could have replaced the core mission of the organization (and perhaps sometimes did). It was not until the TFA management refocused on the core mission that it was able to build a stable base.

The mission must not only be clearly focused, but must also be measured through specific objectives. It is best to create benchmarks, as we have discussed earlier, in order to provide clear indications of whether or not the organization is on track in keeping with its mission. The process of deciding on benchmarks helps to make sure that the members really agree on the mission statement.

TFA has always relied on using clearly measurable goals to guide its policies and decisions. They call these "measures of success," which is really another way of saying "benchmarks." I believe that much of the success of TFA and the appeal the organization has to funders is because its leaders take seriously the need to identify very specific measurable objectives. As shown below, they measure their success for a range of goals over a length of time. Note how the 9/98 figure is given and then a goal set for 9/99. This allows everyone to see where the organization is and where it hopes to go.

Selected Measures of Success Used by Teach for America

Measure of success	Achieved by 9/98	Achieve by 9/99
Percent of alumni accurately tracked through mailing list	76%	85%
Meet funding projection	$6.9m	$7.525m
Number of people to apply to Teach for America	2,747	3,104
Percent of corps members feel the institute prepared them as well as possible to be successful in their first year of teaching responsibilities	94%	95%

You can develop your mission statement with doable objectives using the following three guidelines:

1. **Be clear about the geographical scope.**
   Is the scope local, statewide, or federal? If it is local, what are the exact boundaries? Choosing one locality does not mean that you will not have spin-off impacts at the state or national level, but it does mean that precious resources will not be assigned to efforts outside the locality. This recommendation is merely a logical extension of principle 3.2, "Search for opportunities nearby."

2. **Choose carefully whether your primary mission is to educate, to lobby, or to provide direct service.**
   Educational activities raise awareness and provide information that should change behavior that will eventually remedy the problem. For example, the Partnership for a Drug-Free America seeks to educate people about the dangers of drug abuse. *Lobbying* seeks to get other institutions to provide support for services, which should eventually help to solve the problem. Colin Powell's primary goal is to convince institutions in all three sectors (nonprofit, governmental, and private)

to provide more resources to help at-risk youth. *Direct service* seeks to ameliorate the problem directly. For example, TFA created a service to provide more teachers to disadvantaged school districts. If you are starting a new organization, you need to decide what the primary purpose of the organization is: education, lobbying, or direct service. All three goals may be served but only one should be the primary focus as you start your organization.

3. **Define realistic objectives that are within the group's scope—at least one should be related to resources.** Objectives should be specific goals, stated as benchmarks that can be accomplished by your group within a year. They might be relatively modest, like getting the by-laws written, establishing a corporation, or distributing a monthly newsletter. At least one should be related to resources like an amount of money to be raised or number of members who will have paid dues. You do not want to have too many objectives or objectives that are beyond the scope of your current resource base.

Mission statements are extremely useful in helping to build consensus and to focus efforts on a new organization. The three guidelines provided here are only the beginning of what you will have to do in order to make your mission statement a living document that can direct your organization. You will need to adjust the statement continuously and go back to it frequently in order to keep your new organization on the right track.

Principle 20.3:   Secure the resources to reach goals

Assuming that you have a clearly stated mission, you also have to make sure that you have the resources needed to achieve your objectives and get close to your benchmarks. The resources can be easily divided into different categories like human resources—the people who will do the rowing and steering—and other resources like office space, communication, and record-keeping equipment, and money to pay for products that are consumed in one way or another. The key is to have enough resources to accomplish your objective.

If you are starting an organization, you are probably starting with donated resources, and you must pay close attention to both volunteer and monetary support. You need to recognize the difference between verbal commitments and the actual delivery of the services or the dollars promised. Too many times people make commitments that they eventually fail to keep.

Sometimes, this can be the fault of the organizer who fails to see each promise as a contract. You need to distinguish between those who want to give a relatively small and controllable amount of time to the organization and those who are so committed and so focused that they will step in when the chips are down no matter what. You need more of the former than the latter, and you must take steps not to pressure those who want to make only a partial commitment into pledging an unlimited commitment. That is a recipe for hard feelings.

A group of parents organizing to pressure a city school board, for example, will not succeed if its core members are not willing to meet at least biweekly and for several hours at a time. Difficulty in scheduling meetings and erratic attendance are telltale signs that the chance of survival and impact are low. Another telltale sign of impending failure has to do with money. Usually, members of the organizing group will have to spend some of their own money for start-up funds or give big blocks of their time for phone solicitation. If they show reluctance, the organization is in trouble.

Do not recruit volunteers and members and then have nothing for them to do. This is a common mistake made by the leaders of new organizations. Some of those who come to meetings are happy to do just that, but most would prefer to leave with a defined, doable, useful, and limited task to perform for the new organization.

Develop recruiting campaigns that deliver volunteers within one month before their actions are actually needed. Never recruit new members without asking them for something (usually dues) shortly after they make a commitment. You need to provide multiple opportunities for individuals to show their commitment in a meaningful way.

Principle 20.4:   **Decide whether to institutionalize**

Institutionalization means creating a self-perpetuating basis for the organization so that its activities will continue despite changes in leadership. This usually means that there is a formal legal incorporation of the new organization and a stable stream of human and financial resources.

As a Genuine Do-Gooder, you want to make a significant contribution to improving society, and your decision to work on a problem through a new organization indicates that some type of sustained activity is necessary. If it were not, you would volunteer or become employed at an established organization that already tries to remedy the problem. Kopp wanted to solve the problem of the shortage of teachers in needy areas; she saw no existing institutions where she felt she could make the major kind of change that she thought was necessary. It was her desire to have an immediate impact on the lives of students through their schools by providing a source of additional teachers. Along with this, she wanted the teachers in the corps to benefit from the leadership experience.

It is not inevitable that you need to pursue the path of Kopp. She, however, had no other choice but to institutionalize her organization, given the size and scope of what she wanted to do.

You need not follow this path either in the short term or long term. For example, if you want to provide an after-school program in your neighborhood for students who need help with their homework, you could create a very small organization that accomplishes that purpose. You can ask for space in your local church or even open up your home. You could find three other volunteers to be available to help out. Even an operation on such a small scale could make a very big difference in the lives of some teenagers in your neighborhood.

This direct service activity is only one example. You might also develop a small organization that would lobby your town government to form a comprehensive land-use plan. Such an organization would need only a very small core membership, perhaps as few as 10, as long as it could get the troops out when you needed to have letters written, campaign literature distributed, or people to show up at a meeting. The success of the small core depends on the extent to which they represent a large number of people, so that grassroots activities can be successful.

If your purpose is educational, you could start a newsletter or an Internet newsgroup. For example, you may want to inform people about available child-care resources within your community and create a four-page newsletter that you distribute free. Two or three people could do the work and even cover the expenses. You might want to call yourself an organization for publicity purposes. The organization you established would be informal. It might have no by-laws and even no checking account. However, it could persist for years and help countless people learn about child-care options in the community.

Many of the Points of Light recipients have developed such informal organizations. These groups are small operations that you might think do not deserve the name "organization." However, if they involve two or more people and they operate on a consistent basis, they are organizations in the true sense of the word.

Incorporation is necessary only if you need to raise and spend significant amounts of money, at least in excess of $500 per year. There are several types of nonprofit organization corporation forms. You may also choose the for-profit route if you see a large potential revenue as a key to success. Incorporation is a major step toward institutionalizing your organization because it involves establishing by-laws, membership procedures, and fiscal practices, which are required by both the federal and state governments.

Incorporation does not automatically lead to sustained institutionalization. That can happen only when the incorporation procedures are closely followed and real control is exercised by more than a few people. Whether or not your organization becomes a viable and sustainable institution depends on its success in taking action and obtaining funding. A key factor is the source of funding. As the management of TFA found out, depending on a small number of national funders is not realistic. A long-term source of funding is needed, one that includes government, regional funders, and individuals who are directly solicited.

The preoccupation with funding sources cannot be ignored when discussing institutionalization. Paid staff are required to raise funds, deliver services, explore new strategies, and improve existing ones. The staff should be lean and smart. No organization can maintain itself and provide quality services that have a far-reaching impact without it.

To get funds, the organization must perform well enough to persuade a funder, whether it is the United Way, a foundation, or an individual who is directly solicited, to provide the money. That usually means having a formal board of directors and some continuing evaluation by funding sources. Financial scrutiny by state and federal government agencies is sure to follow. The paid staff is needed, in part, to provide documentation to these groups. However, the requirements for funding also help to ensure that the organization is doing what it is supposed to be doing. It may not always work out that way, as we saw in principle 5.3 ("Big givers need to steer"), but in this case money is the root of responsibility. You need to make sure your new organization respects the Donor's Bill of Rights.

The ultimate size, scope, and even longevity of the organization you start should not be considered the measure of whether or not you are a Genuine Do-Gooder. Rather, the degree to which your mission has been accomplished is the defining standard. Your organization may find its mission completed if some existing nonprofit, business, or government program "picks up" responsibility for the problem. In fact, your institutionalization strategy might be for a bigger and more established organization to incorporate your program and its ideas into its programs.

Your organization should grow slowly and deliberately. You should not seek more publicity and more members than you actually need. Many new groups are too obsessed with press coverage and pronouncements by pundits. That is a path to more fluff and less substance. Press coverage should be sought as part of an overall plan to raise money, gain members, and influence other players. It should not be viewed as an end in itself.

It is also important that you form alliances with agencies that provide similar or complementary services. Try not to get involved in turf wars. Take advantage of what are always scarce resources. You may find out that in working with other groups, you do not need to transform your organization into a new institution. If you can stick to your mission and obtain more resources through joining formally with an existing institution, take that path. If you do, the organization you start may not develop into a permanent institution, but it will still accomplish its mission.

While there are many examples of failed attempts to establish a new organization, there are also thousands of examples of successes. One valuable source of information on those successes can be obtained by visiting the Web site of the Brick Award, which gives $10,000 each year to 10 winners and $100,000 to the top winner. The top winner in 1998 was Mark Levine, who created a nonprofit organization that promotes economic empowerment for low-income immigrant families in upper Manhattan through the creation of a community development credit union in the area. Other winners created a bus riders' union in L.A., a nonprofit cultural arts center to display the work of people with disabilities and special needs in St.

Petersburg, an organization to stimulate the building of affordable housing in Chicago, and an organization to tutor Asian immigrant children in Oakland. The Web site provides profiles of the winners, which serve to both inspire and guide those who seek to establish new organizations.

Do Something BRICK Award
423 W. Fifty-Fifth Street, 8th floor
New York, NY 10019
Tel. 212 523-1175
e-mail: brick@dosomething.org
http://www.dosomething.org

QUIZ RESULTS

1. It is better to start a new organization than to get an existing institution to help remedy a problem you have identified.
Answer: No. Given the failure rate of new organizations and the damage they can do to existing organizations, it is always better to get an existing nonprofit, business, or government organization to remedy your problem if you can. You need to thoroughly study what organizations already exist that might be addressing the problem or could be persuaded to do so before you take on the very difficult task of starting a new organization. The difficulty in working with existing organizations is that they may already be over-committed or may not see your problem as a high priority. In that case, your thorough study of the option of working with an existing organization will make your planning better and also will help you when you go to funders, since the first thing they ask is what existing organizations provide the activities you are planning to undertake.

2. A useful mission statement should lead to a list of doable and measurable objectives.
Answer: Yes. Although mission statements are a list of general goals to achieve over the long run, they should permit you and your supporters to agree on measures of success. If you cannot get this agreement, you do not have a mission statement that is meaning-

ful and shared by the founding supporters. You
may also not have the right mix of people. You should
seriously think about starting over if this problem
persists.

3. Make sure that you build up a large membership
and volunteer base before you begin to plan your short-
term objectives.

Answer: No. You do not want to solicit members
and volunteers until you have specific tasks in mind and
donation requests. They are too precious a resource
to be asked to attend a meeting or even read information about the organization without being asked
for something.

4. An organization has been institutionalized when
it can survive and function effectively without the
founding leadership.

Answer: Not sure. Several other requirements include
stable funding sources, incorporation, and evidence
that the mission is being accomplished. You may also
want to join forces with other institutions.

Appendix

I. Resources: Contact organizations

ACCESS
1001 Connecticut Ave., NW #838
Washington, DC 20036
Tel. 202 785-4233
Fax 202 785-4212
http://www.accessjobs.org

Action Without Borders
350 Fifth Ave., Suite 6614
New York, NY 10118
Tel. 212 843-3973
Fax 212 564-3377
http://www.idealist.org

Activism 2000 Project
PO Box E
Kensington, MD 20895
Tel. 800 KID POWER
Fax 301 929-8907
http://www.youthactivism.com

AIDSACTION—Capitol Hill Votes
1906 Sunderland Place, NW
Washington, DC 20036
Tel. 202 530-8030
Fax 202 530-8031
http://www.aidsaction.org/
hillvotes.html

Alcoholics Anonymous
A.A. General Service Office
475 Riverside Drive
New York, NY 10015
Tel. 212 870-3400
Fax 212 870-3003
http://www.alcoholics-anonymous.
org

Alzheimer's Disease and Related
Disorders Association
919 N. Michigan Ave. #1000

Chicago, IL 60611-1676
Tel. 800 272-3900
http://www.alz.org

American Association of Retired
Persons (AARP)
601 E Street, NW
Washington, DC 20049
Tel. 202 434-3200 or
800 424-3410

AARP Volunteer Talent Bank
Tel. (202) 434-3219
http://www.aarp.org

American Civil Liberties Union–
National Freedom Scorecard
125 Broad Street, 18th floor
New York, NY 10004
Tel. 212 549-2585
http://scorecard.aclu.org

America's Promise–The Alliance
for Youth
909 N. Washington Street,
Suite 400

Alexandria, VA 22314-1556
Tel. 888 55-YOUTH or
703 684-4500
Fax 703 535-3900
http://www.americaspromise.org

Americorps
1201 New York Ave., NW
Washington, DC 20525
Tel. 800 942-2677
http://www.americorps.org

The Appleseed Foundation
910 Seventeenth Street
Washington, DC 20006
Tel. 202 331-7436

Fax 202 331-7437
http://www.appleseeds.net

Arthritis Foundation
1330 W. Peachtree Street
Atlanta, GA 30309
Tel. 800 283-7800
http://www.arthritis.org

Association of Community
Organizations for Reform Now
(ACORN)
88 Third Ave., 3rd fl.
Brooklyn, NY 11217
Tel. 718 246-7900
Fax 718 246-7939
http://www.acorn.org

Big Brothers/Big Sisters of
America
203 N. Thirteenth Street
Philadelphia, PA 19107
Tel. 215 567-7000
Fax 732 544-2260
http://www.bbbsa.org

Business for Social Responsibility
609 Mission Street, 2nd floor
San Francisco, CA 94105-3506
Tel. 415 537-0888
Fax 415 537-0889
http://www.bsr.org

Campus Compact
Box 1975
Brown University
Providence, RI 02912-1975
Tel. 401 863-1119
Fax 401 863-3779
http://www.compact.org

Canadian Association of Retired
Persons
27 Queens St. E, Suite 1304
Toronto, ON, M5C 2M6, Canada
Tel. 416 363-5562
Fax 416 363-7394
http://www.fifty-plus.net

Canadian Centre for Philanthropy
425 University Ave., 7th fl.
Toronto, ON, Canada, M56 1T6
Tel. 416 597-2293
Fax 416 597-2294
http://www.ccp.ca

Canadian Non-Profit Resource
Network
68 Queen St. N.
Kitchener, ON, Canada, N2H 2HZ
Tel. 416 597-2293
http://www.waterlooregion.org/
cnrn/

Caring Institute/National Caring
Awards
228 Seventh Street, SE
Washington, DC 20003
Tel. 202 547-4273
http://www.caring-institute.org

Center for Auto Safety
1825 Connecticut Ave., NW,
Suite 330
Washington, DC 20009
Tel. 202 328-7700
http://www.autosafety.org

Center for Community Change
1000 Wisconsin Ave., NW
Washington, DC 20007
Tel. 202 342-0567
http://www.communitychange.org

Center for Science in the Public
Interest
1875 Connecticut Ave., NW,
Suite 300
Washington, DC 20009
Tel. 202 332-9110
http://www.cspinet.org

Center for Study of Responsive
Law
PO Box 19367
Washington, DC 20036

Tel. 202 234-5176
http://www.csrl.org

Children of Aging Parents (CAPS)
1609 Woodbourne Ave.,
Suite 302A
Levittown, PA 19057
Tel. 800 227-7294

Christian Coalition–Congressional
Election Scorecard
1801-L Sara Drive
Chesapeake, VA 23320
Tel. 757 424-2630
Fax 757 424-9068
http://www.cc.org/score-
cards/98ES/es98.html

Chronicle of Philanthropy
1255 23rd Street, NW
Washington, DC 20037
Tel. 800 728-2819
http://www.philanthropy.com

Coalition for Environmentally
Responsible Economics (CERES)
11 Arlington Street
Boston, MA 02116-3411
Tel. 617 247-0700
Fax 617 267-5400
http://www.ceres.org/

Common Cents of NY
104 W. Eighty-Eighth Street
New York, NY 10024
Tel. 212 PENNIES
Fax 212 579-3488

Community Foundations of
Canada
301-75 Albert Street
Ottawa, ON, Canada, K1P5E7
Tel. 613 236-2664
Fax 613 236-1621
http://www.community-fdn.ca

Congress.org
c/o Capital Advantage
PO Box 2018
Merrifield, VA 22116

Tel. 703 289-4670
Fax 703 289-4678
http://www.congress.org

Co-op America
1612 K Street NW, Suite 600
Washington, DC 20006
Tel. 800 58-GREEN or
202 872-5307
Fax 202 331-8166.
http://www.coopamerica.org/

Consumer Alert
1001 Connecticut Ave., NW
Washington, DC 20036
Tel. 202 467-5809
http://www.consumeralert.org

Consumer Federation of America
1424 Sixteenth Street, NW
Washington, DC 20036
Tel. 202 265-7989
http://www.consumerfed.org

Consumers Union of the US, Inc.
1666 Connecticut Ave., NW,
Suite 310
Washington, DC 20009
Tel. 202 462-6262
http://www.consunion.org

Corporation for National Service-
RSVP and Learn & Serve Projects
1201 New York Ave., NW
Washington, DC 20005
Tel. 202 606-5000
http://www.cns.gov

Council for Excellence in
Government
1301 K Street, NW,
Suite 450 West
Washington, DC 20005
Tel. 202 728-0418
Fax 202 728-0422
http://www.excelgov.org

Council on Economic Priorities
30 Irving Place, 9th floor
New York, NY 10003

Tel. 212 420-1133
http://www.cepnyc.org

Council on Foundations
1828 L Street, NW
Washington, DC 20036
Tel. 202 466-6512
http://www.cof.org

Do Something BRICK Award
423 West Fifty-Fifth Street,
8th floor
New York, NY 10019
Tel. 212 523-1175
e-mail: brick@dosomething.org
http://www.dosomething.org

Energize, Inc.
5450 Wissahickon Ave.
Philadelphia, PA 19144
Tel. 215 438-8342
http://www.energizeinc.com

4charity.com
457-13 Sierra Vista Ave.
Mountain View, CA 94043
Tel. 650 496-2457
Fax 650 496-2431
http://www.4charity.com

The Foundation Center
79 Fifth Ave.
New York, NY 10003
Tel. 212 620-4230
http://www.fdncenter.org

Free the Children International
1750 Steeles Ave., West, Suite 218
Concord, ON, Canada, L4K 2L7
Tel. 905 760-9382
Fax 905 760-9157
http://www.freethechildren.org

The Giraffe Project
PO Box 759
Langley, WA 98260
Tel. 360 221-7989
Fax 360 221-7817
e-mail: office@giraffe.org
http://www.giraffe.org

The Genuine Do-Gooder
http://www.genuinedogooder.com

Good Money
370A Granite Road
Ossipee, NH 03864
Tel. 603 539-3852

Good Money
608 Glass Ave.
Spokane, WA 99205
http://www.goodmoney.com

Green Money Journal
608 W. Glass Ave.
Spokane, WA 99205

Green Money Online
http://www.greenmoney.com

Guidestar
1126 Professional Drive
Williamsburg, VA 23185
Tel. 757 229-4631
http://www.guidestar.org

Habitat for Humanity
121 Habitat Street
Americus, GA 31709-3498
Tel. 912 924-6935
http://www.habitat.org

Harry S. Truman Scholarship
Foundation
712 Jackson Place, NW
Washington, DC 20006
http://www.truman.gov

Humane Society of the United
States
2100 L Street, NW
Washington, DC 20037
Tel. 202 452-1100
http://www.hsus.org

I CAN
500 W. Roy, W107
Seattle, WA 98119
Tel. 206 283-4385
Fax 206 283-4046

IGive, Inc.
1890 Maple Ave., Suite 130
Evanston, Il 60201
Tel. 847 328-5293
Fax 847 328-5789
http://www.igive.com

The "I Have a Dream" Foundation
330 Seventh Ave., 12th fl.
New York, NY
Tel. 212 293-5480
e-mail: ihad_national@together.org
http://www.ihad.org

Impact Online
325 'B' Forest Ave.
Palo Alto, CA 94301
Tel. 650 327-1389
Fax 650 327-1395
http://www.impactonline.org/

The Impact Project
2244 Alder Street
Eugene, OR 9740
Tel. 541 343-2420
Fax 541 343-6956
http://www.efn.org/~impact/

Independent Sector
1200 Eighteenth Street, NW,
Suite 200
Washington, DC 20036
Tel. 202 467-6100
Fax 202 467-6101
http://www.indepsec.org

Interfaith Center on Corporate
Responsibility
475 Riverside Drive
New York, NY 10115
Tel. 212 870-2295
Fax 212 870-2023

Investor Responsibility Research
Center
1350 Connecticut Ave., NW,
Suite 700
Washington, DC 20036-1701
Tel. 202 833-0700

Fax 202 833-3555
http://www.irrc.org

Jobs with Justice
501 Third Street NW
Washington DC 20001-2797
Tel. 202 434-1106
Fax 202 434-1477
http://www.jwj.org

Join Together
441 Stuart Street
Boston, MA 02116
Tel. 617 437-1500
Fax 617 437-9394
http://www.jointogether.org

Kinder, Lydenburg, Domini &
Co., Inc.
Russia Wharf, 530 Atlantic Ave.,
7th fl.
Boston, MA 02210
Tel. 617 547-7479
Fax 617 354-5353
http://www.kld.org

League of Women Voters
1730 M Street, NW
Washington, DC 20036
Tel. 202 429-1965
Fax 202 429-0854
http://www.lwv.org/~lwvus/

Literacy Volunteers of America
635 James Street
Syracuse, NY 13203
Tel. 315 472-0001
http://www.literacyvolunteers.org

Live and Let Live/Breast Cancer
Fund
282 Second St., 3rd floor
San Francisco, CA 94105
Tel. 800 487-0492
Fax 415 543-2975
http://www.letlive.com

Make a Difference Day
USA Weekend
1000 Wilson Blvd.

Arlington, VA 22229-0012
Tel. 800 416-3824
http://www.usaweekend.com/
diffday/

National Association of Partners in
Education, Inc.
901 Pitt Street, Suite 320
Alexandria, VA 22314
Tel. 703 836-4880
http://www.partnersineducation.
org

National Association of Town Watch
PO Box 303
Wynnewood, PA 19096
Tel. 610 649-7055
e-mail: NATWNNO@aol.com
http://www.nationaltownwatch.org

National Association of Youth Clubs
5808 Sixteenth Street, NW
Washington, DC 20011
Tel. 202 726-2044

National Center for
Nonprofit Boards
1828 L Street, NW, Suite 900
Washington, DC 20036-5104
Tel. 800 883-6262
http://www.ncnb.org

National Center for Small
Communities
444 N. Capitol Street, NW,
Suite 208
Washington, DC 20001
Tel. 202 624-3550
http://www.natat.org/ncsc

National Center for Tobacco-Free
Kids
1707 L Street, NW, Suite 800
Washington, DC 20036
Tel. 800 284-KIDS
http://www.tobaccofreekids.org

National Charities Information
Bureau
19 Union Square W

New York, NY 10003
Tel. 212 929-6300
http://www.give.org

National Coalition for the
Homeless
1012 Fourteenth Street, NW #600
Washington, DC 20005
Tel. 202 737-6444
Fax 202 737-6445
http://www.nch.ari.net

National Consumers League
1701 K Street, NW, Suite 1200
Washington, DC 20006
Tel. 202 835-0747
http://www.natlconsumersleague.
org

National Council of Nonprofit
Associations
1900 L Street, NW, Suite 605
Washington, DC 20036-5024
Tel. 202 467-6262
Fax 202 467-2621
http://www.ncna.org

National Council on Aging, Inc.
409 Third Street, SW
Washington, DC 20024
Tel. 202 479-1200
http://www.ncoa.org

National Executive Service Corps
(NESC)
120 Wall Street, 16th fl.
New York, NY 10005
Tel. 212 269-1234

National Family Caregivers
Association
10400 Connecticut Ave., Suite 500
Kensington, MD 20895
Tel. 800 896-3650
Fax 301 942-2302
http://www.nfcacares.org

National 4-H Council
7100 Connecticut Ave.
Chevy Chase, MD 20815

Tel. 301 961-2866
http://www.fourhcouncil.edu

National Priorities Project
17 New South Street, Suite 301
Northampton, MA 01060
Tel. 413 584-9556
Fax 413 586-9647
http://www.natprior.org

National PTA
330 N. Wabash Ave., Suite 2100
Chicago, IL 60611
Tel. 312 670-6782 or
800 307-4PTA
Fax 312 670-6783
http://www.pta.org

National Retiree Volunteer Coaltion
(NRVC)
4915 W. Thirty-Fifth Street
Minneapolis, MN 55416
Tel. 612 920 7788 or
888 733-NRVC
Fax 612 920-7711

National Society for Experiential
Education
1703 N. Beauregard Street
Alexandria, VA 22311-1714
Tel. 703 575-5475
http://www.nsee.org

National Society of Fund Raising
Executives (NSFRE)
1101 King Street, Suite 700
Alexandria, VA 22314-2967
Tel. 800 666-3863
http://www.nsfre.org

National Training and Information
Center
810 North Milwaukee Avenue
Chicago, IL 60622
Tel. 312 243-3035
Fax 312 243-3038

Neighborhood Watch Program/
National Sheriff's Association
1450 Duke Street

Alexandria, Virginia 22314-3490
Tel. 703 836-7827
http://www.sheriffs.org

Newtithing Group
Four Embarcadero Center,
Suite 3700
San Francisco, CA 94111
Tel. 415 274-2761
Fax 415 274-2756
http://www.newtithing.org

The Non-Profit Career Network
PO Box 241
Haddam, CT 06438-0241
Tel. 888 844-4870
Fax 860 345-3299
http://www.nonprofitcareer.com

Oprah's Angel Network
PO Box 909715
Chicago, IL 60607
http://www.oprah.com/angelnet_
main.html

Peace Corps
1111 Twentieth Street, NW
Washington, DC 20526
Tel. 800 424-8580
http://www.peacecorps.gov

Philanthropic Advisory Service of
the Council of Better Business
Bureaus, Inc.
4200 Wilson Blvd.
Arlington, VA 22203-1804
http://www.bbb.org/reports/
charity.html

The Philanthropy News Network
5 West Hargett Street, Suite 805
Raleigh, NC 27601
Tel. 919 832-2325
Fax 832-2369
http://www.pj.org/corporate/

Points of Light Foundation
Awards for Excellence in Corporate
Community Service and the

Presidential Service Award
1400 I Street, NW, Suite 800
Washington, DC 20005
Tel. 202 729.8000
Fax 202 729-8100
http://www.pointsoflight.org/

Principle Profits Asset Management
PO Box 2323
Amherst, MA 01004-2323
Tel. 800 972-3289 or
413 256-1528
Fax 413 256-8459
http://www.principleprofits.com

Project America
310 South Blvd.
Richmond, VA 23220
Tel. 800 880-3352
Fax 804 359-8160
http://www. project.org

Project Vote Smart
One Common Ground
Philipsburg, MT 59858
Tel. 406 859-8683 or
888 VOTE-SMART
Fax 406 859-8680
http://www.vote-smart.org

Ronald McDonald House Charities
1 Kroc Drive
Oak Brook, IL 60523
Tel. 630 623-7048
http://www.rmhc.com

Self-Help Sourcebook
Northwest Covenant Medical Center
25 Pocono Road
Denville, NJ, 07834-2995
Tel. 973 625-3037
http://www.mentalhelp.net/
selfhelp

Senior Companions Program
1110 Vermont Ave., NW
Washington, DC 20525
Tel. 202 274-6697

SERVEnet
Organized by Youth Service
America
1101 Fifteenth Street, Suite 200
Washington, DC 20005
Tel. 202 296-2992
http://www.servenet.org/

Service Corps of Retired Executives
(SCORE)
409 Third Street, SW, 6th floor
Washington, DC 20024
Tel. 800 634-0245
http://www.score.org

Socialfunds.com
http://www.socialfunds.com

Social Investment Organization
366 Adelaide Street, E, Suite 443
Toronto, ON M5A3XA
Tel. 416 360-3680
http://www.web.net/~sio/

Social Venture Network
P.O. Box 29221
San Francisco, CA 94129-0221
Tel. 415 561-6501
http://www.svn.org

S-R-Invest
http://www.tbzweb.com/srivest/

Stand for Children
1834 Connecticut Ave., NW
Washington, DC 20009
Tel. 800 663-4032
Fax 202 234-0217
http://www.stand.org

The State Public Interest Research
Groups/US PIRG
218 D Street, SE
Washington, DC 20003-1900
Tel. 202 546-9707
Fax 202-546-2461
http://www.pirg.org

Students for Responsible Business
609 Mission Street

San Francisco, CA 94105
Tel. 415 778-8366
Fax 415 778-8367
http://www.srbnet.org

Teach for America
315 West Thirty-Sixth Street,
6th floor
New York, NY 10018
Tel. 212 279-2080
Fax 212 279-2081
http://www.teachforamerica.org

Twenty/Twenty Vision Education
Fund
1828 Jefferson Place, NW
Washington, DC 20036

U.S. Department of
Education/America
Goes Back to School
400 Maryland Ave., SW
Washington, DC 20202
Tel. 800 USA-LEARN
http://www.ed.gov/Family/agbts/

U.S. Department of Housing and
Urban Development/Neighborhood
Networks
9300 Lee Highway
Fairfax, VA 22031-1207
Tel. 888 312-2743
http://www.hud.gov/nnw/
nnwindex.html

United States Student Association
1413 K Street, NW, 9th floor
Washington, DC 20005
Tel. 202 347-USSA

Fax 202 393-5886
http://www.essential.org/ussa

United Way of America
701 N. Fairfax Street
Alexandria, Virginia 22314-2045
Tel. 703 836-7100
http://www.unitedway.org

VolunteerMatch
325 "B" Forest Ave.
Palo Alto, CA 94301
Tel. 650 327-1389
Fax 650 327-1395
http://www.volunteermatch.org/

Women's Voting Guide
PO Box 20594
New York, NY 10021
Tel. 212 396-3457
http://www.womenvote.org

Working Assets
701 Montgomery Street, 4th floor
San Francisco, CA 94111
Tel. 800 788-0898
http://www.workingassets.com

YMCA Earth Service Corps
909 Fourth Ave.
Seattle, WA 98104
Tel. 800 733-YESC
http://www.yesc.org

Youth Volunteer Corps
#720, 640 Eighth Ave., SW
Calgary, AB, Canada, T2P 1G7
Tel. 403 266-5448
Fax 403 264-0266
http://www.childfriendly.ab.ca

II. Suggested Readings

Active Citizenship Today Handbook. Alexandria and Los Angeles: Close Up Foundation and Constitutional Rights Foundation, 1994.

Alinsky, Saul. *Rules for Radicals: A Pragmatic Primer for Realistic Radicals.* New York: Vintage Books, 1971.

Archer, Jules. *Special Interests: Lobbyists Influence Legislation.* Millbrook, 1997.

A Snapshot of America's Nonprofit Boards. Washington, DC: National Center for Nonprofit Boards, 1997.

Botros, Reham and Nancy R. Bailey. *National Directory of Internships* (1998-1999 Edition). Needham Heights: Simon & Schuster, 1998.

Brill, Jack. *Investing from the Heart: The Guide to Socially Responsible Investments and Money Management.* Crown Publishers, 1993.

Brill, Hal, Jack Brill and Cliff Feigenbaum. *Investing with Your Values: Making Money and Making a Difference.* Bloomberg Press, 1999.

Carnegie, Dale. *How to Win Friends and Influence People.* New York: Simon and Schuster, 1964.

Carroll, Andrew. *Golden Opportunities: A Volunteer Guide for Americans Over 50.* Peterson's Guides, 1994.

————. *Volunteer USA.* New York: Fawcett, 1991.

Center for Community Change. *How and Why to Influence Public Policy.* Washington, DC: Center for Community Change, 1996.

Cohen, Lilly and Dennis R. Young. *Careers for Dreamers and Doers: A Guide to Management Careers in the Non-Profit Sector.* The Foundation Center.

Colvin, Donna. *Good Works: A Guide to Careers in Social Change*, Fifth Edition. Barricade Books.

Council on Economic Priorities. *The Corporate Report Card.* NAL/Dutton, 1998.

————. *Shopping for a Better World.* San Francisco: Sierra Club Books, 1994.

Dass, Ram and Paul Gorman. *How Can I Help?: Stories and Reflections on Service.* New York: Alfred A. Knopf, Inc., 1985.

DiGeronimo, Theresa Foy. *A Student's Guide to Volunteering.* Franklin Lakes: Career Press, 1995.

Ellis, Susan J. *Volunteer Management Audit.* United Way of America, 1992.

Ellis, Susan J. and Katherine H. Noyes. *By The People: A History of Americans as Volunteers.* San Francisco: Jossey-Bass, 1990.

Ellis, Susan J. and Anne Weisbord. *Children as Volunteers: Preparing for Community Service.* Philadelphia: Energize, 1990.

Galbraith, John Kenneth. *The Good Society: The Human Agenda.* New York: Houghton Mifflin Co., 1995.

Golliver, Joy J. *300 Creative Ideas for Community Involvement*. Seattle, WA: Ignite the Community Spirit, 1991.

Golliver, Joy J. and Ruth Hayes-Arista. *301 Ways to Turn Caring into Action*. Seattle, WA: Ignite the Community Spirit, 1997.

Grobman, Gary M. *Non-Profit Handbook*, National Edition. White Hat Communications.

Hamilton, Leslie and Robert Tragert. *100 Best Non-Profits to Work For*. Macmillan General Reference.

Hollender, Jeffrey and Linda Catling. *How to Make the World a Better Place: 116 Ways You Can Make a Difference*. New York: W.W. Norton & Company, 1995.

Hopkins, Bruce R. *A Legal Guide to Starting and Managing a Non-Profit Organization*, Second Edition. John Wiley & Sons, 1993.

Hummel, Joan M. *Starting and Running a Non-Profit Organization*, Second Edition. University of Minnesota Press, 1996.

I CAN. *The I CAN Ignite the Community Spirit Newsletter*. To order, visit http://www.gstch.com/ignite/need2read.htm

Independent Sector. *Nonprofit Almanac: Dimensions of the Independent Sector*. San Francisco: Jossey-Bass, 1996.

Janowitz, Gayle. *Helping Hands: Volunteer Work in Education*. Chicago: University of Chicago Press.

Kielberger, Craig. *Free the Children: A Young Man's Personal Crusade against Child Labor*. New York: Harper Collins, 1999.

King, Richard M. *From Making a Profit to Making a Difference: Careers in Non-Profits for Business Professionals*. Planning/Communications Publishing.

Kouri, Mary. *Volunteerism and Older Adults: Choices and Challenges*. ABC-CLIO.

Krannich, Ronald L. and Caryl Rae Krannich. *Jobs and Careers with Non-Profit Organizations: Profitable Opportunities with Non-Profits,* Second Edition. Impact Publications.

Kroloff, Rabbi Charles A. *Fifty-four Ways You Can Help the Homeless*. Southport: Hugh Lauter Assoc., 1993.

Lauber, Daniel. *Government Job Finder*. River Forest: Planning/Communications, 1992.

———. *Non-Profits and Education Job Finder*. Planning/Communications, 1997.

Lawson, Douglas M. *Volunteering: 101 Ways You Can Improve the World and Your Life*. San Diego: ALTI Publishing, 1998.

Leadership Directories. New York: Leadership Directories, Inc., annual.

Leifer, Loring and Michael McLarney. *Younger Voices, Stronger Choices: Promise Project's Guide to Forming Youth/Adult Partnerships*. Kansas City: Kansas City Consensus, 1997

Lesko, Wendy Schaetzel and Emanuel Tsouounis, II. *Youth: The 26% Solution*. Information USA, Inc., 1998.

Levine, Michael. *The Address Book: How to Reach Anyone Who Is Anyone*. Perigree Books, updated annually.

Lewis, Barbara A. *The Kid's Guide to Service Projects*. Minneapolis: Free Spirit Publishing, 1995.

———. *The Kid's Guide to Social Action*. Minneapolis: Free Spirit Publishing, 1998.

Mancuso, Anthony. *How to Form a Non-Profit Corporation*, Fourth Edition. Nolo Press, 1998.

McAdam, Terry W. *Doing Well by Doing Good: The Complete Guide to Careers in the Non-Profit Sector*. The Taft Group.

McCurley, Steve and Sue Vineyard. *Handling Problem Volunteers*. Heritage Arts Publishing, 1998.

McIlnay, Dennis P. *How Foundations Work*. San Francisco: Jossey-Bass, 1998.

McMillon, Bill. *Volunteer Vacations*. Chicago: Chicago Review Press, 1997.

Mogil, Christopher. *Welcome to Philanthropy*. Available from the Impact Project—e-mail: impact@efn.org. Eugene: Impact Project.

Mogil, Christopher and Anne Slepian. *We Gave Away a Fortune*. Available from the Impact Project—e-mail: impact@efn.org.

Mother Teresa. *Mother Teresa: A Simple Path*. New York: Ballantine Books, 1995

Nader, Ralph. *Civics for Democracy*. Washington, DC: Essential Books.

The Non-Profit Handbook. The Chronicle of Philanthropy, 1998.

O'Connell, Brian and E.B. Knauft. *Financial Compensation in Voluntary Organizations*. Washington, DC: Independent Sector, 1993.

Osborne, David and Ted Gaebler. *Reinventing Government: How the Entrepreneurial Spirit Is Transforming the Public Sector*. New York: Penguin Books, 1993.

Richan, Willard C. *Lobbying for Social Change*. Binghamton: Haworth Press, 1993.

Rockey, Sherry and Alice L. Hughey. *A Citizen's Guide to Community Education on Global Issues*. Washington DC: League of Women Voters Education Fund, 1988.

Sandak, Cass R. *Lobbying*. 21st Century Books, 1995.

Steckel, Richard and Jennifer Lehman. *In Search of America's Best Non-Profits*. San Francisco: Jossey-Bass, 1997.

Szanton, Peter L. *Board Assessment of the Organization: How Are We Doing?*. Washington, DC: National Center for Nonprofit Boards, 1992.

Tell It to Washington: A Guide for Citizen Action. Washington DC: League of Women Voters Education Fund, 1987-88.

Warren, Chris Robin. *How to Compete and Cooperate at the Same Time: A Guide for Non-Profits Working Together in This Dog-Eat-Dog Day and Age*. Adolfo Street Publications.

Weeden, Curt. *Corporate Social Investing: The Breakthrough Strategy for Giving and Getting Corporate Contributions*. San Francisco: Berrett-Koehler Publishers, Inc., 1998.

Zack, David. *Active Citizenship Handbook Today*. Alexandria and Los Angeles: Close-up Foundation and Constitutional Rights Foundation, 1994.

III List of more than 100 approved charities

These evaluations were valid as of February 15, 1999. For the latest list contact NCIB at

National Charities Information Bureau
19 Union Square West
New York, NY 10003
Tel. 212 929-6300
http://www.give.org

Action on Smoking and Health

Accion International

Advocates for Youth (formerly Center for Population Options)

Africa Fund (American Committee on Africa)

African Wildlife Foundation

Africare

ALM International (American Leprosy Missions)

ALS Association—Woodland Hills, CA (NSC)

ALSAC-St. Jude Children's Research Hospital

Alzheimer's Disease and Related Disorders Association (Alzheimer's Association)

AMC Cancer Research Center

America the Beautiful Fund

American Cancer Society

American Civil Liberties Union/ACLU Foundation

American Committee on Africa (Africa Fund)

American Diabetes Association

American Farmland Trust

American Forests (American Forestry Association)

American Foundation for AIDS Research

American Foundation for the Blind

American Friends Service Committee

American Heart Association

American Humane Association

American Indian College Fund

American Indian Graduate Center

American Kidney Fund

American Leprosy Foundation (Leonard Wood Memorial)

American Leprosy Missions (ALM International)

American Liver Foundation

American Lung Association (Christmas Seals)— New York, NY (NSC)

American Near East Refugee Aid

American Parkinson Disease Association

American Red Cross

American Refugee Committee

American Rivers

American Social Health Association

American Symphony Orchestra League

AmeriCares Foundation

Amnesty International of the USA

Animal Protection Institute of America

Animal Welfare Institute

Arc of the United States

Arthritis Foundation

Asia Foundation

Association on American Indian Affairs

AVSC International (formerly Association for Voluntary Surgical Contraception)

Big Brothers/Big Sisters of America—Philadelphia, PA (NSC)

Boy Scouts of America—Irving, TX (NSC)

Boys and Girls Clubs of America—Atlanta, GA (NSC)

Business Council for the U.N.

Camp Fire Boys and Girls—Kansas, MO (NSC)

Cancer Care Inc.

Cancer Research Foundation of America

Cancer Research Institute

Catholic Relief Services—United States Catholic Conference

Center for Community Change

Center for Marine Conservation

Child Find of America

Child Welfare League of America

Childreach (PLAN International USA)

Children Incorporated

Children International (Holy Land Christian Mission)

Choice in Dying

Citizens' Scholarship Foundation of America—St. Peter, MN (NSC)

City of Hope

Compassion International

Consortium for Graduate Study in Management

Council on Economic Priorities

Covenant House

Crohn's & Colitis Foundation of America (formerly National Association for Ileitis and Colitis)

Cystic Fibrosis Foundation

Deafness Research Foundation

Direct Relief International

Disabled American Veterans

Doctors Without Borders USA

Doctors of the World USA

Ducks Unlimited

EarthJustice Legal Defense Fund

Easter Seal Society (National Easter Seal Society)

Elizabeth Glaser Pediatric AIDS Foundation (formerly Pediatric AIDS Foundation)

Environmental Defense Fund

Epilepsy Foundation of America

Ethics Resource Center

FAIR (Federation for American Immigration Reform)

Fight for Sight (Prevent Blindness America)

Foundation Fighting Blindness

Friends of Animals

Friends of the Earth

Fund for an Open Society

Fund for Peace

Futures for Children

Gifts in Kind International

Girl Scouts of the U.S.A.—New York, NY (NSC)

Girls Incorporated (formerly Girls Clubs of America)—New York, NY (NSC)

Goodwill Industries International—Bethesda, MD (NSC)

Guide Dog Foundation for the Blind

Habitat for Humanity International

Heifer Project International

Helen Keller International

Hispanic Scholarship Fund

Holy Land Christian Mission (Children International)

Hugh O'Brian Youth Leadership (formerly Hugh O'Brian Youth Foundaon)

Hunger Project

Huntington's Disease Society of America

Immigration and Refugee Services of America (U.S. Committee for Refugees—formerly American Council for Nationalities Service)

Inform

Institute of International Education

INTERACTION: American Council for Voluntary International Action

International Center

International Executive Service Corps

International Institute of Rural Reconstruction

International Planned Parenthood Federation/Western Hemisphere Region

International Rescue Committee

Izaak Walton League of America

Junior Achievement—Colorado Springs, CO (NSC)

Juvenile Diabetes Foundation International

Laubach Literacy International

League of Women Voters Education Fund

Leonard Wood Memorial (American Leprosy Foundation)

Leukemia Society of America

Literacy Volunteers of America—Syracuse, NY (NSC)

Lupus Foundation of America

Make-A-Wish Foundation

March of Dimes Birth Defects Foundation

Medical Education for South African Blacks

Mexican American Legal Defense and Educational Fund

Muscular Dystrophy Association

Myasthenia Gravis Foundation

NAACP Legal Defense and Educational Fund

National 4-H Council

National Action Council for Minorities in Engineering

National Alliance of Breast Cancer Organizations

National Alliance of Business

National Anti-Vivisection Society

National Association for Visually Handicapped

National Audubon Society

National Center for Learning Disabilities

National Center for Missing and Exploited Children

National Childhood Cancer Foundation

National Coalition for the Homeless

National Committee to Prevent Child Abuse—Chicago, IL (NSC)

National Conference for Community and Justice

National Council for Adoption

National Council on Alcoholism and Drug Dependence—New York, NY (NSC)

National Crime Prevention Council

National Down Syndrome Society

National Easter Seal Society

National Executive Service Corps

National Hemophilia Foundation—New York, NY (NSC)

National Hospice Organization

National Jewish Medical and Research Center

National Kidney Foundation

National Medical Fellowships

National Neurofibromatosis Foundation

National Osteoporosis Foundation

National Parkinson Foundation

National Psoriasis Foundation

National Society to Prevent Blindness (Prevent Blindness America)

National Trust for Historic Preservation

National Urban Fellows

National Urban League—New York, NY (NSC)

NationalWildlife Federation

Native American Rights Fund

Natural Resources Defense Council

Nature Conservancy

Near East Foundation

NOW Lega Defense and Education Fund

Our Little Brothers and Sisters

Overseas Development Council

Oxfam America

Pan American Development Foundation

Partners of the Americas

Pathfinder International

Pearl S. Buck International

PLAN International USA (Childreach)

Planned Parenthood Federation of America

Population Action International (formerly Population Crisis Committee)

Population Institute

Populalion Reference Bureau

Prevent Blindness America (National Society to Prevent Blindness)

Project Concern International

Rainforest Action Network

Reading is Fundamental

Recording for the Blind and Dyslexic

Resources for the Future

St. Jude Children's Research Hospital (ALSAC-St. Jude)

Save the Children Federation

Second Harvest

SIDS Alliance—Baltimore, MD (NSC)

Sierra Club Foundation

SOS Children's Villages—USA

Starr Commonwealth (formerly Starr Commonwealth Schools)

Sunshine Foundation

Susan G. Komen Breast Cancer
Foundation

Technoserve

Trickle Up Program

Union of Concerned Scientists

Unitarian Universalist Service
Committee

United Negro College Fund

USO (United Service
Organizations)

U.S. Committee for Refugees
(Immigration and Refugee
Services of America—formerly
American Council for
Nationalities Service)

U.S. Committee for UNICEF

U.S. Olympic Committee

United Way of America—
Alexandria, VA (NSC)

Wildlife Preservation Trust
International

World Concern

World Education

World Emergency Relief

World Learning

World Neighbors

World Wildlife Fund, Inc.

YMCA of the U.S.A.—Chicago, IL
(NSC)

YWCA of the U.S.A., National
Board—New York, NY (NSC)

Youth for Understanding